TROUT UNLIMITED'S
GUIDE TO

AMERICA'S
100
BEST
TROUT
STREAMS

JOHN ROSS

FALCON™

HELENA, MONTANA

A FALCON GUIDE ®

Falcon® Publishing is continually expanding its list of recreational guidebooks. All books include detailed descriptions, accurate maps, and all information necessary for enjoyable trips. You can order extra copies of this book and get information and prices for other Falcon® books by writing Falcon, P.O. Box 1718, Helena, MT 59624 or calling toll free 1-800-582-2665. Also, please ask for a free copy of our current catalog. Visit our website at www.FalconOutdoors.com or contact us by e-mail at falcon@falcon.com.

© 1999 Falcon® Publishing, Inc., Helena, Montana.
Printed in the United States of America.

2 3 4 5 6 7 8 9 10 MG 05 04 03 02 01 00 99

Cataloging-in-Publication Data is on record at the Library of Congress.
Ross, John, 1946–
        Trout Unlimited's guide to America's 100 best trout streams / John
Ross.
            p.   cm. — (A Falcon guide)
        Includes index.
        ISBN 1-56044-830-X (pbk.)
            1. Trout fishing—United States—Guidebooks.   2. United States—
Guidebooks.   I. Trout Unlimited.   II. Title.   III. Title : Guide to
America's 100 best trout streams.   IV. Series.
        SH688.U6R67 1999
        799.1'757'0973—dc21   99-12303
                                                                          CIP

CAUTION

Outdoor recreational activities are by their very nature potentially hazardous. All participants in such activities must assume responsibility for their own actions and safety. The information contained in this guidebook cannot replace sound judgment and good decision-making skills, which help reduce risk exposure, nor does the scope of this book allow for disclosure of all the potential hazards and risks involved in such activities.

Learn as much as possible about the outdoor recreational activities in which you participate, prepare for the unexpected, and be cautious. The reward will be a safer and more enjoyable experience.

♻ Text pages printed on recycled paper.

CONTENTS

ACKNOWLEDGMENTS

Not long after I'd moved to Winona, Minnesota, TUer Joe Lepley introduced me to those fabulous yet fragile spring creeks that drain the bluff country along the Mississippi River. He wooed me with wild browns, re-established there by collaborative work between Minnesota's Department of Natural Resources and a quarter of a century of efforts by the Win Cres and Hiawatha chapters of TU.

Thanks to Joe, I saw the inside of TU firsthand and at its best. The Win Cres chapter works hard to recover habitat trashed by years of mindless neglect. It holds fishing days for youngsters, helping to ensure a supply of future anglers who will carry on TU traditions. It talks with legislators and state agency personnel, encouraging them to pursue action that enhanced coldwater fisheries. And it throws one heck of a banquet. It is like hundreds of TU chapters everywhere.

It's not possible to individually thank each and every TU member who provided me with information for this book. But all have my deepest appreciation. So do Pete Rafle, Christine Arena, and Kenny Mendez at TU's national office, who helped conceive the project, and Charles Gauvin, TU president, who made it possible. Likewise, Larissa Berry and Ric Bourie at Falcon Publishing deserve thanks. Without them, this book would never have come together.

FOREWORD

For more than four decades, Trout Unlimited members have taken pride in the fact that TU is "more than a fishing club." Since its founding in 1959 on the banks of the Au Sable in Michigan, TU has espoused the philosophy that if we take care of the fish, and the waters they inhabit, the fishing will take care of itself. Today, TU members from Pennsylvania to Oregon bristle at the implication that TU is a "sportsman's group" and will explain with more than a hint of pride that Trout Unlimited is a conservation group first— representing the interests of the environment first, and those of the angler a distant second.

And yet, after a genuine concern for our fragile environment, the one thing that unites TU members from California to Connecticut is a love of fishing. At the risk of over-generalizing, TU members represent some of the most devoted, expert, and experienced anglers you'll ever hope to meet. In my travels around the country, I've fished with dozens of TU members, and I can honestly say that I've learned something about the art and craft of fishing from every one of them. And that's where this book comes in.

Ten years ago, on the occasion of TU's 30th birthday, *TROUT* magazine - TU's quarterly — published a remarkable special issue featuring America's "100 Best Trout Streams." The magazine, which was so popular that even our national headquarters has only two jealously-guarded copies remaining, presented eloquent, literate paeans to each of 100 rivers by some of the most talented writers in the business. There was some marvelous writing in that issue, and the list of authors read like a "who's who" of the fishing litterati.

In the intervening years, *TROUT*'s "100 Best Streams" has become something of a touchstone; no one else has attempted anything like it. In fact, *TROUT*'s staff have sent photocopies of that compendium to countless angling enthusiasts, and every month or so, someone calls to ask for it. We are more than happy to oblige them.

Nevertheless, I can't help thinking that at least some of them are a little disappointed when they open the envelope. For what they get is only a taste of what it's like to fish those fabled waters. There isn't a map, or even much of a clue as to how or where to fish when you finally make the pilgrimage to the Madison, the Henry's Fork, or the Delaware.

This book, published in part to mark the completion of Trout Unlimited's 40th year, aims to bridge that gap. In a very basic sense, this is a guidebook like many others. But there are a couple of crucial differences that set it apart from the run of the mill.

First, this time the 100 rivers have been chosen by nomination and vote of TU's membership at large. This has led to some surprising choices (I'll let you decide which ones they are) but it means this is a guide not just to the 100 best streams in America (many have carried over form the 1989 list), but to Trout Unlimited members' 100 favorite streams. Every one of these streams is someone's "home waters," the one stream to which one returns season after season, with the assurance that he'll be welcomed like a lifelong friend.

In addition, virtually every one of these streams has benefited from the friendship of Trout Unlimited members and other conservationists in some meaningful way. Most have been restored or repaired by TU volunteers, and more than a few have been saved outright from death by shopping malls or gold mines. Every entry includes some hint at what conservation-minded anglers can do to safeguard the future of our sport and the delicate ecological resources on which it depends.

As Trout Unlimited embarks on its fifth decade, our ranks have passed the 100,000 mark, and conservation-minded anglers are steadfastly working to protect and restore streams in every state of the Union. Their work takes many forms: some organize campaigns to protect a threatened watershed, others raise funds, and others teach young people about the importance of clean water and wild trout. In all these ways, and countless others, we "give something back" to the resources that have given us so much pleasure.

Ultimately, any list of 100 best streams is arbitrary and subjective, but there's nothing wrong with that. That you can catch wild trout in these 100 streams and countless others is testament in itself to the dedication, perseverance, and passion of TU conservationists nationwide.

Charles F. Gauvin
President and CEO, Trout Unlimited
Arlington, VA 1999

Introduction

A guide to the *best* 100 trout streams in the United States? Pretty presumptuous, I'd say. But more than 1,200 members of Trout Unlimited (TU) cast ballots for the streams that they felt are the best in the country. They made their choices on the quality of the fishing, particularly on the number of catchable wild trout, salmon, or steelhead. They selected streams based on the amount of public access—waters that have at least some stretches that you and I can fish regardless of the thickness of our wallets. The overall scenic beauty of the rivers counted, too. And so did the involvement of TU chapters in preserving and enhancing each fishery.

Are these the best streams in the United States? Hard to tell. For some anglers, the best stream is one of superb technical challenge like the Letort or Williamson where fly, tippet, and presentation must be precisely matched to the water, or the trout simply will not take. For others, the best stream is the one they take their kids to and drift worms through the cobble-bottomed depths on the chance that a rainbow may be home. There are anglers who favor the great tailwaters of the Southeast, where spinners and spoons and crankbaits call up browns of trophy proportions. Still others prefer high mountain streams where native brook trout are as colorful as the forget-me-nots along the bank. And some of us dream all summer of those bitter days of winter when snow blows through the trees and steelhead lie coiled in blackwater holes.

The stream that's best for me today may be the little spring creek near my house where, if I only have an hour to fish, I can count on a wild trout, maybe two. On other days it may be a stream where I'll enjoy the camaraderie of anglers I've never met before. And there are times, as we all know, when another angler is the last thing you want to meet. The stream that's best for you may not be best for me with my errant casts. Each of us has our own sense of "best." The streams in this guide, then, may not be the best streams in the United States, but they are pretty good.

Most of the trout stream guides on bookshelves today are written by fly fishers for their colleagues. They do so, not for money lord knows, but because they really enjoy sharing information with others of like mind. I do not know of a richer trove of information for any individual sport. Spin and bait anglers can take advantage of all this knowledge. Not only do regional guides—and there are several listed in the chapters in this book—provide accurate where-to-go, what-to-use, and how-to information, but you'll also find scores of titles on fly-tying, tackle craft, and technique. The regional guides provide a wealth of very specific information on local streams and their eccentricities, information that's far too detailed to be included in this guide. Here you'll find a broad brush profile, setting forth the basics and providing a bit of context to distinguish each stream from the others. The information contained in each short profile is an introduction. For greater depth, check out the regional guides, talk with staff at tackle shops, read the most current state regulations, and surf the Web. This book should help get you started

John Ross
Upperville, VA 1999.

Locator Map

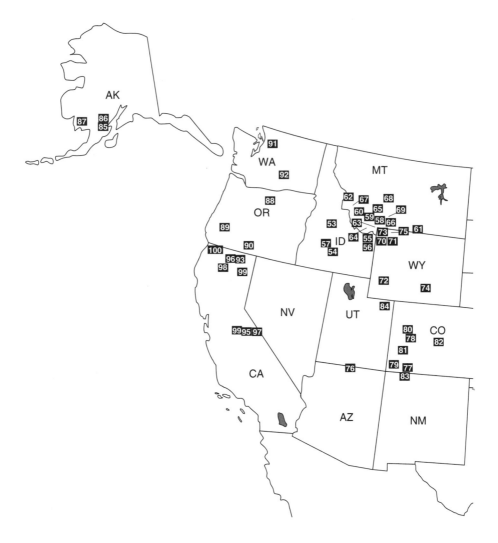

Map Legend

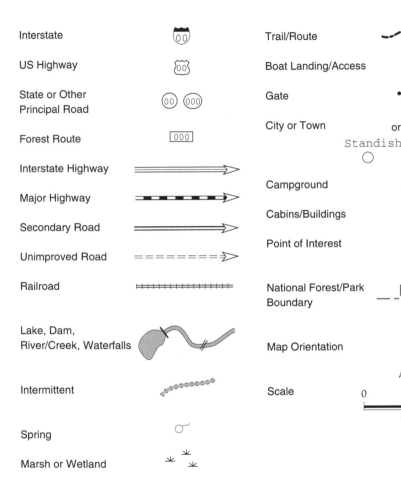

Interstate

US Highway

State or Other
Principal Road

Forest Route

Interstate Highway

Major Highway

Secondary Road

Unimproved Road

Railroad

Lake, Dam,
River/Creek, Waterfalls

Intermittent

Spring

Marsh or Wetland

Trail/Route

Boat Landing/Access

Gate

City or Town   or

Standish   Standish

Campground

Cabins/Buildings

Point of Interest

National Forest/Park
Boundary

Map Orientation   N

Scale   0   0.5   1

Miles

A Century of Trout

The Angler

With greenheart rod in hand, the angler crouches behind the granite boulder and casts the bait—a hellgrammite on a thin wire hook—up into the run. Clusters of blossoming laurel, each white flower perfectly striped with pink, nod above the frothing cataract. Framing the laurel are butts of huge hemlock and their feathery tops form a green cathedral over the stream. At the rapid's tail, the water slows, eddying and turning dark behind a ledge that juts into the pool. The cast is good, and the current carries the bait into the hole where a moment later, the angler feels a tug. With a deft flip of the rod, he pulls the fish, a gaily colored brook trout of six inches or so, from the pool and slips the fish through the top of his wicker creel onto the bed of ferns that cradles a dozen others. He rebaits and casts again, eagerly anticipating the congratulations of his camp mates for catching the most fish this day. A creel of 30 ought to do it, he says to himself, as another eager brook trout takes the bait.

The Mogul

Stretching across the shoal, the log and stone dam is a marvel. Behind it pools a smooth and tranquil lake, rippled by a faint breeze that flutters the leaves of white birch along the shore. Below the dam is the new mill where wool will be spun into yarn and then woven into cloth for blankets and coarse yardgoods from which the trousers and jackets of lumbermen will be cut. The mill will employ many in the town and others nearby whose hardscrabble farms no longer sustain a family. With a mighty tug, the chairman of the board pulls the lever that opens the gate allowing a mighty current to sluice down the race and across the veins of turbine to drive the mill. A generation later, the crest of the dam would be raised. Dynamos would be installed to convert the mechanical energy from the water-spun turbine into electricity to power new looms. And another board chairman would throw another lever, this time a breaker, that would release new power to the plant. After accepting congratulations from the mayor and other of the growing city's leaders, he would then board his railroad car for the overnight run to northern New Brunswick, to fish where salmon still ran in unfettered rivers.

The Farmer

At first, the rains of early summer were welcome. The corn was in and coming up. Spring, though, had been dry. Sure, the plow bit deep and the rows were long and straight from fence to fence, down across the swale in the middle of the field and back up the other side. He had put as much of his bluff country farm in corn as he had land. Corn was as good as cash, though not as good as it had been. Now, standing on the porch of his white frame house he looked west

1

across the prairie, he saw yet another line of dark clouds rolling toward his farm. This was troubling. Mud clung to his gum-rubber boots this morning as he checked the corn, and he noticed that the creek under the bridge was running bank-full and light brown, on the verge of another flood.

In the twentieth century, the economy of the country was based primarily on extraction of natural resources, agriculture, and manufacturing. The sporting tradition was grounded in consumption of wildlife, a heritage of hunting and gathering with roots reaching all the way back to the decks of those caravels that carried the first settlers to the New World. We claimed dominion over all things, and we were surprised that each, in turn, became exhausted. It is too easy to blame anglers who killed 50 trout in a day, the farmers and loggers whose plows and saws stripped soil-retaining plants from the land and allowed silt to suffocate trout in creeks and rivers they feed, and the moguls who dammed the rivers and used them to power mills and then carry away foul by-products of manufacturing. We bought their produce and products and invested in their companies. We sought fish and game as if it were ours by divine right, and chuckled up our sleeves at the valiant efforts of wardens who attempted to enforce seasons and creel limits.

It wasn't until the middle of this century—when ducks were nearly all shot, salmon next to extinct, and wild trout close to gone—that individuals acting in the tradition of Aldo Leopold took stock of what was happening. They realized that conservation was not a matter of dumping hatchery raised trout in streams plagued by pollution and erosion. That was the first lesson, and more were to follow, many of them conceived in the living room of George and Helen Griffith's comfortable old log house overlooking the Holy Waters of Michigan's Au Sable. The first meeting, on July 18, 1959, of what would become Trout Unlimited got off to a rather inauspicious beginning. Of 60 anglers invited, only 16 showed up—and some of those were summer guests who'd tagged along out of curiosity with their hosts. Still it was enough to get the job done. Vic Beresford, deposed editor of *Michigan Out-of-Doors,* was hired for the princely sum of $350 per month as half-time executive director. With $815 in the bank, Griffith at the helm, and Beresford spreading the word, TU took off like a rocket.

A year later, nascent TU had 175 members and its first chapter—Illinois—outside Michigan. Its board of scientific advisors considered questions and recommended solutions on everything from stream improvement to special regulations and protection for wild trout. In 1964, TU's North American Trout Management Policy was adopted. It was a landmark document because it postulated that the keys to effective management are trout and their habitats rather than only attempting to regulate the behavior of anglers. TU began to flex its considerable political muscle. Concerned that a proposed Bureau of Reclamation dam would flood ten miles of Montana's Big Hole—a fine trout fishery—TU fought the proposal and it was killed. TU chapters cropped up in other states, and legions of volunteers began taking to streams to stabilize banks, install needed structure, and improve flow over prime spawning areas. At TU's urging, states began to phase out the stocking of hatchery-reared fish in streams that could support wild trout populations.

The '70s saw TU come of age. It was among the first organizations to propose a total ban on high-seas fishing for Atlantic salmon, and it stepped up advocacy for "catch and release," a conservation measure championed by Lee Wulff and other legendary coldwater anglers. It fought and lost battles to halt the construction of Tellico Dam on the Little Tennessee and a dam on the Teton River in Idaho, prime waters for threatened native cutthroat. The Teton Dam collapsed, but Tellico Dam stands as a monument to environmental folly. Not built was a proposed dam that would have flooded Paradise Valley of the Yellowstone above Livingston, one of the last free-flowing rivers in the country. TU battled that project and continues to promote preservation of the Yellowstone.

Grassroots lobbying and continuing habitat improvement took center stage during the 1980s. The Mellon Foundation gave TU $300,000 to underwrite Embrace-A-Stream, which provides small grants to chapters to support local stream enhancement projects. On the national level, at the urging of the Sport Fishing Institute, TU, and others, Congress passed the Wallop-Breaux Amendment to the Federal Aid in Sport Fish Restoration Act. The national organization, following the Colorado state council's lead, entered into a partnership with the USDA Forest Service to enhance coldwater fisheries. The agreement is the model for future working relationships with the Bureau of Land Management and Bureau of Recreation. And during the 90s, TU moved more forcefully into the international sphere with support for a treaty between the United States and Canada to protect Pacific salmon from overharvest and agreement with the All Russian Union of Hunters and Fishermen for scientific and recreational exchange.

Relicensing of hydroelectric projects became a major issue in the early 1990s. Victories on the Clyde in Vermont—where a permit to rebuild a dam washed out in a torrential storm was rescinded, thus opening the river to spawning salmon—and the pending removal of Edwards Dam on Maine's Kennebec signaled that the heretofore virtually automatic relicensing of hydroelectric projects by the Federal Energy Regulatory Commission was no longer a certainty and that environmental and economic impacts on recreational fisheries must be considered. Implemented in 1993, TU's Coldwater Conservation Fund underwrites scores of research projects that provide scientific bases for decisions regarding fisheries management. The 1990s also saw the initiation of comprehensive analysis of trout fisheries, not only in terms of the quality of habitat and ability to support wild trout, but also of the economic impacts associated with trout fishing. The first of these studies, the Home Waters Initiatives, was an in-depth assessment of the Beaver Kill, Willowemoc, and surrounding communities; the second is the Kickapoo project in Wisconsin.

While initiatives in state, national, and international venues continue, they often attract attention away from the week-in and week-out work of local chapters (nearly 500 of them) and 100,000 members. Many members gather on Saturday mornings laboring alongside regional staff of state departments of natural resources to clean up stream banks, hammer together cribs that will become lunker structures, and otherwise improve the quality of streams. Members work with schools, providing mini-aquariums where salmon fry are raised before the students stock them in local rivers. They publish stream guides to raise money for habitat projects, and run banquets where everyone goes home a winner. And they forge partnerships with state, agricultural and national organizations to solve specific problems that plague local streams.

The last half of the twentieth century has been good for coldwater fisheries, and the future—with a couple of exceptions—looks bright. Cooperative efforts such as the Home Waters Initiatives are bringing together diverse economic and recreational interests to preserve and enhance the quality of a number of watersheds and the fisheries they host. Other collaborations such as that forged by the Henry's Fork Foundation to balance water rights among angling and agricultural interests, a model partnership, are extremely promising. Cooperation and collaboration are on the upswing and are proving more effective than the old paradigm of contention and competition. That policy leaders are beginning to understand the regional economic impact of coldwater fisheries has moved their preservation and enhancement from the single-issue perspective of the angler to a broader question of jobs and communities.

Fishing for trout has burgeoned in the waning years of this century. The number of anglers is increasing daily and placing phenomenal pressure on streams and their trout. Given the relative affluence of the past 25 years, more anglers are seeking second or vacation homes along prime trout waters, resulting in exploding development and degradation of the very habitat they seek to enjoy. And some anglers, new to fishing, come to it with the same competitive spirit that they bring to sporting clays or racquetball. Public access to streams is increasingly limited, though states and local TU chapters are working diligently and effectively to secure easements.

For the past few decades, the future of trout fishing has been largely a matter of enlightened public policy, forged by the advocacy of TU, the Federation of Fly Fishers, and a number of other organizations. This will continue, of course, because new challenges arise every day, and only through vigilance can we and our partners preserve hard-won gains. We must continue to focus our efforts on protection of our watersheds because stewardship of land is the key to the quality of water that flows in the streams. We must redouble efforts to ensure that, while safeguarded against flooding, streams and rivers are free flowing allowing the unfettered migration and spawning of native species. And we must do more to encourage the establishment of wild and native fish as the foundation of sport fisheries. TU plans to move forward along these broad vectors as it enters the new millenium.

Yet, underlying issues of politics and policy, is the behavior of us individual anglers. To a large degree, the future of trout and salmon fishing lies in the hands of the anglers—much as it did at the opening of the 1900s. Anglers who trespass on posted land, who continue to fish when waters are too low and too warm, who wade through spawning beds, who ignore creel and season limits, and who refuse to respect the rights of other anglers, do more to jeopardize the sport than those who pollute the streams. How we demonstrate the ethic of angling today determines the attitudes and beliefs of future generations of anglers and of those who control access to the waters we love to fish. In the mid-1900s we focused on preserving wild trout. In the twenty-first century, through education programs such as those initiated by TU, the Atlantic Salmon Federation, the Federation of Fly Fishers, and others, and through our instruction of our daughters and sons, we have an opportunity—more than that, a responsibility—to create a culture of ethical angling that is worthy of the streams and the wild trout and salmon we have all worked so hard to preserve.

How to Use this Guide

The profiles in this book are arranged and numbered in a geographical order; that is, the rivers are grouped with other streams that flow in the same TU regions.

Each profile opens with a few basic facts to give the reader, at a glance, the primary characteristics of the stream. This is the briefest of shorthand, filed under the following headings:

Location: Where the river flows.

Short take: A description, in 50 words or less, of why the stream is worth visiting with a rod and reel.

Type of stream: General character of the water, but it may change from spring creek, to freestone, to tailwater over the length of its run.

Angling methods: Most streams are open to use of spinning, casting or fly-fishing tackle. Bait and lures may be used, but often streams include mileage that's specially regulated for one technique or the other. And this changes from year to year. Read current state regulations carefully.

Species: The kind of trout you'll find in the stream, from brookies, to cutthroat, to browns, to all the rest.

Access: How easy is it to make your way to the water's edge? On some rivers, like the Middle Fork of the Salmon in Idaho, little of the river can be reached without a long float trip or a hike of exhaustive proportions. It's difficult to access to say the least. Other rivers are so easy, you can park, rig your rod, and be fishing in less than five minutes.

Season: Some rivers are open for fishing all year but only fish well during specific periods. Others have closed seasons. Fishing is permitted year-round on many rivers in this book, but technique and creel limits may vary. Check current fishing regulations before you buy a license.

Nearest tourist services: The closest place to find supplies and services that you'll need during a fishing vacation.

Handicapped access: We have made a modest attempt to note which streams have some access for physically challenged anglers. It is a difficult topic because the nature and impact of physical handicaps varies so widely from individual to individual. While some streams such as the Beaver Kill and Willowemoc boast extensive and well defined facilities for the physically challenged, and you'll find others on Henry's Fork and the Upper Madison, special ramps and platforms are largely non-existent on many trout streams. However, many whose physical condition permits can enjoy fishing from drift boats. Other wheel-chair bound anglers may find the boat launching ramps or low flat grassy banks offer angling opportunities. The best sources of information for any stream are the tackle shops and state fisheries departments that serve specific watersheds.

Closest TU chapter: With nearly 100,000 members and close to 500 chapters, TU is a vast network of anglers who are committed to coldwater fishing. Many of the profiles contain the name of a nearby chapter, but because presidents of the chapters change with some frequency, I did not include addresses. Those, along with phone numbers and addresses are readily available on TU's website, www.tu.org. If you're thinking about fishing one of the streams in this book, call the local TU chapter for first-hand, up-to-date, and accurate information.

Along with each profile is a map showing the most popular reaches of each stream, the roads that will get you there, and directions to nearby cities and towns of importance. These maps provide a general view, but more detailed maps are available in regional guides, USGS quadrangles and similar topos, from the Forest Service and state agencies, and tackle stores. Maps change: unpaved roads leading to favorite mileage are opened or closed depending on ownership, aging bridges are sometimes washed out and not rebuilt, tracks may be taken up from railroad rights-of-way creating trails that may by open to vehicles. Once you get to the closest town, ask in the tackle shop for the best map, or go to the county seat and buy a county highway map—one of the best (and least well-known) sources of accurate info about local roads. Atlases like DeLorme's—the map people in Maine — are also very useful tools.

At the close of each chapter is a list of sources for more information: fly and tackle shops or outfitters who can help with your **Gearing up;** chambers of commerce, tourism offices, and visitor centers that can provide information about **Accommodations;** and **Books** that can provide more detailed information about the streams we touch on here. Check with the publishers of the books; revised editions and new titles appear almost daily. These referrals must not be construed as an endorsement of those businesses or products listed by Trout Unlimited. Rather, they are offered as references which should make your visit to each stream more enjoyable.

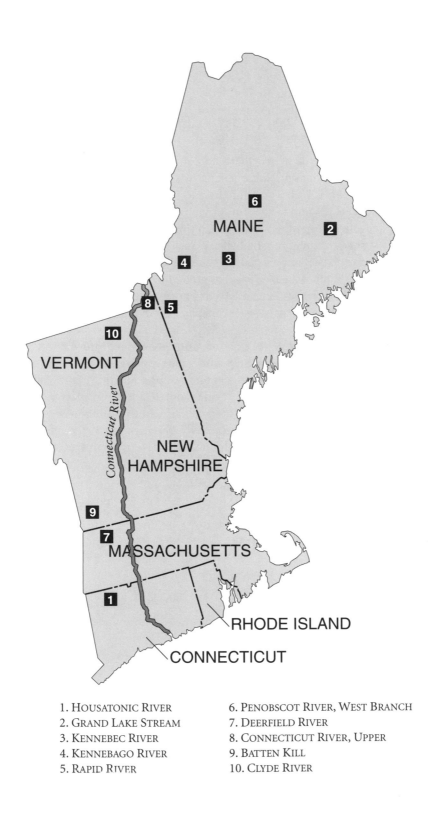

MAINE

2

6

4 3

8 5

10

VERMONT

Connecticut River

NEW
HAMPSHIRE

9

7

MASSACHUSETTS

1

RHODE ISLAND

CONNECTICUT

1. HOUSATONIC RIVER
2. GRAND LAKE STREAM
3. KENNEBEC RIVER
4. KENNEBAGO RIVER
5. RAPID RIVER

6. PENOBSCOT RIVER, WEST BRANCH
7. DEERFIELD RIVER
8. CONNECTICUT RIVER, UPPER
9. BATTEN KILL
10. CLYDE RIVER

NEW ENGLAND

CONNECTICUT

MAINE

MASSACHUSETTS

NEW HAMPSHIRE

VERMONT

1 HOUSATONIC RIVER

Location: Western Connecticut.
Short take: Bucolic river valley in the midst of eastern bustle. Cooperative rainbows and selective browns, but unscheduled releases from dams pose problems for fish and anglers.
Type of stream: Tailwater.
Angling methods: Fly, spin, bait.
Species: Rainbow, brown.
Access: Easy.
Season: Year-round.
Nearest tourist services: West Cornwall.
Handicapped access: None.
Closest TU chapter: Northwest Connecticut.

THE SIGN, TACKED ON AN ELM on the river says legions, "Housatonic River Trout Management Area—All Trout Must Be Returned Without Avoidable Injury."

For about nine miles, from the bridge carrying Routes 112 and 7 across the Housy near Lookout Point downstream to Cornwall Bridge, the river is a rarity among the rare: a marvelous trout stream flowing through a tranquil and historic farming valley within an hour's drive of a quarter of the population of the United States. To be sure, the Housatonic would not be the fishery it is were it not for PCBs, GE, and TU. The PCBs (polychlorinated bihenyls) spilled into the upper river from the General Electric plant near Pittsfield, Massachusetts. The spill occurred in the 1960s, and it rendered all fish downstream inedible. At the time, the Connecticut Division of Environmental Protection closed the river to all fishing, but a few years later at the petition of TU and others, the DEP began to manage the stretch downstream from the Falls Village Dam as a catch and release coldwater fishery. It flourished beyond expectations. In the mid-1980s, one could fish its gentle, bouldry course, and reasonably expect to tussle with a 24-inch brown.

Then came the late 1980s. The river ran low and warm. Trout took refuge in spring seeps and the mouths of coldwater tributaries (where fishing is *verboten* during July and August). But heavy releases of warm water from upstream dams, releases that can raise the water level in the trout management area by a foot to 18 inches, flush trout out of their sanctuaries, and in effect, cook them. Fish kills were and are common. Local TUers, serving as members of the Housatonic Coalition, are fighting pro-forma relicensing of the two offending hydro projects, arguing for run-of-river as opposed to peak flow releases. By maintaining pool level of the impoundments and then discharging only as much water as enters the lakes, the Housatonic will receive a more consistent flow and the trout habitat will be stabilized. The EPA is also in the preliminary process of developing a remedy for the PCBs in the upper river.

HOUSATONIC RIVER

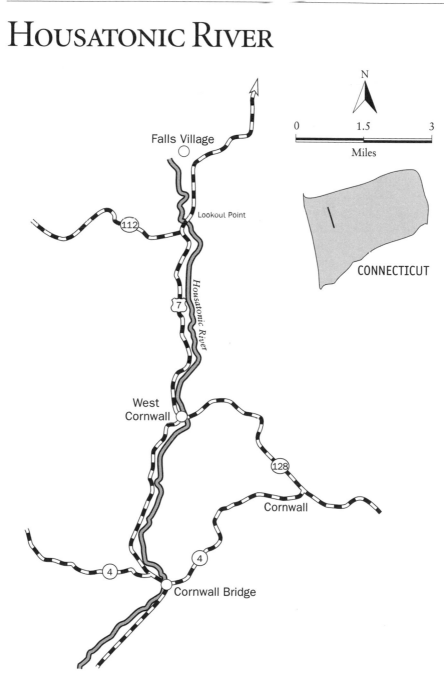

Route 7, a heavily traveled north-south byway, follows the trout management Area waters. Above the town of Cornwall Bridge, the highway runs through Housatonic Meadows State Park, which provides some access to the west bank of the river. Route 128 crosses a covered bridge into West Cornwall. Just before reaching the railroad tracks, a small road that's paved at first but rapidly becomes dirt, leads north and south along the river's east bank. From this road you'll find access to such famous holes as Push 'em Up Pool, the Doctor's Hole, and the Elms. To the south are Garbage (natural, not human, flotsam), Horse, Carse Brook, Cellar, Rainbow Run, and the list continues.

In the main, the Housatonic's bottom is of limestone rock, and, for a small river, it is easily wadeable. To some, it resembles a western stream. Browns, generally in the 10- to 15-inch class, constitute the bulk of the fishery, though rainbows up to 18 inches are also encountered. Blue-Winged Olives produce from spring through fall; green and brown drakes come off in the Horse Hole in late May and early June. You'll also find tricos and sulphurs. Caddis, such a staple on other streams, are limited to May and mid-June on the Housy. Unlike most trout management waters, bait fishing is permitted, logic being that if you can't eat the fish anyway, what's the difference how you catch them? A 3.5-mile section of fly-fishing-only water runs from the Meat Hole down to Cornwall Bridge. Bed-and-breakfasts and country inns provide nice alternatives to motel chains, and one of the better river-front Bed-and-Breakfasts—Housatonic Anglers— is run by angler Rob Nicholas and his wife Nell.

RESOURCES

Gearing up: Housatonic River Outfitters, Rt. 128 at the Bridge, West Cornwall, CT 06796; 860-672-1010. Wilderness Shop, 85 West St., Litchfield CT 06759; 860-567-5905.

Accommodations: Northwest Connecticut Chamber of Commerce, 333 Kennedy Dr., Torrington, CT 06790; 860-482-6586.

Books: *Great Rivers & Great Hatches*, Charles Meck and Greg Hoover, Stackpole, Mechanicsburg, PA, 1992.

2 GRAND LAKE STREAM

Location: Eastern Maine.
Short take: Popular for landlocked salmon from April to mid-June and mid-September to mid-October. Otherwise, a fine brook trout river.
Type of stream: Freestone, tailwater.
Angling methods: Fly.
Species: Landlocked salmon, brook.
Access: Easy.
Season: April to mid-October.
Nearest tourist services: Grand Lake Stream.
Handicapped access: None on the stream, but a pier above the dam provides wheelchair-bound anglers a reasonable chance of hooking a landlocked salmon in the first two weeks of October.

SHORT BUT OH, SO SWEET. That sums up Grand Lake Stream, a three-and-a-half mile fly-fishing-only run from West Grand Lake to Big Lake, known for its marvelous stocks of landlocked salmon and brook trout. Not only does this piece of water provide nice-sized fish—trout of a pound or two and salmon, occasionally, of three pounds-plus—but public access is ample and anglers of varying skill can find suitable beats.

As far as landlocked salmon are concerned, Grand Lake Stream has two distinct seasons. Opening on April 1, smelt imitations including streamers and tube flies fished with sink-tip lines or intermediate lines and a short, three-foot section of 3X tippet will produce. Salmon are foraging on needle smelt, about two inches long. Fish are holding close to the bottom, and it's imperative that you get down to them, but adding weight is prohibited. This early in the season, the typical drill is to cast across, throw a mend, and work the fly as slowly as you dare among the cobble and occasional boulders where fish lie. Since water temperatures may be in the 40s, early season fish may not be overly aggressive with their take. Rest assured; you'll know when you have a hook-up.

As the season progresses toward May, fish become more active but less interested in streamers. Bead head Prince, Hare's Ear and stonefly nymphs—even Brassies—work well. Bigger is definitely not better. Often the #18 Brassie fished on a dropper behind a #12 bead head Pheasant Tail, is the fly that takes the fish. By mid- to late May, action reaches the top of the water column as the first of the Dark Hendricksons and Blue-Winged Olives appear. Adams is always a popular and effective pattern on this river. Three days of good sunshine, which puts a real damper on mayfly hatches, brings out stoneflies.

By mid-June, water temperature in West Grand Lake is rising into the 60s and when it reaches 64 degrees F, salmon return to the depths of Big Lake. Still in the river, though, are brook trout, and they provide gay sport throughout the summer.

GRAND LAKE STREAM

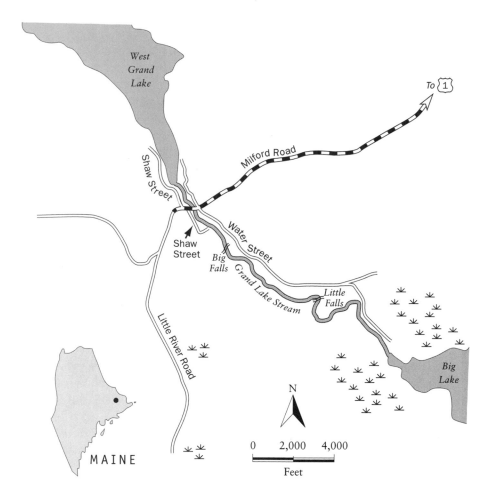

West
Grand
Lake

To 1

Shaw Street

Milford Road

Shaw
Street

Water Street

Big
Falls

Grand Lake Stream

Little
Falls

Little River Road

Big
Lake

MAINE

N

0   2,000   4,000

Feet

RICHARD V. PROCOPIO

Landlocked salmon in the three-pound class draw anglers to Grand Lake Stream.

Caddis, of course, play a major part in the trout diet. Elk Hair Caddis are good in summer and for fall you'll want to add little black caddis in sizes #16 to #18 to your box. Ants and hoppers—particularly in late July and August—attract attention as do Wulffs of various flavors. Dropping temperatures in late August and early September bring landlocked salmon back into the flowage. They'll hit Yellow Sallies from #14 to #16, and caddis from #12 to #20.

When the river volume is steady at 400 or so cfs, fishing is at its best. In many places, especially during autumn when the river is at its clearest, you can see salmon in their lies and can cast to them. If the water is running above 800 cfs, you'll find better sport fishing the Big Lake for smallmouth or nearby ponds for brook trout.

Recognized as an outstanding sport fishery for more than a century, the river is divided into a series of named beats and pools. Just downstream from the dam (fishing within 150 feet of it is prohibited) is Upham's Corner. Here you're likely to find Bob Upham, well known in these parts for his excellent streamer ties. Water below the dam but above the bridge fishes best in April. Hatchery Pool is known for its easy access and consequently may be crowded. A better bet is the run along the Wall. If you're the first to fish it in the morning, the odds favor your success. In the middle of the upper half of the stream are three pools that seem to be most productive in May: Evening Pool, The Glide, and Gowdy's Point—so named because Curt Gowdy would fish all day in that one spot. Fishing is good above Big Falls, a stony 10-foot or so drop below Cable Point. Little Falls constricts the river at the top of the lower section, but then the river broadens through The Bathtub and The Meadows—here the approach is swampy, but the bottom is firm gravel—before entering the upper reaches of Big Lake. These lower beats can be good in mid- to late June, and again in mid-August into September, when the first waves of landlocked salmon return to the river. At both times during the year, fish the edges of the heaviest current.

A road runs along the north side of the river and numerous paths provide access from the south. Most of the stream is obscured by a mature forest of 100-year-old firs with stands of birch here and there on the fringes. Much of the river, however, is open. If you must fish when the sun is high, you'll find trout collected in shadows cast by the few overhanging trees.

RESOURCES

Gearing up: Pine Tree Store, Grand Lake Stream, ME 04637; 207-796-5027. Northeast Anglers Inc., Gary D. Scavette, Registered Maine Guide, 551 Atlantic Highway, Northport, Maine 04849; 800-558-7658.

Accommodations: Weatherby's, Box 69, Grand Lakes Stream, ME 04637; 207-796-5558.

3 KENNEBEC RIVER

Location: Central Maine.
Short take: Primarily smallmouth water. Upper section below Moosehead known for landlocked salmon and brook trout. TU-championed removal of Edwards Dam at Augusta will aid in restoring small Atlantic salmon runs.
Type of stream: Freestone with many dams.
Angling methods: Fly, spin, bait.
Species: Brook, brown, and rainbow trout, landlocked and Atlantic salmon, smallmouth.
Access: Easy.
Season: April through mid-October.
Nearest tourist services: Waterville, Fairfield.
Handicapped access: None.
Closest TU chapter: Kennebec Valley.

THE BIGGEST NEWS ON THE KENNEBEC is the pending removal of Edwards Dam, a precedent-setting effort to restore migratory coldwater fisheries. After several years of intense work by the Kennebec Valley Chapter of TU and a coalition of allied state and federal organizations, the Federal Energy Regulatory Commission recommended that Edwards Dam, built in 1837, be eliminated to enhance spawning of nine anadromous species including Atlantic salmon and sea-run brown trout. Much of the credit for the effort rests with Steve Brooke, a former president of the local TU chapter who coordinated the work of the coalition leading to the planned removal of the dam in 1999.

In 1997, the Federal Energy Regulatory Commission recommended that the dam be removed after its owner, Edwards Manufacturing Company of Augusta, refused to ante up $8.9 million to install the fishway proposed by the U.S. Fish and Wildlife Service. Taking out the dam and implementing related fish restoration projects are expected to cost $7.25 million, which will come from Bath Iron Works, one of the nation's primary naval contractors, and the Kennebec Hydro Developers group, a coalition of operators of dams upstream from Augusta.

Draining more than 6,000 square miles, the Kennebec was a rich Atlantic salmon fishery during the eighteenth and early nineteenth centuries. Indeed today, the river sees small runs. With the removal of Edwards Dam, 17 miles of the river will be open to migratory fish, and biologists believe that spawning can only increase. Still, the river is a long way from becoming a first-class salmon river, though its upper reaches offer excellent fishing for *salmo salar*'s landlocked cousin. The significant fishery of rainbows and browns below Shawmut Dam should also improve after Edwards Dam is removed.

Come spring and fall, the three-mile East Outflow from Moosehead Lake to Indian Pond is one of the top landlocked salmon fisheries in the state. This section is accompanied by a road on the west and a path on the east. While the water is

KENNEBEC RIVER

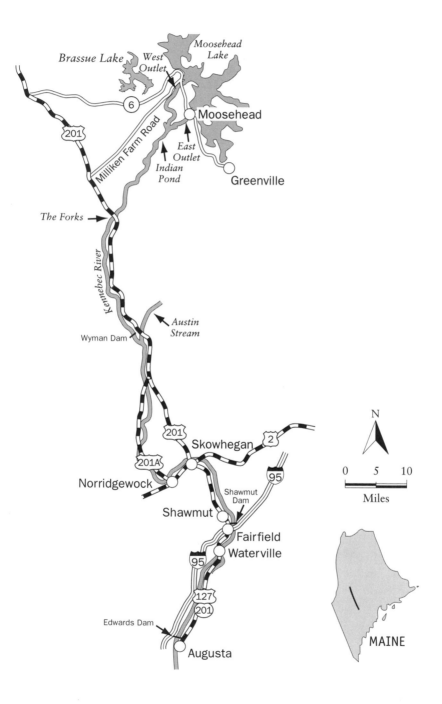

Brassue Lake

West Outlet

Moosehead Lake

Moosehead

6

201

Milliken Farm Road

East Outlet

Indian Pond

Greenville

The Forks

Kennebec River

Austin Stream

Wyman Dam

201

2

Skowhegan

N

0 5 10

Miles

95

201A

Norridgewock

Shawmut Dam

Shawmut

95

Fairfield

Waterville

127

201

Edwards Dam

Augusta

MAINE

classic pool, boulders, runs, and pockets, levels are controlled by releases from the dam at Moosehead Lake. Below 2,000 cfs, the river is fishable, but above that a canoe becomes a better bet than wading. If you're floating the river, pay special attention to class III rapids at Beech Pool and a mile or so farther down at Ledge Falls. The prudent angler portages.

The section between Ledge Falls and Indian Pond is known for good-sized brook trout and the half-mile above the pond is worth special attention. To the west, a second and slower outlet runs from Moosehead Lake to Indian Pond. This is better smallmouth water, though some brook trout and landlocked salmon are occasionally caught. The best time to fish these waters for landlocked salmon is early in the season, as soon after opening day as you can make it. Standard streamer patterns will work here, but you'll need to dredge them along the bottom. Later, as the water warms, salmon will be more apt to go for smaller flies, particularly bead headed nymphs of one sort or another. These fish are not really choosy.

Warming in Indian Pond, the Kennebec becomes more of a smallmouth stream. To be sure, a few landlocked salmon move up from impoundments to the tailwaters of the next dam upstream where they can be caught with conventional fly or spinning gear (depending on the law, which changes with enough frequency you'll want to read the latest regs before you fish). Brook trout hold near the mouths of mountain streams such as Cold and Moxie which enter the Kennebec a couple of miles north of The Forks. Running alongside the river south of The Forks is Route 201, but it's of little interest to coldwater anglers until you reach Wyman Dam, about two miles north of Bingham.

Best fished from boat or canoe, the tailwater of the dam holds rainbows, one of the few self-sustaining populations in Maine. The secret is not only cold water released from the dam, but the presence of an icy feeder, Austin Stream, where the 'bows spawn. There's no wading below the dam, but Old Railroad Road follows Austin Stream up to the height of land between the Austin and Moxie drainages. Below Bingham, the river is divided by a series of cobbly islands with swift runs on either side. Good-sized rainbows, as well as landlocked salmon, are taken here early in the season and also in September.

The river slows below Wyman. Brown trout cohabitate with ubiquitous smallmouth, and a canoe float from riffle to riffle can be quite productive. Most success will be had with nymphs and streamers fished deep. Below Shawmut Dam above Fairfield, fishing for browns picks up dramatically thanks to the tailwater, inflows from the Sebasticook, an uncommonly high number of baitfish, and more good habitat improvement work from the Kennebec Valley Chapter of TU.

As for patterns for the Kennebec, Mike Holt of Fly Fishing Only, a trout shop in Fairfield just upstream from Waterville, puts it this way: "There's nothing unusual about the hatches on the Kennebec." Blue-Winged Olives are the staple fly on the river. Hatches begin in April and continue sporadically, generally in periods of heavy cloud cover, into September. Little black stoneflies, best fished as #12 to #16 nymphs, appear in May and continue throughout the season. Quill Gordons begin coming off in June and July brings little back caddis and some Hendricksons. March browns, yellow stones, and light cahills finally make it in late July, and there are even some tan caddis in September. Woolly Buggers, Gold Ribbed Hare's Ears, Zug Bugs, Tellicos, black and brown stones, as well as Mickey Finns and Black Ghosts all belong in an angler's fly box. Spin fishers will find inch-and-a-half crank baits, Mepps, and Panther Martins all to be good bets where legal.

Most anglers arrive over-rodded for the Kennebec. A 9-foot, 6- is more than adequate. A sink-tip line will pay big dividends in spring. Spin fishers will find ultra-light gear hard to beat.

RESOURCES

Gearing up: Fly Fishing Only, 230 Main St., Fairfield, ME 04937; 207-453-6242; www.maineflyfish.com. Charlie's Log Cabin, 5 Pleasant St., Oakland, ME 04963; 207-465-2451.

Accommodations: Mid-Maine Chamber of Commerce, 1 Post Office Sq., Waterville, ME 04901; 207-873-3315; www.mid-mainechamber.com.

4 KENNEBAGO RIVER

Location: Northwestern Maine.
Short take: A very good brook trout and salmon fishery throughout the season, but you'll have to walk a ways to reach the river.
Type of stream: Freestone, with dams on lower section.
Angling methods: Fly, spin.
Species: Brook, brown, landlocked salmon.
Access: Limited.
Season: April 1 through September 30.
Nearest tourist services: Rangeley.
Handicapped access: None.

SOME RIVERS ARE DEMANDING. They roust you out of bed at "Oh:dark:thirty" and have you in the car and pounding the highway to reach the water by first light. Not so with the Kennebago north of Maine's Rangeley Lakes. The river fishes consistently throughout the day. In wet years, when there's good run-off, the landlocked salmon for which this stream is justly noted will stay in the river all year. However, if summers are hot and flows are low, come July, salmon will move out of the main channel into the depths of the closest, coolest lake. Even then, you'll find brook trout, though they may be concentrated near springs or coldwater seeps. After summer heat breaks, usually by mid-August, trout return to the main stream, and salmon will follow a week or two later. During summer and fall, spates of rain will trigger action.

The Kennebago can be divided into two large sections and a short tail. Rising in a handful of ponds between White Cap and Snow Mountains near the Maine-Quebec border, the river flows about a dozen miles through a riffly, pool-and-pocket course interspersed with long stretches of boggy wetland until it reaches Little Kennebago Lake above Otter Camps on Tim Pond Road. This upper section carries wild brook trout and some landlocked salmon, but it is a relatively modest fishery when compared to the section below Kennebago Lake. A graded logging road, maintained for the use of camp and lodge owners, follows the course of the upper section. Only the lower four miles are accessible.

There's also a road along the middle 10-mile section of the river, but it too is locked off below Little Kennebago Lake. Most likely, you'll park at a gate four miles north of Route 16 and walk in. Lack of access to the runs and classic pools of this middle section limits fishing pressure; here, if you hike in far enough, you can find solitude and tranquility. Heavy forest serves as a backdrop to stands of alder that line the river. The gradient is not nearly as steep as that of the Rapid River to the southwest. And, while the current can be heavy, in most places edges of the river afford good wading and access to a number of named pools along its route. Along with your six-weight rod, pack in a wading staff, and you're set.

KENNEBAGO RIVER

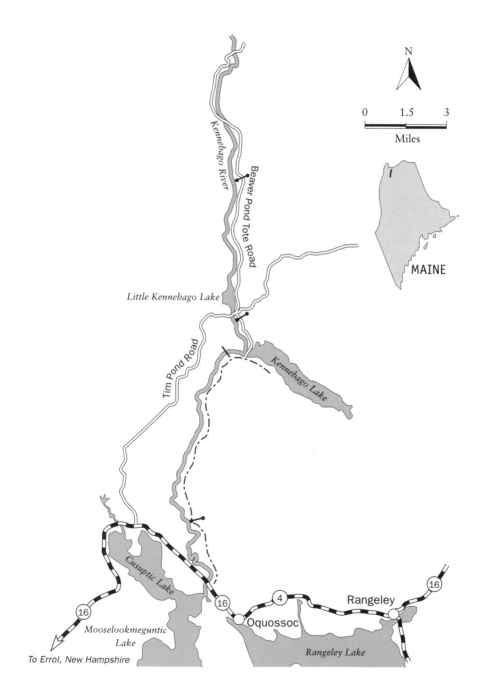

Why is the Kennebago so highly regarded as a salmon stream? First, its cold waters are relatively free of pollution. It's a tremendous nursery of salmon parr—some 15,000 per season. High (and protected) smelt populations in the lakes provide forage for juvenile salmon. Twice during the season, first in June and July, and again in September, salmon move up to the river from Cusuptic Lake. The first run does not spawn immediately, but holds in the river until fall. Also, reasonably light angling pressure and the river's catch-and-release designation limit mortality. The combination equals a fine sport fishery. Most landlocked salmon run in the 14- to 17-inch class with occasional specimens of 22 inches. Brook trout of a pound or so are common, and fish of three to five pounds are caught every year, mostly during the fall run.

The season seems long when you look at it on paper, but in fact it's quite short. Ice hangs around into May in these parts. While the season opens April 1, the fishing in the river doesn't really pick up until two months later on Memorial Day weekend. This is fly-fishing-only water. Anglers are permitted one salmon of 14 inches-plus and two trout. Both trout must be at least 10 inches long, but only one can be more than 12. Salmon fall for the Black Ghosts and similar streamers, and the Kennebago Muddler fished as an emerger just under the surface takes lots of fish. Carry #4 and #6. Woolly Buggers also produce. The river also spawns an excellent green drake hatch. The hatch tends to be strongest under drizzling, misty skies. A six-weight system is ideal, and carry a sink-tip line with 100 yards of backing on a reel with a smooth drag. Early in the season, shorter leaders will allow you to reach more fish. Later, as water lowers and warms, lengthen your tippet.

RESOURCES

Gearing up: Rivers Edge Sport Shop, Rt. 4, P.O. Box 347, Oquossoc, ME 04964; 207-864-5582. Rangeley Region Sport Shop, P.O. Box 1118, Rangeley ME 04970; 207-864-5615.

Accommodations: Rangeley Lakes Area Chamber of Commerce, P.O. Box 317, Rangeley, ME 04977; 207-864-5364.

5 RAPID RIVER

Location: Western Maine.
Short take: Probably the best wild, big brook trout river in the United States. Requires at least a mile's walk or hour's boat trip to reach fishable water.
Type of stream: Freestone, tailwater.
Angling methods: Fly.
Species: Brook, some landlocked salmon.
Access: Moderate to difficult.
Season: April through September.
Nearest tourist services: Rangeley, Oquossoc.
Handicapped access: None.

THIS MAY BE THE SHORTEST and best brook trout river in the world. While only 3.2 miles long, the Rapid River consistently produces brook trout of five pounds or so. Why? Nobody, not even Forrest Bonney, state fisheries biologist, knows. He suspects the reason may have something to do with the genetic pool from which these lunkers come. Another factor may be an abundance of smelt fed into the river from Richardson Lake. And eliminating ice fishing at the Big Hole, where the Rapid discharges into Lake Umbagog on Maine's border with New Hampshire, may also have had an impact. Before the stream was designated as catch-and-release water in 1996, the average size of Rapid's brookies was declining and had dropped to three pounds. Now, two years later, the average is back up. If you want to wrestle square-tails of near-Labrador size on fly fishing tackle in the lower 48, here's the place to do it.

A bumpy trek over 13 miles of gravel road or an equally interminable boat ride down Richardson Lake brings you to the headwaters of this pristine river. If you drive the road, you'll park at a locked gate and then hoof it another mile or so to the river. The boat will take you directly to Middle Dam and you can start fishing from there. You can also boat in from Lake Umbagog.

At the outflow of Richardson Lake at Middle Dam, the Rapid lives up to its name. Here the river crashes and brawls over ledges and boulders of granite, cascading into deep pools, before swirling a time or two and moving on. This is classic big pocket water; some of it is wadeable and some of it is not. While rafters occasionally float the river (and some discharges are timed to accommodate floaters, especially on weekends from mid-July to mid-August), few anglers try to fish it from canoe or drift boat. Under most conditions, a kayak would be lucky to make it through the turbulent drops.

About a quarter of the way down the river, the river slows at Pond in the River, a wide spot of about 500 acres impounded by Lower Dam. The mileage just upstream and downstream from the dam provides outstanding fishing, particularly early in the season and again in September. Not to be overlooked is the lower end of the river. Anglers in the know will boat up the river's channel from Umbagog to Cedar

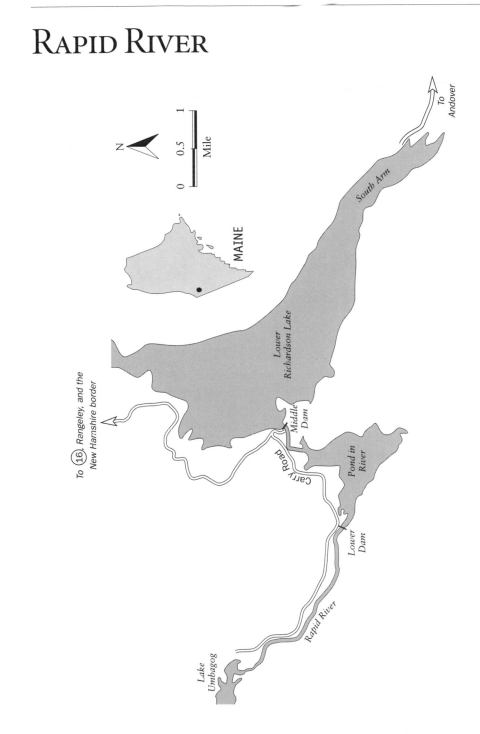

RAPID RIVER

To Andover

South Arm

MAINE

N

1

0.5

0

Mile

Lower
Richardson Lake

To (16), Rangeley, and the
New Hamshire border

Middle
Dam

Carry Road

Pond in
River

Lower
Dam

Rapid River

Lake
Umbagog

RICHARD V. PROCOPIO

The Rapid River is a proven and dependable fishery for trophy brook trout.

Campsites and cast for brook trout, salmon, and smallmouth (three to six pounds!). The action is good from mid-May to mid-June and from mid-August to the end of September.

The quality of fishing on the Rapid River is dependent on water flows; 800 cfs is ideal. If you can time your trip so that you arrive just as the water has been reduced, the fishing will pick up, says Bonney. On the other hand, fish take a couple of days to establish new holds when water changes levels. Though the river stays reasonably cool throughout the six-month season, fishing slows after the Fourth of July and picks up again in mid-August. Streamers, primarily Gray and Black Ghosts, are very effective here as are caddis patterns. Though stands of pine, spruce, and fir hem in the river, few anglers here have taken to two-handed Spey rods. A six-weight, nine-footer seems to do fine for most folks, though if you're bent on tossing streamers of #2 or #4, a ten-foot 8-weight might be welcome.

While some rivers face a series of threats from development, pollution, and over-fishing, the Rapid River seems to be in pretty good shape, thanks in part to baseline river studies underwritten, in part, by TU's Coldwater Conservation Fund. Recent agreements with the Federal Energy Regulatory Commission have resulted in the establishment of adequate minimum flows for the river, though there's considerable pressure from rafters and kayakers for absurdly high summer releases. Union Water Power, which controls dams on the Rapid, understands the delicate balance between its need to provide enough water to insure the viability of paper companies downstream in Berlin, New Hampshire, and the need to maintain the viability of the Rangeley Lake fishery, which is an increasingly important element in the economy of the region. Union has a reputation as a good neighbor, according to folks who live in the region, and that's refreshingly unusual among dam operators. Most recently, Union has entered into a new conservation easement that prohibits additional development and permits angler access to a length of ten rods on each side of the river. How long is a rod? About 16 feet. In Maine, the King's English meets no bounds.

RESOURCES

Gearing up: Rivers Edge Sport Shop, Rt. 4, P.O. Box 347, Oquossoc ME 04964; 207-864-5582. Rangeley Region Sport Shop, P.O. Box 1118, Rangeley ME 04970; 207-864-5615.

Accommodations: Rangeley Lakes Region Chamber of Commerce, P.O. Box 317, Rangeley, ME 04970; 207-864-5364.

6 Penobscot River, West Branch

Location: Central Maine near Baxter State Park.
Short take: One of Maine's premiere landlocked salmon fisheries. Holds up all season, but is best in late spring and early fall.
Type of stream: Freestone, tailwater.
Angling methods: Fly, spin.
Species: Landlocked salmon, brook.
Access: Easy to moderate.
Season: April through September.
Nearest tourist services: Millinocket.
Handicapped access: None.

WHEN A PAVED ROAD RUNS alongside a section of water no matter how beautiful, I have a tendency to thumb my nose at it. Obviously it gets hammered by too many anglers, and for me that means spooky and usually small fish. But such is not the case with the West Branch of the Penobscot River. Golden Road, a private paper company toll road, follows the valley of the West Branch for about 35 miles from the town of Millinocket to the headwaters at Ripogenus "Rip" Dam on the outflow of Ripogenus Lake. To the north, in Baxter State Park, rises Mount Katahdin, still snowcapped when the first salmon run.

Flows in the river are, of course, controlled by the Rip Dam. However, unless heavy rains have saturated the central part of the state, the river is normally fishable. Guides run McKenzie River drift boats on the West Branch so you can fish it as you would the Yellowstone when it's flowing high, wide, and handsome. Canoeists are equally at home here, picking their paths down the river and working its myriad pockets and runs. Scores of trails penetrate the forest of firs and spruce leading to the river's shore. Anglers who wade will be able to work good areas of the river more thoroughly than drift-boaters. The campground at Big Eddy plus a number of sporting lodges in the region provide accommodations for West Branch anglers. Unless you float the river, odds are you won't be alone. But the beauty of the West Branch is that there's enough water and fish to go around.

Top flight landlocked salmon fishing begins just below the dam at the head of Ripogenus Gorge. The gorge is deep and treacherous, yet in its bowels lie some of the largest salmon in the river. Hire a guide like Ian Cameron and let him run you through the rips in his reinforced raft. You'll toss through class 5 rapids on a wild, whirling ride, and you'll tail out in tan-foamed eddies where the biggest salmon in the river are apt to lie. A minimum keeper in this stretch is 26 inches, but who's counting?

PENOBSCOT RIVER, WEST BRANCH

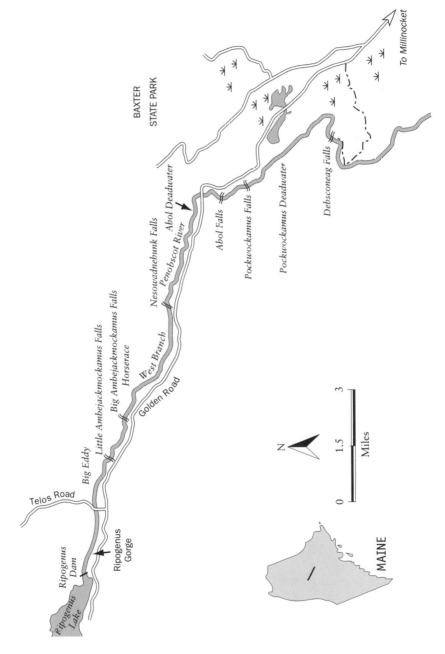

At the base of the gorge, Telos Road crosses the river and from the bridge down to Debsconeag Falls, anglers are permitted one salmon of at least 18 inches and a general limit of trout. This is artificial lure, single-hook (single point or treble) water from April 1 through August 15. After that, it's fly-fishing-only through the end of September. Park at the Telos Road bridge and make your way to the river. Probe all pockets and pools carefully. Some knowledgeable anglers like David Klausmeyer work up one side of the river fishing nymphs and caddis larvae, and then fish back down throwing streamers and caddis pupae.

No matter how densely packed the campground, don't overlook the water at Big Eddy. While you can't be certain which rock or bit of still water will hold a fish, you can rest assured that some of them do. Work it early in the morning. Below Big Eddy are Little and Big Ambejackmockamus Falls and then the Horserace, all swift pools and runs that defy access by any conveyance other than shank's mare or waterborne craft. Below the Horserace, the river pools up in the Nesowadnehunk Deadwater, which isn't dead early in the season; salmon and trout abound in its upper end at that time of year. Downstream of this long flat, the river gains speed and hustles through a series of pools and runs. The Abol Deadwater, also a misnomer, marks the end of the best section of the West Branch, though there's some trout and salmon action all the way down to Ambajejus Lake.

Fly selection here is reasonably routine. Streamers may do the trick in April, but nymphs take over toward the end of the month and hatches begin in mid-May—Blue-Winged Olives, Red Quills and Hendricksons. By the end of June you may also see some Green Drakes. Caddis are a staple of these fish, so stock up on varying hues in sizes #12 to #16 and don't overlook caddis larvae and pupae as well. Even in mid-summer, anglers who work fast currents in the center of the river will find success with traditional Maine streamer patterns: Mickey Finn, Gray Ghost, and White Ghost. Remember, these landlocked salmon are feeding, and we've got a civic responsibility to give them what they want.

The main event here is the river, and it's best fished with a 6-weight system. A floating line will handle most chores, but bringing a sink-tip or intermediate line will put you in good stead. If you tote along a canoe or belly boat, you can put it to good use in the river and access outstanding ponds for brook trout. In that case, toss in a 3-weight. Despite the paved road and pair of campgrounds, this region is fairly secluded. You're apt to see moose and bear, eagles and ospreys and, without a doubt, black flies. Maineacs will tell you that the black fly season ends in mid-June. Guys from Brooklyn will sell you a bridge. Fly dope helps.

RESOURCES

Gearing up: Maine Guide Fly Shop, Main St., Greenville, ME 04441; 207-695-2266. Eddie's Flies and Tackle, 303 Broadway, Bangor ME 04401; 800-649-3225.

Accommodations: Katahdin Area Chamber of Commerce, 1029 Central St., Millinocket, ME 04462; 207-732-4443; www.mainerec.com/millhome.

7 DEERFIELD RIVER

Location: Northwestern Massachusetts.
Short take: Fish early. Let floaters ride the crest. Fish late.
Type of stream: Tailwater.
Angling methods: Fly, spin.
Species: Brown, rainbow, occasional brook.
Access: Easy to moderate.
Season: Year-round.
Nearest tourist services: Charlemont.
Handicapped access: Limited.
Closest TU chapter: Deerfield/Millers.

IT SEEMS THAT EVERY FEW MILES of the Deerfield River carries a small hydro dam operated by Northeastern Utilities. At one time these dams, and the early nuclear generating plant near Rowe with its unslakable thirst for cooling waters, were the curse of the river. Now that the plant is closed and TU and other organizations have negotiated minimum flows for the Deerfield, the river is cooler and better habitat for stocked rainbows and browns, some as large as 26 inches. These bruisers were stocked, to be certain, but when dumped into the river they were, maybe, 14 inches in length. Holdovers are increasingly common in these fast, cold waters, especially in the two runs designated for catch-and-release.

While the Deerfield rises in Vermont's Green Mountains and joins the Connecticut below Greenville, the portion of the river that attracts most interest is the eight-mile stretch from the Route 2 bridge at Mohawk Campground upstream to Fife Brook Dam. The river follows a riffle, run, and pool pattern through a narrow gorge with low mountains rising 1,400 feet on either side. Spruce, hemlock, and birch climb the hillsides and ferns carpet the forest floor. In spring, pick a basket of fiddleheads, fish the catch-and-release sections, keep maybe one or two trout from the put-and-take section, and enjoy a New England dinner as fresh as the breath of spring.

Retaining fish is, of course, *verboten* in the catch-and-release areas where only artificial lures may be used. The uppermost, and the one favored by many anglers, runs from the base of Fife Brook Dam down to the trestle that carries the Boston & Maine Railroad into the Hoosac Tunnel. This stretch begins in the boulder-strewn pool called the Aquarium. Long pools and flows of pocket water characterize this 1.6 miles of river. The lower mileage, about two miles from Pelham Brook to the campground is similar, but bigger, water. Known mainly for its caddis, Blue Quills, tricos, Light Cahills and the ubiquitous Adams also produce. You may fare better with nymphs and streamers. And hoppers, ants, and beetles cast under overhanging vegetation turn the trick in late summer.

While TU was instrumental in negotiating minimum flows during the relicensing of the dams on the river, summertime releases are scheduled to facilitate commercial

DEERFIELD RIVER

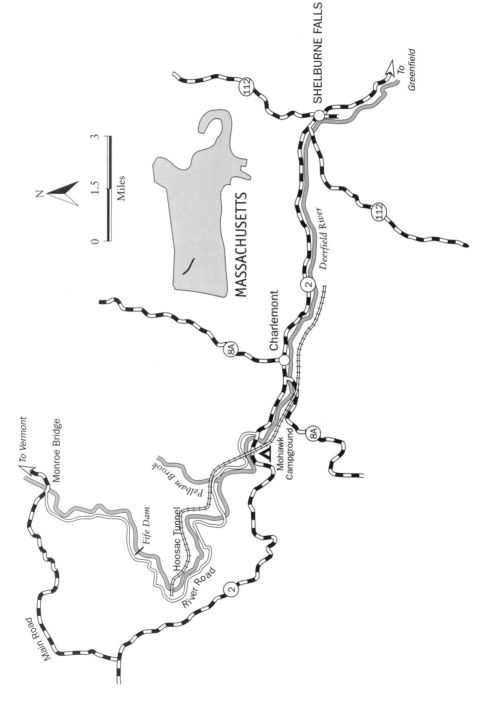

rafting. Coldwater surges can add two feet of water to the river in a few minutes. If you're fishing, you must pay attention and head for higher ground at the first sign of rising water. Normally, releases for floaters occur in mid-morning and by mid-afternoon the crest has passed below the Route 2 bridge. While fish in some systems would be turned off by daily river level fluctuations, these fish don't appear to be. They'll begin taking again once flows return to normal. In the meanwhile, anglers tell lies to each other over burgers at the Charlemont Inn a few miles east of the lower catch-and-release area.

Efforts are underway to reintroduce Atlantic salmon to the Deerfield, and the Deerfield/Millers chapter of TU has established a model program with elementary schools along the river's course. In partnership with the Massachusetts Division of Fisheries and Wildlife, U.S. Fish and Wildlife Service, and others, TU has set up aquariums in eight fifth- and sixth-grade classrooms to raise salmon from eggs. When the fry reach an inch or so in length, students go on a field trip to release the fry in rivers. Accompanying the project arc lessons on the life-cycle of salmon and the river. The project shows promise of rearing both salmon and a new crop of informed anglers for the Deerfield.

RESOURCES

Gearing up: Points North Fly Fishing Outfitters, 1111 Forest Park (mail); 68 Park (shop) Adams, MA 01220; 413 743-4030. Rick Moon, 107 Stockbridge Road, Great Barrington, MA 01230; 413-528-4666.

Accommodations: Oxbow Resort, Rt. 2. Mohawk Trail, Charlemont, MA 01339; 413-625-6011.

Books: *Anglers Guide to Trout Fishing In Massachusetts,* Brian Tucholke, ed., Massachusetts/Rhode Island Council TU, 1988.

8 CONNECTICUT RIVER, UPPER

Location: Northern New Hampshire.
Short take: Landlocked salmon, early. Otherwise you'll have to make do with trout.
Type of stream: Tailwater.
Angling methods: Fly, spin.
Species: Landlocked salmon, brown, brook, rainbow.
Access: Easy to moderate.
Season: January 1 through mid-October.
Handicapped access: Very limited.
Nearest tourist services: Pittsburg.

INDEPENDENT IS THE MIDDLE NAME of the folks of New Hampshire's North Country; they're as staunch as the granite mountains and they take their angling seriously. But nothing fancy. If your flybox contains a handful of Sulphurs and Yellow Sallies, Elk Hair and Black Caddis, a few hex, some Adams and Royal Wulffs you'll be pretty much set. For wet flies try Gray Ghosts, Magog Smelt, Putt's Favorite, and a gray Woolly Bugger. Those, and a 6-weight system, will prepare you for fly fishing. Ultra-light's the way to go for spinners who should carry along the usual run of Mepps, Roostertails, Panther Martins, and Kamloop spoons.

The Connecticut River is broad and beamy where it enters Long Island Sound at Old Lyme, Connecticut, but below the Fourth Connecticut Lake, a click south of New Hampshire's border with Quebec, you can stand comfortably with one foot on each bank of the river. While you'll find wild, native brookies lurking in the deeper holes of this water, they're not much bigger than a few inches. The river only becomes fishable, really, below the second of the four lakes in the Connecticut chain. Fishing from the outlet of the lake down to the Magalloway Bridge can be good. Spawning smelt draw landlocked salmon and bigger brook trout up from the First Connecticut Lake into classic pocket water runs. Among the best spots to fish are the mouths of three feeder brooks: Dry, Smith, and Big. The tailwater below the First Connecticut Lake is set aside as catch-and-release, fly-fishing water. Depending on temperatures, salmon runs may start as early as late April. Normally mid-May marks the opening of the best runs.

Below the lowest of the lakes in the chain, Lake Francis, you'll encounter an occasional salmon, but here the fishery is heavily stocked with brook trout and rainbows. Boulders are fewer on this mileage which begins to take on the character of a meadow stream. The gravel bottom makes wading easy. Fishing these waters is good year-round. Downstream from Pittsburg, the river deepens and pools become defined as those deep sloughs on the outside of river bends. Most anglers elect to float portions of this mileage, which stretches down to Colebrook, and below. A popular stretch, you'll see all kinds of watercraft from canoes, to kick-boats, to drift boats that belong out west.

CONNECTICUT RIVER, UPPER

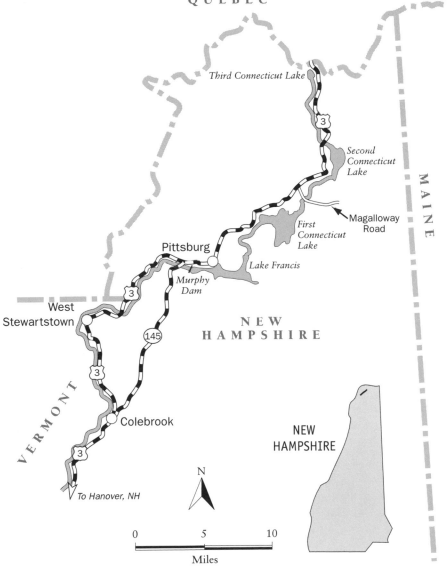

QUEBEC

Third Connecticut Lake

3

Second
Connecticut
Lake

← Magalloway
Road

First
Connecticut
Lake

Pittsburg

Lake Francis

Murphy
Dam

3

West
Stewartstown

145

NEW
HAMPSHIRE

VERMONT

3

Colebrook

3

To Hanover, NH

NEW
HAMPSHIRE

MAINE

N

0   5   10

Miles

Ice-out traditionally marks the best time to fish landlocked salmon flowages, but trying to guess that date is iffy at best. Unless salmon are your primary quarry, go for the color, when autumn sets the wood's maples and birches aflame, and air carries a bite as crisp as hard cider and sharp cheese. You can fly into this area, but it's better and cheaper to fly into Hartford, rent a car and drive up the bucolic river valley. Forgo Interstate 91, and pick instead the little river roads of New Hampshire that carry you though the country of Daniel Webster and Robert Frost. You'll be tempted to stop and poke around. Don't do it. Remember, you've come here to fish.

RESOURCES

Gearing up: Lopstick Lodge and Outfitters, First Connecticut Lake, Pittsburg, NH 03592; 603-538-6659.

Accommodations: Tall Timber Lodge, 231 Beach Rd., Pittsburg, NH 03592; 800-835-6343.

9 BATTEN KILL

Location: Western Vermont, eastern New York.
Short take: If the Beaver Kill was the cradle of fly fishing, you'll find its soul on the Batten Kill.
Type of stream: Freestone.
Angling methods: Fly, spin.
Species: Brown, brook, rainbow.
Access: Moderate.
Season: Mid-April through mid-October.
Nearest tourist services: Manchester.
Handicapped access: None.
Closest TU chapter: Clearwater (NY); Batten Kill (VT).

LADEN WITH SPRUCE, PINE, and occasional larch, the Green Mountains roll through central Vermont spawning scores of trout streams, but none so famous as the Batten Kill. The river is not long, barely 50 miles divided evenly with New York, west of the border. A dairy region turned resort area by the middle of the 1800s, the gentle valley of the Batten Kill drew thousands who came for its cool and healthy healing airs. In 1836, Charles F. Orvis was born in Manchester on the Batten Kill. The company he founded has revolutionized angling and its shops in Manchester attract legions of anglers. Few, however, fish the river that runs behind the store.

Overshadowed by western big-fish waters, the Batten Kill is taciturn, reticent, a bit like New England itself. You'll find no rapacious pods of stocked trout here; none have been introduced since the early 1970s. Much of the mileage is held in private hands, though access is not as difficult as it might be. The river itself rises in East Dorset along US Highway 7 and plays tag with the railroad and old US 7A until it flows through Manchester. Below the center of town, Union Street crosses the creek at the head of a mile of fly-fishing-only water. Obtain a permit at the Orvis shop and try this mileage with Sulphurs in June, Blue-Winged Olives from July into August, and tricos and terrestrials from July well into fall. Brookies predominate in this run of pools and riffles, but you'll also encounter browns. Most will be fairly small, but some, especially those sipping in heavy cover near the bank, may be large enough to double your dainty three-weight.

Below Manchester, the Batten Kill picks up water from Lye Brook, Mill Brook, and Roaring Branch, but the gradient does not increase. From the intersection of Richville and River Roads, the Batten Kill dons the persona of a small, narrow pond. Its deep runs, overhung with vines and trailing branches, hold some very respectable browns and a few little brookies. Wading is difficult because the bottom is mud in many places. Drifting in a canoe and roll casting to rising fish is an extremely pleasant way to spend a late evening. As you work through this section, you'll discover the scenes that inspired artists John Atherton and Ogden Pleisnner.

Batten Kill

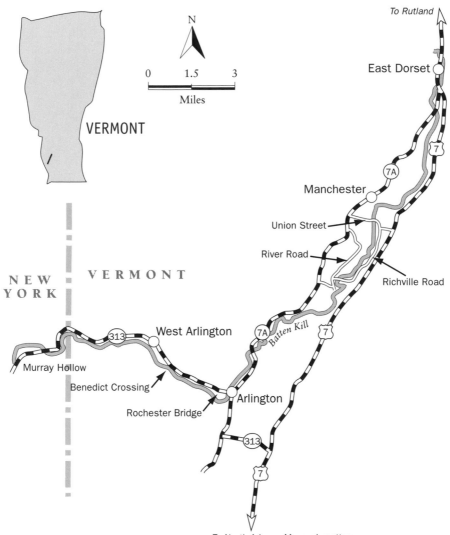

N

0   1.5   3

Miles

VERMONT

To Rutland

East Dorset

7

7A

Manchester

Union Street

River Road

Richville Road

NEW
YORK

VERMONT

313   West Arlington

7A   Batten Kill   7

Murray Hollow

Benedict Crossing

Rochester Bridge   Arlington

313

7

To North Adams, Massachusettes

As autumn touches the stream banks, days shorten and trout appetites quicken.

At Arlington, the Batten Kill changes character. As it bends westward it shallows, broadens, and picks up a little steam. An artificials-only section has been established between Rochester Bridge and Benedict Crossing. Easy riffles separate long pools with an occasional rocky rapid and undercut or rocky bank. Browns in this run, and that to the New York border, tend to be a bit smaller than the denizens which lie in the dark waters above Arlington. Fish the river all the way to the state line.

While the focus of the Batten Kill is surely on fly fishing, spinner fans who toss Panther Martins and little Mepps and who dredge tiny Rapalas through long slow pools will be quite successful. Ultra-light is the name of the game here, two- to four-pound test line, and lures of 1/32 to 1/8 oz. And while the Batten Kill receives most of the press, anglers willing to explore its tributaries will find wild brook trout, some up to a foot in length.

Manchester is a tourist destination and it fills up with vacationers soon after school is out. Lodging at delightful country inns and bed-and-breakfasts, not to mention the Equinox, the Grande Dame of Manchester's historic resort hotels, should be booked well in advance. Guides abound, of course, and you'll want to visit the American Museum of Fly Fishing. Not served by commercial flights, the least expensive way to visit this region is to drive, or fly to Albany and rent a car.

RESOURCES

Gearing up: Orvis, Historic Rt. 7A, Manchester, VT 05254; 802-362-3750. Gloria Jordon's Fly Rod Shop, P.O. Box 667, Manchester Center, VT 05255; 802-362-3186.

Accommodations: Manchester and the Mountains Chamber of Commerce, 5046 Main Street, Suite 1, Manchester Center, VT 05255; 802-362-2100.

Books: *Fishing Vermont's Streams and Lakes,* Peter F. Cammann, Backcountry Publications, Woodstock, VT, 1992.

The Batten Kill, John Merwin, Lyons Press, New York, NY, 1993.

10 CLYDE RIVER

Location: Northern Vermont.
Short take: TU, with an assist from Mother Nature, takes out dam and salmon return to the river.
Type of stream: Freestone.
Angling methods: Fly, spin.
Species: Brown, brook, landlocked salmon.
Access: Easy.
Season: Mid-April through October.
Nearest tourist services: Newport.
Handicapped access: None.
Closest TU chapter: Northeast Kingdom.

FOR FIVE YEARS, the Northeast Kingdom chapter of TU fought Citizen's Utilities' efforts to obtain relicensing for Number 11 dam which dewatered the Clyde River at the height of the landlocked salmon and walleye spawns. The dam flooded 0.75 mile of prime spawning ground, and when power demands were low, another 0.75 of a mile below the dam would simply cease to run, often stranding fish that had come in during periods of normal flow. Gathering opposition to the relicensing from U.S. Fish and Wildlife and the state of Vermont, TU was poised for a final battle with the Federal Energy Regulation Commission (FERC) when, heavy rains on the winter's snowpack raised the Clyde to flood stage and it breached the left abutment of the dam. That was in May 1994, and TU thought Mother Nature had come off the bench and hit a grand slam. Not so; the shot caromed of the left field post and was ruled a foul by FERC, which authorized the utility to repair the dam. But after the Vermont Agency of Natural Resources notified federal officials that the utility was violating the Clean Water Act during construction, FERC voted to remove the dam from the river.

The dam was demolished in 1996, and that fall a few landlocked salmon returned to the river to spawn for the first time in nearly 40 years. Before the dam, salmon stacked up in the river twice each year—during the fall spawn and in the spring, when they gorge on smelt and pinhead minnows. Back then, anglers arrived by train, booked all rooms in hotels and guest houses, and engaged area residents to guide them on the stream. The Clyde was known as one of the finest landlocked salmon rivers in the East. The fish are coming back. Last year, TU's Frank Smith, chair of the Vermont Council, landed a 10-pounder on a Pistachio Pudding streamer, which he'll tell you about, with some embarrassment, if you ask. Walleye, too, are back in the system, but Smith and others admit that it will take a long time, maybe 10 years, to reestablish anything like the numbers of salmon that once ran in this section of the river.

The salmon section of the stream runs only about 1.5 miles from Lake

CLYDE RIVER

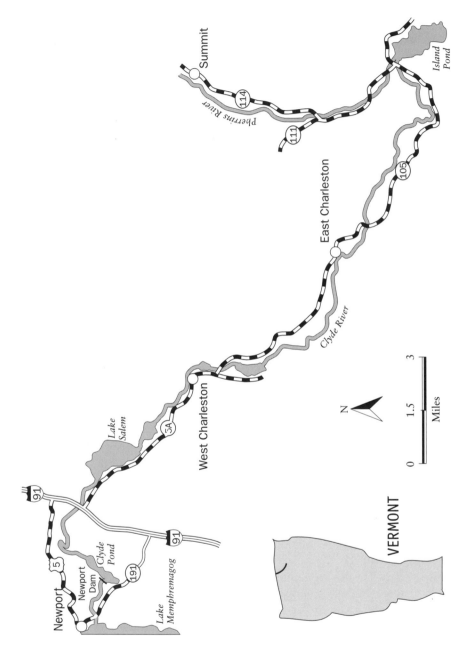

Memphremagog in Newport to the steep runs just below Clyde Pond Dam. Above the dam, for nearly 40 miles, the river winds through a shaded and boggy valley, interrupted here and there by ponds and little lakes. Still waters tend to hold brown trout and walleye. The river beyond the lakes is primarily brook trout water, best fished as a long and lazy canoe trip. Deep holes harbor large brook trout, some in excess of two or three pounds. The farther upstream one goes, the better the angling for brook trout. The tributaries above the Clyde's headwaters at Island Pond, particularly the Pherrins River, are well known as fine brook trout streams, which will occasionally yield fish weighing more that two pounds.

The Clyde is not a technically difficult river to fish. A 6-weight and a small box of half a dozen flies: caddis, trico, Adams, Wulffs, and Stimulators will normally get you through. Spinners also work on trout. Nor is the river unduly discolored while in spate. The marshes and a number of dams allow sediment to filter out. But as the water gets skinny at Island Pond and later on Pherrins, stealth and careful presentation are essential.

RESOURCES

Gearing up: Wright's Enterprises, 10 Community Dr., Newport, VT 05855; 802-334-6115. Great Outdoors, 181 Main St. Newport VT 05855; 802-334-2831.

Accommodations: Vermont's Chamber of Commerce, The Causeway, Newport, VT 05855; 802-334-7782.

Books: *Fishing Vermont's Streams and Lakes,* Peter F. Cammann, Backcountry Publications, Woodstock, VT, 1992.

11. AUSABLE RIVER, WEST BRANCH
12. BEAVER KILL
13. DELAWARE RIVER
14. ESOPUS RIVER
15. NEVERSINK RIVER
16. WILLOWEMOC CREEK
17. FISHING CREEK
18. LETORT SPRING RUN
19. PENNS CREEK
20. SLATE RUN
21. SPRUCE CREEK

NORTHEAST

NEW YORK

PENNSYLVANIA

11 Ausable River, West Branch

Location: Northeastern New York, in the Adirondacks.
Short take: Big stocked trout and stunning scenery.
Type of stream: Freestone.
Angling methods: Fly, spin.
Species: Brown, brook, rainbow.
Access: Easy.
Season: Year-round.
Nearest tourist services: Wilmington, Lake Placid.
Handicapped access: The "lake" in Wilmington.
Closest TU chapter: Lake Champlain.

RISING IN THE SHADOW of the ski jump for the 1980 Olympics, just to the east of the town of Lake Placid, the West Branch of the Ausable flows some 30 miles to its junction with the East Branch at Ausable Forks. Then, according to Fran Betters, author and owner of Adirondack Sports, the West Branch of the Ausable has all the ingredients of a fine trout stream: clean, cold, unpolluted water that's well oxygenated; ample food; and good cover. From its headwaters, the river slides lazily through four miles of meadows. Riffles and runs are rare here. Instead, banks are undercut and the water flows deep, and it is said that these runs hold some of the largest trout in the river. The slick stretch continues until it's crossed by State Route 86. As if awakening with its increasing gradient, the river tosses over boulders and through pools for a mile before jumping off 100-foot Monument Falls into a gorge of turbulent pool and pocket water. From a mile above the Route 86 bridge down to Wilmington Notch, the river is governed by catch-and-release, artificial-lures-only regulations.

About a mile above the village of Wilmington, the river crashes down a steep set of rapids called The Flume and into a pool that bears Betters' name. This is a big fish pool, very popular with anglers fishing nymphs and streamers. After this pool, the river tails out into a small lake backed up by a little dam in the town. There is some water reserved for physically challenged anglers at the lake in Wilmington, and the pool below the dam yields big fish in the spring just after ice-out, and on those deep evenings of summer when big stoneflies—try a #6 Stimulator—hatch sporadically. From this plunge pool, the river keeps up its pool, pocket water, pool constitution for a pair of miles that is Betters' favorite fly water on the river. Downstream from this mileage is a posted section of a mile or so followed by five miles where fishing is again permitted.

First Little Black Brook and, a mile further, Great Black Brook enter the West Branch from the north. Together they denote the head of the final good fishing flowage of the river. Access is via old logging roads, but, alas, this area seems to be

AUSABLE RIVER, WEST BRANCH

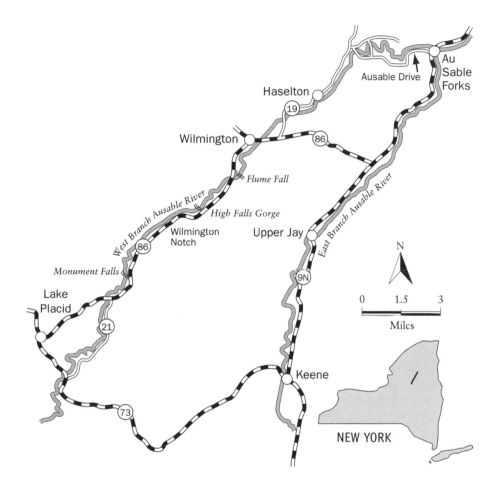

slated for subdivison, and permission to cross private land is increasingly difficult to come by. Because the land is flatter, the river is slower, and the pools less pronounced than in the upper reaches. The final fishable run of this branch comes in a small ponding of the river above the crossroads of Ausable Forks, and in the waters immediately upstream of the confluence of the East Branch. Below, the water shallows and the sun's rays warm it too much to hold significant populations of good trout.

Spin and bait fishers do well on the West Branch of the Ausable as do fly fishers. With straightforward modesty, Betters' says that the Ausable Wulff, which he designed in 1964, accounts for 90 percent of the big trout caught on the river. Even if he's off by a magnitude of 10, it's worth having a few of these ties in your box if you're fishing this mileage. The river is known for its Hendricksons, Light Cahills, Green Drakes (June), and *Isonychia* from mid-August on. Caddis are probably the most prevalent hatch with the first coming off in May and varieties continuing well into September.

As you'd suspect, this is high resort country so accommodations are ample and sometimes pricey. You can stay, for instance, at The Point for $850 to $1,350 per night, or check into the West Branch Fly Fishing Club for $25 per night for two. And you'll find everything in between including the Hungry Trout Motor Inn where fly fishing is spoken fluently. Commercial air carriers serve Lake Placid.

RESOURCES

Gearing up: Adirondack Sports, Wilmington, NY 12997; 518-523-4875. The Hungry Trout Fly Shop, Rt. 86, Whiteface Mountain NY 12997; 518-946-7418.

Accommodations: Lake Placid/Essex County Visitor's Bureau, 216 Main St., Lake Placid, NY 12940; 518-523-2445; www.lakeplacid.com.

Books: *Good Fishing in the Adirondacks*, Dennis Aprill, Ed., Backcountry Publications, Woodstock, VT, 1996.

Ausable River, Paul Marriner, River Journal Series, Frank Amato, Portland, OR, 1994.

12 BEAVER KILL

Location: Southern Catskills, Southeastern New York.
Short take: Excellent fishery, though apt to be crowded. Home water of American dry-fly fishing. Best fished spring and fall. Lower sections below Roscoe are often too warm to fish in August.
Type of stream: Freestone.
Angling methods: Fly, spin.
Species: Brown, rainbow, brook.
Access: Easy.
Season: Year-round.
Nearest tourist services: Roscoe.
Handicapped access: Excellent.
Closest TU chapter: Beamoc.

THE BEAVER KILL HAS BEEN eclipsed by western rivers as far as the "big fish-big waters" crowd is concerned. But you don't make the pilgrimage to Roscoe, the quintessential trout town, on New York's Route 17, for big fish. The journey is more spiritual. In the pools and riffles of this most classic freestone stream, the art and science of American dry fly fishing was hatched in the late 1800s. The sense of history is palpable in the river valley. Here and there, neat white frame farm houses hold forth on the flood plain, flanked by barns which once held dairy cows and fields once tilled for corn, but now given over to hay and wildflowers. Here too are the old fly fishing clubs like the Theodore Gordon and a score of others, and the quaint country fly shops of Darbee and Dette, and their disciples, who gave us so many of the patterns we enjoy with such success today.

Rising in the Beaver Kill Range, a rather grand appellation for a trio of glacially rounded 3,800-foot mountains, the kill (the word for "river" used by the Dutch who settled this region in the early 1600s) is a tiny stream populated with native brook trout. The uppermost two miles of stream cross public forest and are therefore accessible. Trout are small, delightful, and readily take almost any small dry; use an Adams or a little tan caddis of #12 or #14. You can hike to the upper water from Round Pond Trailhead, but the river below is almost exclusively private. Students at the Wulff School of Fly Fishing, presided over by Joan Wulff, a preeminent fly caster and leader in the effort to adapt fly gear for women, and guests at the Beaver Kill Valley Inn at Lew Beach, have access to a mile or so of outstanding pocket water.

You'll find a mile of public access at the state's Covered Bridge Campground, and another two and a half miles running from where Route 206 crosses the Beaver Kill down to the famed Junction Pool downstream from Roscoe. As you'd suspect, these two public sections of the upper river get hammered in the summer. Weekdays in early spring, particularly in early May during Hendrickson and Green Drake hatches, can be very productive for brown trout up to 18 inches, though most are in the 10- to 12-inch range. Terrestrials (tiny black ants, particularly) tan and dark

BEAVER KILL

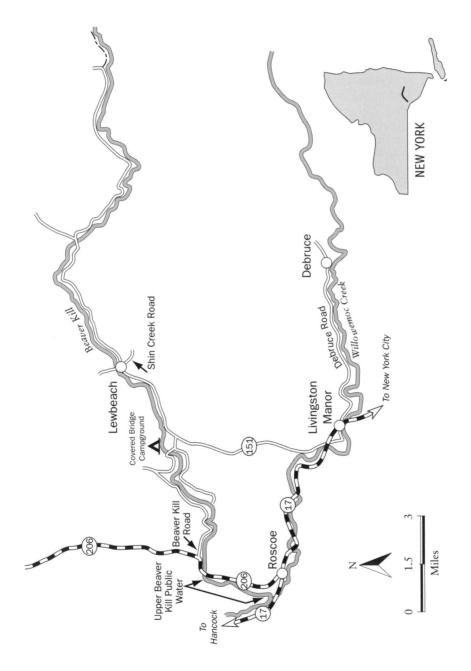

caddis, and blue-winged olives are among the most productive patterns for late summer.

The lower stretch of the river below Roscoe is much larger than the upper because the Willowemoc enters at the Junction Pool. From there, roughly 15 miles to its confluence with the East Branch of the Delaware is some of the most celebrated trout water in America. To say that it's easily accessible is an understatement; Route 17, the Quickway from New York City to Binghamton, runs along the river's course. Parking spots are ample and the water can be fished with lure or bait—your choice. Every pool has a name and the list marches on down the stream. And every pool sees heavy concentrations of anglers, particularly those in the no-kill sections. Barnharts, Hendrickson's, Cairns, and School House are among the most popular pools in the upper 2.6-mile section a couple miles west of Roscoe. Further west is a second, similar sized no-kill section where fishing is best in the Acid Pool, or just below it.

In years of ample rainfall and moderate summer temperatures, the lower reaches of the Beaver Kill can be wonderful. It is heavily stocked by the state. Hatches are prolific, Blue-Winged Olives early, then Quill Gordon and Hendricksons, March Browns in May and Sulphurs and Drakes in June. Drakes continue into July along with cahills. Tricos come in the height of summer. Yet, in years when precipitation is at a minimum, the lower section of the river warms like bath water. Fishing here at times like this is seldom productive and if you do happen on a fish, taking it can stress it to death. Under those circumstances, it's much better to head for the nearby

BARRY AND CATHY BECK

The Beaver Kill provides anglers a brush with the origins of American dry fly fishing.

East Branch of the Delaware with its monstrous tailwater browns, or to hit the uppermost public water on the Beaver Kill or its sibling stream, the Willowemoc.

Drought and watershed degradation posed such a serious threat to the Beaver Kill and Willowemoc that TU proposed a comprehensive plan to protect and restore the Beamoc. Working with TU's national staff, grants from the Richard King Mellon Foundation, the National Fish and Wildlife Foundation, and Orvis totaling about $250,000 were secured to fund intensive research of the watershed and the economic impact of the fishery. The first data, the economic impact study, was an eye-opener for local officials. With lumbering and agriculture fading as primary industries, the towns along the two rivers face increasingly stringent times. But data from the TU survey suggested that recreational fishing brings about $9.6 million annually into local economies, about $2.3 million of it in wages from 177 fishing-related jobs. Town and county leaders now understand that trout-related tourism is a major industry in these tight hills and valleys, and that the rivers must be managed wisely to sustain the economic benefit to the region. The second phase of the study is designed to strengthen long-term management and conservation of the fishery. Phase three, implementation of restoration and conservation plans, is under way. Thanks to this unusual partnership involving New York's Department of Environmental Conservation, private foundations, Orvis, TU, and hosts of volunteers, America's most hallowed dry fly fishery will be there for anglers for generations to come.

RESOURCES

Gearing up: Beaverkill Angler, P.O. Box 198, Roscoe, NY 12776; 607-498-5194; Fax: 607-498-4740. Fur, Fin, Feather Sport Shop, DeBruce Road, Livingston Manor, NY 12758; 914-439-4476.

Of special interest: Catskill Fly Fishing Center and Museum, 5447 Old Rt. 17, P.O. Box 1295, Livingston Manor, NY 12758; 914-439-4810.

Accommodations: Roscoe-Rockland Chamber of Commerce, c/o Stone Realty, P.O. Box 900, Roscoe NY 12776; 607-498-6055. Livingston Manor Chamber of Commerce, P.O. Box 950, Livingston Manor, NY 12758; 914-439-4859.

Books: *The Beaverkill: The History of a River and Its People,* Ed Van Put, The Lyons Press, New York, NY, 1997.

Good Fishing in the Catskills, Jim Capossela, The Countryman Press, Woodstock, VT, 1992.

13 DELAWARE RIVER

Location: Southeastern New York near Pennsylvania border.
Short take: The easternmost "western" river in the United States.
Type of stream: Tailwater.
Angling methods: Fly, spin.
Species: Rainbow, brown.
Access: Moderate.
Season: Year-round.
Nearest tourist services: Hancock.
Handicapped access: None.
Closest TU chapter: Binghamton.

AVID ANGLER BY PASSION and railroad brakeman by profession, Dan Cahill had slipped a few milk cans of McCloud-strain rainbows on the run from Matamoras to Deposit. His plan on this day in the 1880s was to stock the cool waters of West Branch of the Delaware, but the train broke down in Calicoon, about 40 miles south. Rather than see the prize fingerlings suffocate, he dumped them in the main river, hoping that these warm-water tolerant rainbows would survive. Even a gambler wouldn't have taken the bet. High and cold with Catskill runoff in spring, the river became low and turgid in summer, fit mainly for walleye, smallmouth, and catfish. What trout there were—native brookies and renegade browns escaped from the private waters of the wealthy—washed into the river from feeder streams. Not until the 1950s with the construction of two bottom-draw dams, Pepacton on the East Branch and Cannonsville on the West, did the progeny of old Dan's rainbows spread out from the springholes where they'd taken refuge and begin to gorge themselves on an incredible array of aquatic insects.

You'll find them all here. Every major species and many of the subspecies of caddis, mayfly, and stonefly found in the East hatch on this river. Small fish are abundant as well: minnows, shad, and the fry of spawning trout. Upstream flowages, particularly on the East Branch, support large populations of crustacea. Ann McIntosh is right when she writes that for trout, the Delaware is an extensive smorgasbord and, to be successful, anglers must match the hatch with precision that's rarely necessary elsewhere. Its rainbows, browns, and brook trout roam the waters of the river, migrating from the deeper waters of the main stem up into the branches and feeder streams to spawn. TU's Binghamton Chapter and the New York State Department of Environmental Conservation partnered in a study of the migration habits of Delaware River trout.

In reality, the Upper Delaware is three rivers: the West Branch from Deposit to Hancock, the East Branch from Downsville to its confluence with the Beaver Kill at East Branch, and the main river from Hancock to Callicoon. After stepping down a set of bouldery rapids below the dam above Deposit, the West Branch turns south

DELAWARE RIVER

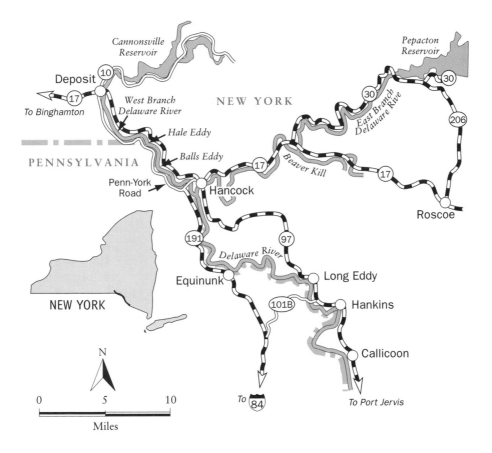

into a modest valley floored with glacial till. In the upper reaches, the water flows through occasional clutches of islands before coalescing into one stream of fairly consistent gradient. The run is broken by riffly shallows. Generally the bank is brushy, an automat delivering ants, crickets, hoppers, and beetles into the jaws of waiting browns. State Route 17 runs up along the east side of the river and a number of county and township roads—most paved, but some not—run up the west side. While many anglers float this section, you really don't need to. In fact wading is best. That may not be the case with the run of the East Branch from Downsville to Shinhopple. With the exception of a stretch or two of riffles, most of this mileage flows cold and slow. In late summer, dense stands of aquatic grasses wave beneath your canoe, the only craft that makes any sense here. While you can walk in to a number of pools, you'll find better ones by drifting and can move through concentrations of anglers to runs where there are few. Big browns dominate the lower portion of this run; brook trout dominate the upper. At Shinhopple, the East Branch trips down a series of rapids and into a lovely valley. Pull-offs from Route 30 on the west bank and Harvard Road on the east offer access. Much of the land is private and permission is obligatory.

While SR 17 roars along above the East Branch and the water looks very inviting from the State Route 30 junction to Hancock, it is a poor trout fishery. By the time it reaches East Branch, the Beaver Kill's waters are too warm and releases from Pepacton Reservoir cannot cool it enough. This mileage fishes reasonably well into June, but then the low flows commence and by August fish are badly stressed. Besides, there's no reason to focus on the lower East Branch when the main river below Hancock holds such promise. It's big water. It runs from long, deep pool, through gravel channels, into another pool of similar size and structure. Where the river cuts against the base of a ridge, trout hold among large, angular boulders. On sunny days you'll find them sipping under the shade of forest along the banks. On cloudy days, they'll key on pockets of emerging insects. The most effective patterns are Blue-Winged Olives, tricos, and Spotted Sedges. But remember, hatch-matching is a high art here. The best way for the uninitiated to begin to learn the hatches is to hire a guide and float the river in a McKenzie drift boat. While you can wade the river below high water marks, many of the old, popular, private access points, sadly, have long been closed to the public. On a brighter note, a new public access has opened just downstream from the confluence of the two branches on the Pennsylvania side near Hancock. This is great water and a fine place to meet the "Big D."

RESOURCES:

Gearing up: Al Caucci's Delaware River Club Fly Shop, HC1 Box 1290, Starlight, PA 18461; 800-662-9359. Al's Wild Trout, HC 89 Box 666, Rt. 30, Downsville, NY 13755; 607-363-7135; www.catskill.net/alstrout.

Accommodations: Hancock Area Chamber of Commerce, P.O. Box 525, Hancock, NY 13178; 800-668-7624.

Books: *Mid-Atlantic Budget Angler,* Ann McIntosh, Stackpole, Mechanicsburg, PA, 1998.

14 Esopus River

Location: Southeastern New York.
Short take: A challenging stream, with lots of trout and a glowing future.
Type of stream: Freestone.
Angling methods: Fly, spin.
Species: Brown, rainbow, brook.
Access: Easy.
Season: April through November.
Nearest tourist services: Kingston.
Handicapped access: None.
Closest TU chapter: Ashokan-Pepacton.

HEAVY STOCKING AND HEAVY discharges from the Shandaken Tunnel, which carries water from the Schoharie into the Esopus and eventually into the taps of New York City's residents, have made this river something of an enigma. Rising across the gap from the West Branch of the Neversink— another classic Catskills river— the Esopus encircles Panther Mountain as it flows down into Ashokan Reservoir. The rep on this river is this: lots of trout, many of them wild, and a great place to fish with spinners or bait.

Tubes and kayaks float the river on summer weekends when the portal is running. That's the down side. On the other hand, heavy rainbows and browns of five pounds and more run up out of the reservoir to spawn in the Esopus and its tributaries. 'Bows do it in spring, browns in the fall, and some rainbows migrate with the browns. Finding these spawners is more like hunting than fishing. Being able to think like a big trout is a must. Seeking out holes at the mouth of feeder streams, or up the streams if the water is high, and then working large (#6 or #4) nymphs through each probable lie in a manner so patient that even birds won't be disturbed, will occasionally connect you with a behemoth. And that, along with 3,000 to 5,000 trout per mile and the tranquil charm of its upper reaches, is why anglers bother with the Esopus.

Jim Capossela, author of *Good Fishing in the Catskills*, divides the river into three sections: headwaters at Lake Winnisook to Big Indian, Big Indian to the mouth of the tunnel at Allaben, and the reach from Allaben to the reservoir. The uppermost mileage is very small, but contains deeply shaded pools and pockets that hold lovely native brook trout, some of eight inches or more. Much of this run is private, but a few gaps between posted parcels provide limited access. It's dainty, delicate fishing. Dappling drys or leading nymphs through the dark runs will often produce strikes. Fluttering spinners also do the job. Below Big Indian, the river increases in size, swelled by Birch Creek. For five miles, the river works its way through a series of pools and runs and very good pocket water. The river is not wide here, 30 to 40 feet at most; there's not much room to wave a fly rod. Ultra-light anglers may see more

ESOPUS RIVER

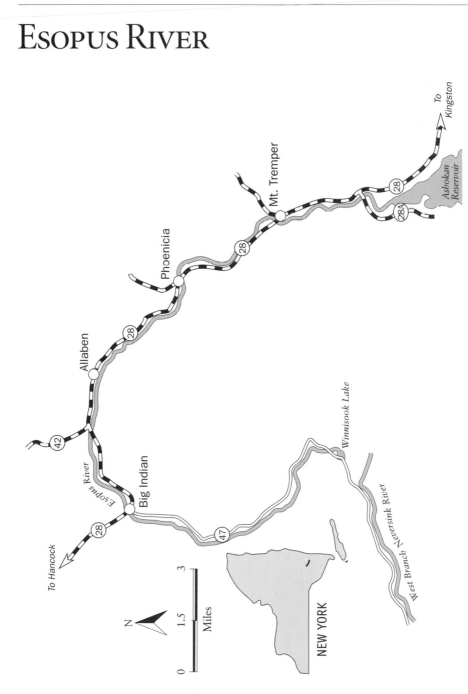

success. The 12-mile reach from Winnisook to the portal is entirely free flowing, and the watershed is small. In mid-summer water levels begin to shrink, and angling becomes more difficult.

From Allaben down to the reservoir, the river is best known for its "rubber hatch" of tubers who bounce gaily on the whitewater. But most of these folks are seldom on the river before 10 A.M. and they're usually gone by 7 P.M. or so. The best water of summer is still available to anglers. Pools and pockets abound as do large angular boulders all creating holds for fish. On bright sunny days, fish are spooky; fish the tributaries then for brookies. But on days when the sky is gray and drizzle threatens, this river can fish as well as any in the Catskills. And no matter when you fish this section, there's a chance you'll catch one of the moving spawners.

Though it's one of the historic trout streams of the Catskills, the Esopus is not a destination river like the Beaver Kill or other branches of the Delaware watershed. Still, if you happen to be in that neck of the woods, particularly in May or October, a trip over the mountain might just be productive. Accommodations are found in Phoenicia and Kingston.

RESOURCES

Gearing up: Don's Tackle Service, 69 S. Broadway, Red Hook, NY 12571; 914-758-9203.

Accommodations: Chamber of Commerce of Ulster County, 7 Albany Ave. #63, Kingston, NY 12401; 914-338-5100; www.ulsterchamber.com.

Books: *Good Fishing in the Catskills,* Jim Capossela, Backcountry Publications, Woodstock, VT, 1992.

15 NEVERSINK RIVER

Location: Southeastern New York, South-central Catskills.
Short take: Still the hallowed waters of American dry-fly fishing.
Type of stream: Freestone, tailwater.
Angling methods: Fly, spin.
Species: Brook, rainbow, brown.
Access: Moderate.
Season: April through November.
Nearest tourist services: Livingston Manor.
Handicapped access: None.
Closest TU chapter: Beamoc.

THERE ARE ANGLERS WHO COME to the Neversink today just for the fishing. They come for furtive, brightly colored brook trout high up in the headwaters of the East and West Branches in the Catskill Preserve. They seek brookies and browns in the mileage from Claryville to the top of Neversink Reservoir. They chase browns below the dam and through the gorge and all the way down to the Delaware River at Port Jervis. Those who come just for the fishing leave with no more than half a loaf. Sure, at the end of the day, their hands may smell of trout, and they may feel quite satisfied at overcoming challenges presented by water and wind and vegetation—to say nothing of the trout. But to wade the Neverskink without some knowledge of Theodore Gordon or George LaBranche or Edward R. Hewitt who, in fishing this river, learned the secrets of its trout and passed them on, is akin to going home for lunch just as the main hatch of the day begins. Fortunately, the slim volume *Fishless Days, Angling Nights* by Sparse Grey Hackle (Alfred W. Miller) can be found in many good used bookshops, and Lyons Press has brought forth a fine volume, *An Honest Angler: The Best of Sparse Grey Hackle.* Reading his prose carries you back to the days of greenheart rods, leaders of gut, and the first American dry flies which danced on the riffles of the Neversink.

East and West Branches are mostly posted, private water, with the exception of a stretch above Denning on the East Branch where Erts Brook comes in from the north. You may find little brook trout up to seven inches or so in this water. Slim most of the time, it gets thinner as summer progresses and nearly vanishes in dry years. When they are hitting, these trout are not particularly choosy. On the West Branch, consider the water at the Frost Valley YMCA camp, which permits overnight guests to fish three private miles of stream. From the confluence of the two branches at Claryville to the upper reaches of the reservoir is some of the finest and most historic water in the stream. It is tightly held and access is limited to club members and their guests.

In 1955, waters rising in Neversink Reservoir drowned forever the old farm house where Theodore Gordon lived his last years. Flooded, too, were the great pools on

NEVERSINK RIVER

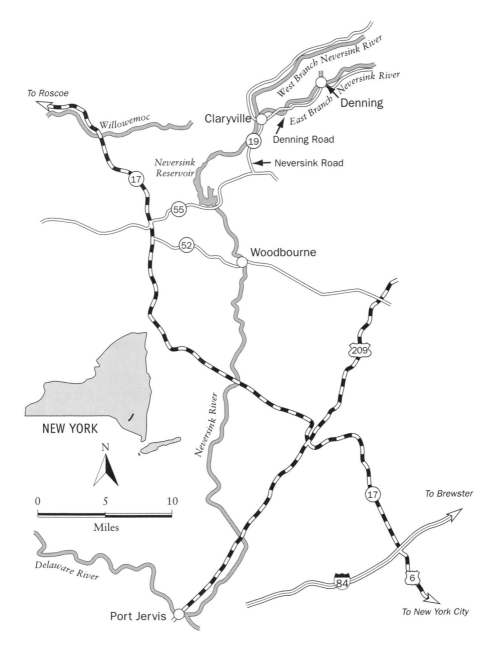

To Roscoe

Willowemoc

West Branch Neversink River

East Branch Neversink River

Claryville

Denning

19

Denning Road

Neversink Road

Neversink Reservoir

17

55

52

Woodbourne

209

NEW YORK

N

0   5   10

Miles

Neversink River

17

To Brewster

Delaware River

84

6

Port Jervis

To New York City

the Hewitt property where so many of the fly fishing truths we know today were first discovered. But the dam created four miles of tailwater where flows are fairly consistent, and brown trout respond to typical mayfly, caddis, and limited stonefly hatches. The effects of the cold water are fairly well mitigated by the time the river reaches Route 42. The river slides under State Route 17, the Quickway, and heads for a 3.5-mile run of the river included in the Neversink Gorge State Unique Area. Home to a number of pairs of nesting bald eagles, the rugged terrain embraces a gorge that cools and oxygenates the river as it tumbles down little rapids into plunge pools. Fishing rights to this mileage are still divided, somewhat, between public and private parcels. Checking in with New York's Region 3 office will provide up-to-date information.

Is it worthwhile to fish this river? Sure, if only to put a landscape to its heritage. But, alas, like the Esopus, the Neversink is not a destination river. Still, a week on the Upper Delaware and the Beamoc wouldn't be complete without a trip over the mountain to the waters where American trout may have seen their first dry flies.

RESOURCES

Gearing up: Beaverkill Angler, P.O. Box 198, Roscoe, NY 12776; 607-498-5194; Fax: 607-498-4740. Fur, Fin, Feather Sport Shop, DeBruce Road, Livingston Manor, NY 12758; 914-439-4476.

Accommodations: Chamber of Commerce of Ulster County, 7 Albany Ave. #63, Kingston, NY 12401; 914-338-5100; www.ulsterchamber.com.

Books: *Good Fishing in the Catskills,* Jim Capsule, Backcountry Publications, Woodstock, VT, 1992.

An Honest Angler: The Best of Sparse Grey Hackle, Gloria Miller, Nick Lyons, New York, NY, 1998.

The Dry Fly in Fast Water, George LaBranche, Greycliff, Helena, MT, 1998.

16 WILLOWEMOC CREEK

Location: Southeastern New York, Southern Catskills.
Short take: Sibling of the Beaver Kill, more public water.
Type of stream: Freestone.
Angling methods: Fly, spin.
Species: Brown, rainbow, brookie.
Access: Easy.
Season: Year-round.
Nearest tourist services: Roscoe, Livingston Manor.
Handicapped access: Ample.
Closest TU chapter: Beamoc.

WHEN IT COMES TO CATSKILL STREAMS, the Beaver Kill gets most of the glory. But its primary tributary, the Willowemoc, has a larger share of public water and fishes almost as well. Touring trouters, when visiting this region, should plan to spend some time on both. However, if your travels will take you into the area any time from the second week in August into mid-September, you may be better off fishing the tailwaters of the East and West Branches of the Delaware. Unless this section of the Catskills receives three or four days of steady rain—not torrential downpours that provoke flooding, but enough to soak the ground and spawn a little run-off—streams in the Beaver Kill-Willowemoc drainage tend to become very low and quite warm. Even though you release the fish, playing a trout under these conditions may kill it.

Brookies, with spring-time bellies as bright as trout lilies, lie in pockets and tiny plunge pools in the heavily shaded stretches of the reaches of the Willowemoc above the hamlet by the same name at the junction of County Roads 82 and 84. Access is limited, but between Fir Brook, a reasonable small fishery for brooks and some browns which comes in from the southeast, and Butternut, which joins the Willowemoc from the north about a mile and a half upstream, the state controls much of the river. From the crossroads downstream, publicly-owned easements provide several miles of good, small stream fishing. The mileage in the vicinity of Mongaup Creek is private, but from a mile or so downstream to State Route 17, the state owns a number of easements. Flowing under SR 17, the creek enters the little town of Livingston Manor and runs past the Catskill Fly Fishing Center and Museum, well worth a visit. The museum contains a number of excellent displays portraying the contributions of the region's legendary anglers and fly-tiers: Walt and Winne Dette, Harry and Elsie Darbee, Lee and Joan Wulff. It also runs a number of programs on casting, tying, and rod-building as well as environmental education for adults and children. Project Access, a nonprofit group dedicated to providing facilities from which physically challenged anglers can fish, has created a number of such sites on both the Beaver Kill and the Willowemoc. Two are located near the bridge which enters the center.

Willowemoc Creek

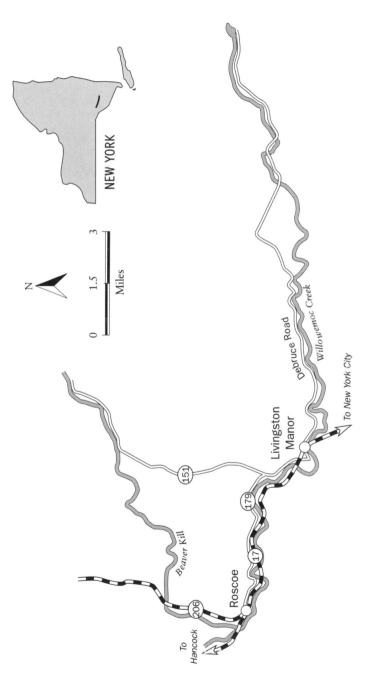

At Livingston Manor, the Willowemoc assumes its adult configuration, coursing through gravel runs and over rocky ledges through patches of forest and meadow. SR 17 shadows the river for most of the mileage to Roscoe where it flows into the Beaver Kill. Two secondary roads out of Livingston Manor, Hazel Road to the south of the creek, and County Route 179 to the north, provide access to fishable pools. The big "Moc," as it's called, is known for its great Hendrickson and March Brown hatches in May and the Green Drakes of June. Lack of shade on much of the lower mileage keeps hatches of mayflies from reaching the intensity found on the Beaver Kill, but still the Moc is one of the most fertile streams in the East. As mentioned, the lower river is subject to low flows in autumn when browns begin to come up from the Delaware to spawn. Fishing in the no-kill sections continues year-round. A couple days of sun playing on the cobble bottom will trigger midge hatches as early as January. There are worse times to be fishing the Willowemoc.

Heavy flooding in January 1996 scoured the river system and pointed to the need for corrective measures to mitigate polluting run-off from SR 17 which threatens trout in the Willowemoc. After extensive advocacy by TU, the organization and the New York State Department of Environmental Conservation have entered into a formal agreement that will rehabilitate sections of stream bed that were bulldozed after the '96 floods, restore the Beaver Kill Campground on the Willowemoc in Livingston Manor, and conduct other restoration projects in the Upper Delaware watershed.

RESOURCES

Gearing up: Frank Kuttner Fly and Tackle, HCR #1 Box 12, Beaver Kill Road, Livingston Manor, NY 12758; 914-439-5590. Beaverkill Angler, P.O. Box 198, Roscoe NY 12776; 607-498-5194.

Of special interest: Catskill Fly Fishing Center and Museum, 5447 Old Rt. 17, P.O. Box 1295, Livingston Manor, NY 12758; 914-439-4810.

Accommodations: Roscoe Chamber of Commerce, c/o Stone Realty, P.O. Box 900, Roscoe, NY 12776; 607-498-6055.

Livingston Manor Chamber of Commerce, P.O. Box 950, Livingston Manor, NY 12758; 914-439-4859.

Books: *Good Fishing in the Catskills,* Jim Capossela, The Countryman Press, Woodstock, VT, 1992.

17 FISHING CREEK

Location: North-central Pennsylvania.
Short take: Fine trout, ample public water. No wonder it's so popular.
Type of stream: Limestone.
Angling methods: Fly, spin.
Species: Brown, brook.
Access: Moderate.
Season: Year-round.
Nearest tourist services: Lock Haven, State College.
Handicapped access: None.
Closest TU chapter: Lloyd Wilson.

EVER SEEN A GREAT TROUT STREAM pull a disappearing act? That's what you get with Fishing Creek, sometimes known as "Big" Fishing Creek to differentiate it from others of the same appellation in Pennsylvania's Columbia and Potter Counties. During warm weather when flows are low, this Fishing Creek slides underground upstream from the Interstate 80 bridge and resurfaces—cleaned, cooled, and refreshed—above Mackeyville where it almost seems to begin anew. If only other streams had this gift.

Rising near Green Gap, Fishing Creek slides southwestward between Nittany Mountain and Big Mountain through Loganton and Tylersville before rounding the Big Mountain's nose south of Lamar and then heading northeast toward its ultimate junction with Eagle Creek south of Lock Haven. Good roads provide reasonable access to some 25 miles of fishable water that look for all the world like a freestone stream. But reach this stream on a sultry day in July to fish Blue Quills or Blue-Winged Olives, and you'll see a faint gray mist hanging a foot or two over the surface. Numerous springs chill the creek during its course to the Eagle. The bottom, too, seems to be more like a freestone creek—beds of cresses and waving aquatic plants are all but absent. Instead the creek's riffles, runs, and pools define its persona.

You'll find nearly all the major caddis, mayfly, and stonefly hatches on Fishing Creek. The river is larger downstream from the state hatchery at Tylersville where big springs augment its flow. Here the special regulations section (artificial lures only) begins its five-mile run through the Narrows, probably the most popular mileage on the stream. Sharp hillsides squeeze the creek into deep shaded pools separated by fast runs. State Route 2002 runs alongside this stretch; access is reasonably easy. Stream-bred browns of 12 to 14 inches and brookies of nine inches or so are the standard bill of fare. As is the case on some of Pennsylvania's premier special regs waters, portions of the Narrows flow across private land and some of it, but not much, is posted.

While the Narrows is the most popular section of the creek, it can become crowded, especially during the green drake hatch on those lovely evenings in June.

FISHING CREEK

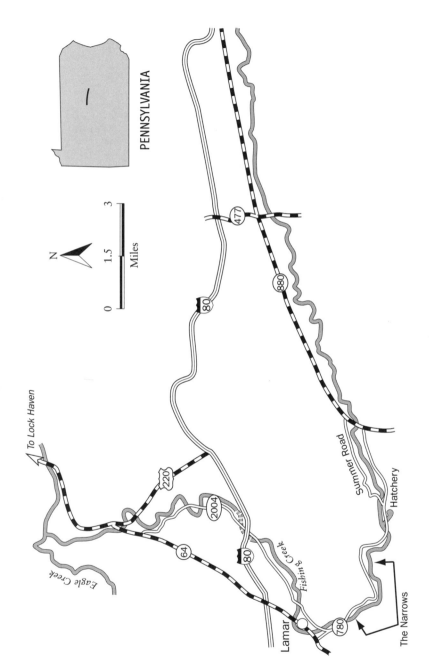

PENNSYLVANIA

N

0   1.5   3
Miles

To Lock Haven

Eagle Creek

220

2004

64

80

80

Lamar

780

Fishing Creek

The Narrows

Summer Road

Hatchery

880

477

80

Look at the water downstream, particularly that stretch running southeast of State Route 2004. It sees much less pressure and sustains good trout populations. Also, the mileage from Mackeysville town to Mill Hall provides action. The big springs at Tylersville really define Fishing Creek. The water above is thin and in some places, intermittent in dry seasons. Those trout that reside in this flowage are small. And, at the head of the watershed, up where I-80 crests the gap in the mountains, you'll find some fishing for wild native brook trout.

In winter months, tiny Blue-Winged Olives, little black stones, white and gray midges and Blue Quills are effective on the larger waters. April adds Quill Gordons, Light Hendricksons, and Grannom Caddis. Sulphurs and Yellow Hendricksons highlight May's prolific hatches, and in June it's Cahills and caddis along with the drakes. Caddis are heavy on evenings in July and August, but tricos seem almost absent. Don't forget terrestrials. It's also important to bear in mind that nymphs account for most of the larger fish taken from this fine spring creek.

Fishing Creek is a destination creek; it's worthwhile to plan to spend a few days deciphering some of its mysteries and moods. State College, less than an hour's drive to the southwest, provides accommodations, fly shops, and an airport with regular commercial flights. And anglers who make that their headquarters in this major university town will find themselves about equidistant from Penns Creek and Spruce Run.

RESOURCES

Gearing up: Uncle Joe's Woodshed, Rt. 150 West, Lock Haven, PA 17745; 717-748-6621.

Accommodations: Clinton County Economic Partnership, 212 North Jay Street, Lock Haven, PA 17745; 717-748-5782.

Books: *Trout Streams of Pennsylvania*, Dwight Landis, Hempstead-Lyndell, Bellefonte, PA, 1995.

TU Guide to Pennsylvania Limestone Streams, A. Joseph Armstrong, Stackpole, Mechanicsburg, PA, 1992.

18 LETORT SPRING RUN

Location: South-central Pennsylvania.
Short take: Quintessential chalk stream filled with hulking browns with attitudes to match.
Type of stream: Limestone spring creek.
Angling methods: Fly, spin.
Species: Brown.
Access: Easy.
Season: Mid-April through February.
Nearest tourist services: Carlisle, Boiling Springs.
Handicapped access: Yes.
Closest TU chapter: Cumberland Valley.

A BLACK MAILBOX WITH RED FLAG raised sits behind an old wooden bench on the run where legendary anglers—Charlie Fox, Vince Marinaro, Ed Koch, and Ed Shenk—pondered the feeding habits of big brown trout. They watched rise forms and the stages of insect life and tied pattern after experimental pattern. Eventually they figured it out, some of it anyway, and developed a core of terrestrial patterns for hoppers, ants, beetles, and jassids that are as important to late-season dry-fly anglers as the hatches of mayflies in spring. Messrs. Fox, Marinaro, et al. did not limit their work to terrestrials. They also pioneered thorax-style duns and patterns that imitate the scuds and sowbugs (crustacea) that constitute such a large share of the diet of spring creek browns. Presentation on this ether-clear creek of little more than 20 feet in width requires the ultimate of finesse. Our boys worked out the science of the long, finely tapered leader for presenting their exquisite patterns with nary a ripple or a trace of drag. But there's much more to be learned here, and that's why George Hagn put up the mailbox so anglers could leave notes for others about what works and what doesn't, and what they think they'll try next. Hagn owns one of the meadows where Marinaro, Fox, and company ran their lab.

The meadow is across from an old railroad trestle south of Interstate 81. The railroad grade, now a bike and walking path, follows the creek for much of the length of its upper mileage. Park in Letort Park on East Pomfret Street and walk upstream. The fly-fishing-only section of catch-and-release water begins at the abandoned railroad bridge at the south end of the park and continues upstream for a mile and a half of the most challenging water you'll ever fish. Tall stands of grass mark the boggy bank, which quakes with each step. The creek is slick and strong, thanks to a number of large springs that feed it, even in the deepest drought. Beds of cress become more prevalent as you fish upstream. After I-81 bridges the Letort, it broadens for a bit, then narrows back down. You'll find some fast water and shade at Bonny Brook Quarry. Above that run the Letort enters an extremely cressy stretch which extends up past the little parking area near the bridge on Bonny Brook Road where the creek forks. Parking is also available at the TU's pavilion on Spring Garden Street

LETORT SPRING RUN

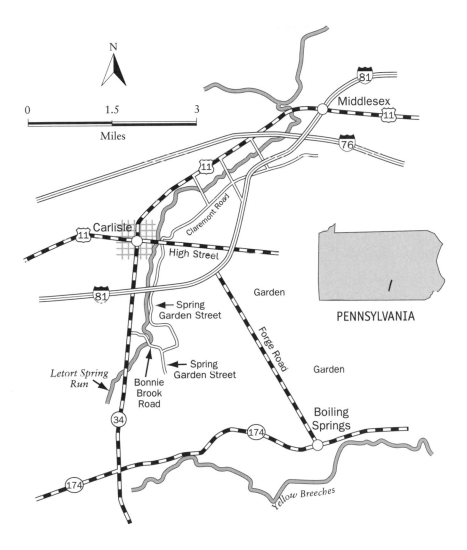

next to Hagn's about half a mile north of the quarry. Here you'll also find two monuments honoring Fox and Marinaro.

If there's a signature hatch on the Letort, it would have to be Sulphurs that come off at dark from early May into June. You'll also find tiny Blue-Winged Olives in early spring and late fall.

Public access is assured to the fly-fishing-only section known as the Heritage Waters, but a lower run of the river below the town of Carlisle flows through private lands. Permission is required to fish this mileage. Often a gentle knock at a

Tiny insects and large fish make the Letort Spring Run a perfect brown trout laboratory.

landowner's door is all that's required. Those who fish without permission jeopardize public access. The lower end is well worth fishing. In the main, the creek holds less cress than the upstream section; grassy undercut banks flowing through large, open meadows are more the norm. Because this portion of the creek is not catch-and-release, numbers of sizeable fish are fewer. But there's more structure. Runs and pools are more clearly defined, and the stream tends to be deeper. Thus the lower run may be more easily fished than the upper. The best angling is found below Carlisle Barracks and above the Pennsylvania Turnpike bridge. Below the bridge, the creek flows through backyards before tumbling down a rocky run to join with the Conodoguinet.

RESOURCES

Gearing up: Cold Spring Anglers, 419 East High Street, Suite A, Carlisle, PA 17013; 717-245-2646; www.coldspringangler.com. Yellow Breeches Outfitters, 2 First St., Boiling Springs, PA 17007; 717-258-6752.

Accommodations: Greater Carlisle area Chamber of Commerce, 212 N. Hanover St., Carlisle, PA 17014; 717-243-4515.

Books: *Trout Streams of Pennsylvania*, Dwight Landis, Hempstead-Lyndell, Bellefonte, PA, 1995.

TU Guide to Pennsylvania Limestone Streams, A. Joseph Armstrong, Stackpole, Mechanicsburg, PA, 1992.

19 Penns Creek

Location: North-central Pennsylvania.
Short take: Famous for great green drakes and big browns.
Type of stream: Limestone/freestone.
Angling methods: Fly, spin.
Species: Brown.
Access: Easy.
Season: Year-round.
Nearest tourist services: State College.
Handicapped access: None.
Closest TU chapter: Spring Creek.

PENNS CREEK IS A LONG DRINK OF WATER. Rising in Penns Cave, the creek cuts down across a broad farming valley before colliding with the flank of Big Poe Mountain. The height of land turns the stream to the northeast but at Coburn it finds a rift in the mountains. Here it enters a tight and very scenic valley, the lower stretch of which is inaccessible by road but followed by an abandoned railroad grade. Emerging from the mountains at Cherry Run, Penns begins to wind and warm as it courses through a Weikert on its way to the Susquehanna River at Selinsgrove. The mileage from Spring Mills to Cherry Valley is considered to be Penns Creek's best trout water due to the rejuvenating powers of numerous limestone springs and spring-fed creeks that cool the flow and add to the volume. Most of the distance is accessible to anglers, but little, excepting the course upstream from Cherry Run, is in public hands. Permission to fish may not be required on all private land, but it never hurts to ask.

The main event on Penns Creek is the hatch of green drakes which typically occurs around Memorial Day and lasts through the first week in June. These big mayflies—*Ephemera guttulata*—are called shad flies (because the hatch coincides to some degree with the spring run of shad in the large rivers of the Mid-Atlantic states) locally, and they attract platoons of anglers from throughout the East. Though different in genus and species, the Green Drake hatch is as important on Penns Creek as it is on Henry's Fork in Idaho and the Metolius in Oregon. On Penns Creek, the heaviest hatches of Green Drakes may not be the best time to fish big dry spinners or duns. Fish may have a difficult time selecting the artificial. But after the primary hatch has passed, sporadic emergences will occur and trout seem to take imitations more readily. Green Drake nymphs are also very productive. This hatch often begins late in the day and continues into the night. Some of the best fishing is found after dark. Caddis, particularly Grannon Caddis are also very productive in mid- to late April, as are the Sulphurs of June and July.

Pine Creek, itself a fine trout fishery, joins Penns Creek at Coburn significantly mitigating the effects of the long flow across farm country. You'll find nice browns

PENNS CREEK

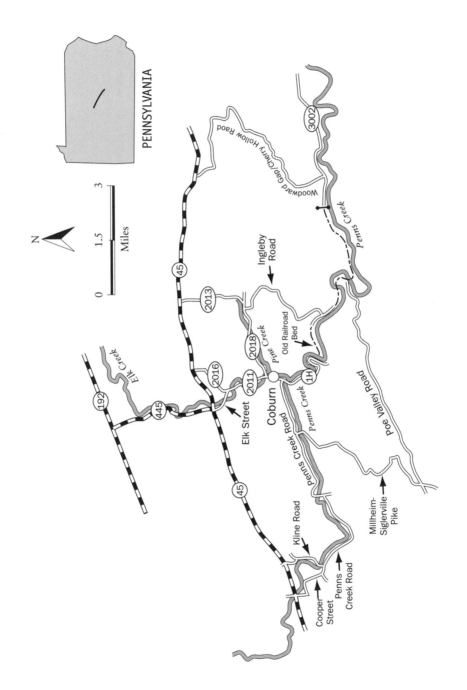

On Penns Creek, anglers flock to the emergence of the Green Drakes in early June.

in the pools and runs below the village. A gravel road shadows the creek, but after a mile or so it ends at a parking lot where a trail leads to the railroad grade, bridges Penns, and works its way through the mountains along the stream. Walking the grade is easy and the creek's pocket water holds good fish. Continuing past a cluster of cabins at Ingleby (reachable by car via the Pine Creek Road and then Ingleby Road), the railroad bed follows the creek crossing the creek again about a mile below Ingleby. The lower stretch of this mileage through the mountains can be reached from the Poe Paddy State Park. Below the park, the railroad grade crosses another trestle and passes through a short tunnel. Across Penns Creek from the tunnel's lower portal, Swift Run adds its waters to the stream, marking the start of about four miles of catch-and-release water. Here the creek is broad, running down riffles, across flats and through pools. Not stocked like other sections, this mileage holds wild brown trout of 12 to 14 inches. The catch-and-release area ends below the confluence with Cherry Run, best reached by car from State Route 3002 running west out of Weikert. The catch-and-release section of Penns Creek sees some pressure to be sure. But most is concentrated within the first mile of either end.

Together with Pine Creek, and its tributary, the shorter Elk, the Penns Creek drainage makes up the longest run of wild trout water in Pennsylvania. A plan to expand a limestone quarry near Aaronsburg was approved by the Pennsylvania Department of Environmental Protection (DEP), but outcries by the Penns Valley

Conservation Association and TU's local chapters and state council that mining would pollute or otherwise jeopardize the streams resulted in an agreement not to quarry below the water table and for ongoing monitoring by DEP.

RESOURCES

Gearing up: Flyfisher's Paradise, 2603 E. College Ave., State College, PA 16801; 814-234-4189.

Accommodations: Centre County Visitors Bureau, 1402 S. Atherton St., State College, PA 16801; 800-358-5466.

Books: *Penns Creek*, Daniel Shields, River Journal Series, Frank Amato, Portland, OR, 1996.

Trout Streams of Pennsylvania, Dwight Landis, Hempstead-Lyndell, Bellefonte, PA, 1995.

TU Guide to Pennsylvania Limestone Streams, A. Joseph Armstrong, Stackpole, Mechanicsburg, PA, 1992.

20 SLATE RUN

Location: North-central Pennsylvania.
Short take: Perhaps the loveliest of Pennsylvania's freestone mountain streams with browns and brook trout to match.
Type of stream: Freestone.
Angling methods: Fly, spin.
Species: Brown, brook.
Access: Moderate.
Season: Year-round.
Nearest tourist services: Slate Run, a village of 18 people.
Handicapped access: None.
Closest TU chapter: Lloyd Wilson.

IN THE EAST, GETTING AWAY FROM IT ALL ain't easy, but there's one hamlet up in the area of Pennsylvania's Grand Canyon where people are few. Though Slate Run has been a famous and popular trout stream for a century, its ruggedness naturally limits the number of anglers you'll find working its pocket water and pools. The reputation of this seven-mile stream extends far beyond the Keystone State. You'll hear it discussed wherever trout fishers gather—Idaho, Alaska, California—to swap stories about those that got away and lies about those that didn't. Slate Run, so named for the horizontal beds of shale that outcrop along its banks, flows through a very narrow flood plain in the bottom of a gorge that's 1,000 feet below the flat tableland atop the mountains. Oaks and pines timber the steep slopes along the river's course. Up high, where brook trout play, mountain laurel blooms in late May and seem to put the wild native brook trout in a rapacious mood. Most anglers come to fish the lower reaches for browns and a few venture into the upper reaches for brookies which grow quite large.

Proclaimed "Heritage Trout" water by the Pennsylvania Fish Commission, Slate Run is open all year to angling, but it's entire length is restricted to fly fishing with barbless hooks. Torrential floods have taken their toll on Slate Run's pools over the past couple of decades and some of the old, well-known pools have been shallowed by cobble washed in from upstream. Still, the run produces a prodigious crop of new browns every year. You'll find them in the riffles; larger fish lie in miles of pocket water, punctuated here and there with an occasional pool. Because the drainage is small, run-off is not normally a problem. But low water in late summer can be. Because the creek is deeply shaded, Slate Run does not warm as much as other streams of similar size. In fact, trout stocked in Pine Creek (not the one that feeds Penns Creek, but another) move up into Slate Run when rising temperatures make the Pine untenable.

The lower reaches of Slate Run are best accessed either from below, in the village by the same name, or at the confluence with Manor Fork. A mile above the fork,

SLATE RUN

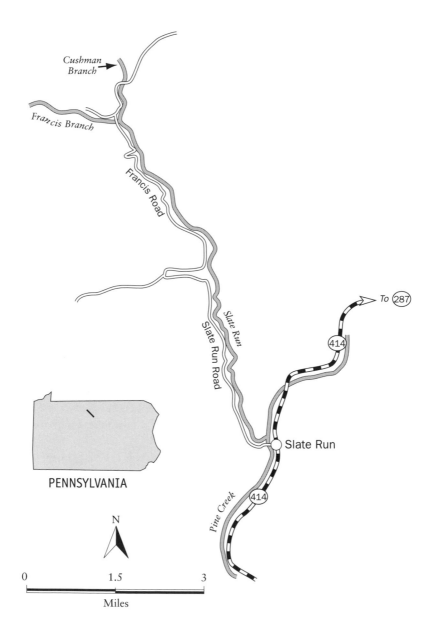

Cushman Branch

Francis Branch

Francis Road

Slate Run

Slate Run Road

To 287

414

Slate Run

414

Pine Creek

PENNSYLVANIA

N

0   1.5   3

Miles

Morris Run Road crosses the Slate providing some additional access. Roads tend to crab high along the sides of these mountains, and anglers who wish to fish must scramble down steep paths to the water. This is not a good place to fish solo. Among critters commonly seen are rattlesnakes, particularly when the dryness of late summer draws them toward the stream. Access to the upper reaches is easier. The gradient is shallower, roads are more prevalent, and brook trout of good size, up to 10 or 11 inches, inhabit these waters. Along with the Blue Quill hatch in April, fish Sulphurs and Slate and Green Drakes in May. By June, most of the major hatches have passed—though there is some action on Blue-Winged Olives early in the day, and maybe a few Yellow Sallies or Light Cahills in the evening. Crickets and ants come into their own, and, after summer spates, small nymphs work reasonably well. With water flowing clear as iced vodka, tippets need to be long and fine to fish fall runs of spawners in the wooded gorge which riots with the reds and oranges of turning leaves.

Accommodations in Slate Run, a town of 18 people, are not as scant as you'd expect. You can choose from three hotels (none of them more than a few rooms), or you can opt for Wellsboro, a mountain resort and lumbering town 40 miles to the northeast. For about 25 years, Tom and Debbie Finkbinder have run a general store, deli, and tackle shop in Slate Run. "We'll sell you anything from a bamboo rod to a steak, but you gotta cook the steak yourself," says Tom. They're good folks and important sources of information. If you're heading to Slate Run, add a couple of days to fish Cedar Run in the next drainage north. Access is a bit easier and the water and hatches are essentially the same.

RESOURCES

Gearing up and accommodations: Wolf's General Store and Slate Run Tackle Shop, P.O. Box 1, Slate Run, PA 17769; 570-753-8551. The Finkbinders, owners of the store, can also provide information on accommodations.

Books: *Trout Streams of Pennsylvania*, Dwight Landis, Hempstead-Lyndell, Bellefonte, PA, 1995.

21 SPRUCE CREEK

Location: Central Pennsylvania.
Short take: What's open to the public is very good, but there isn't much of it.
Type of stream: Limestone creek.
Angling method: Fly.
Species: Brown.
Access: Very limited.
Season: Year-round.
Nearest tourist services: Spruce Creek, Altoona.
Handicapped access: No.
Closest TU chapter: Spring Creek.

LONG BEFORE JIMMY CARTER drifted a dry fly on its cold and clear waters, Spruce Creek earned a reputation for excellent hatches. You'll find them all here with sulphurs and green and gray drakes being the most famous. You'll also find lots of huge brown trout—many of them stocked, and in some stretches fed chow to help them grow quickly. What you won't find is a great deal of public access. Spruce Creek is tied up in private ownership and leases. With the exception of a short stretch managed by Penn State University, you'll pay to fish Spruce Creek. An average day on the river will cost roughly $300 for two. You'll pay that much to drift any of the premier rivers out West.

Rising at the base of Tussy Mountain in the Rothrock State Forest, the upper section of Spruce Creek wanders through open fields and some patches of woods before moving against the base of the mountain about four miles southwest of its origin. From there, the stream plays tag with the edge of the forest along the mountain until it empties into the Little Juniata at the crossroads called Spruce Run. The stream is never wide, but its pools are shaded and landowners such as Wayne Harpster have added lots of structure to provide cover and aeration. The wildness of these trout comes not from the accident of their breeding, but from their ability to strip line off little reels mounted on light rods.

The half-mile Penn State section is 0.6 miles northeast of the mouth of the creek. The mileage begins in a large pool and then divides into a series of braids which coalesce near the end of the run. Trout in this section are, by and large, wild by birth, but they're not as large as those in the private waters. In October, bigger browns begin to move up out of the Little Juniata to spawn in Spruce Run and its feeders. They begin working their way downstream in late October or early November. Fishing slows in winter, but takes off with stonefly hatches in March. It runs into high gear with a fabulous hatch of grannon caddis in late April, then moves on into sulphurs, drakes (both green and slate), tricos and Blue-Winged Olives.

Because of its springs, the river never really runs low and warm in the fall, although the lower reaches—some 15 miles or so from major springs—are a bit more

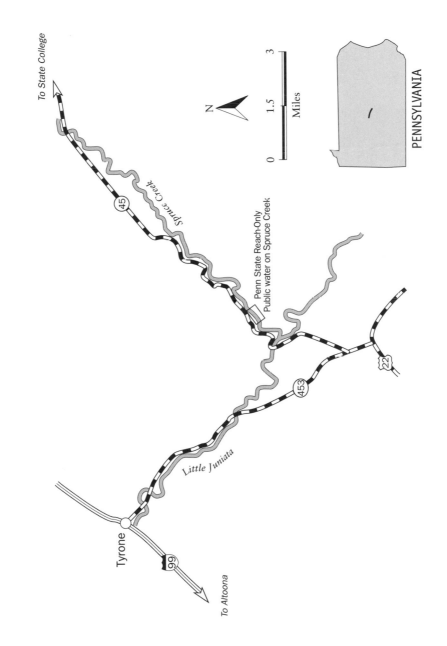

SPRUCE CREEK

tepid come August. And unless the region receives 100 inches or more of snow, spring run-off is seldom a problem. Is Spruce Creek worth a visit? Sure, what great trout stream isn't? On the other hand, unless you plan to lay out a thousand dollars or so for three days of fishing, take a look at the Penn State section. If it's fishing well, give it a whirl. If it's too crowded, check out the Little Juniata. It has all of the hatches, many more access points, and a good deal of the charm of its exclusive cousin.

RESOURCES

Gearing up: Spruce Creek Outfitters, Rt. 45, P.O. Box 36, Spruce Creek, PA 16683; 814-632-3071.

Accommodations: Raystown Country Visitors Bureau, Seven Point Rd., RD#1, Box 222A, Hesston, PA 16647; 814-627-1261.

Books: *Trout Streams of Pennsylvania*, Dwight Landis, Hempstead-Lyndell, Bellefonte, PA, 1995.

TU Guide to Pennsylvania Limestone Streams, A. Joseph Armstrong, Stackpole, Mechanicsburg, PA, 1992.

MID-ATLANTIC

MARYLAND

VIRGINIA

WEST VIRGINIA

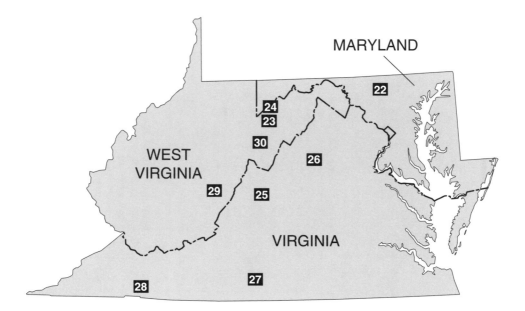

22. Big Gunpowder Falls River
23. Potomac River, North Branch
24. Savage River
25. Jackson River
26. Rapidan River
27. Smith River
28. Whitetop Laurel Creek
29. Cranberry River
30. Seneca Creek

22 Big Gunpowder Falls River

Location: Northeastern Maryland.
Short take: Wildflowers, wild trout, and maybe a bit of seclusion (but only mid-week) on the cool green pools of a river 15 miles north of the Baltimore beltway.
Type of stream: Tailwater.
Angling methods: Fly, spin.
Species: Brown.
Access: Easy.
Season: Year-round.
Nearest tourist services: Tackle shops, accommodations.
Handicapped access: Yes.
Closest TU chapter: Maryland.

FOR TEN MILES, BIG GUNPOWDER FALLS RIVER ambles through the countryside of north-central Maryland virtually unnoticed by hundreds of thousands of passengers in vehicles pounding their way along Interstate 83 between Baltimore and York, Pennsylvania. The exit to the river does not announce its presence. The sign says "Hereford," referring to a crossroad community a mile to the east. As you drive this section of the interstate, you get the feeling that you're crossing remnants of a plain, as indeed you are. The river has cut its way down below the general lay of the land, and that's why it's hidden from view.

But a turn off the highway takes you onto roads that are, at once, country. Turn west on Mount Carmel Road, then right after a mile onto Evna Road, and right again onto Falls Road, and the road winds down through a forest of oaks and hickory and hemlock, past moss-covered outcrops of limestone rock, down to the uppermost bridge over the river. Park in the little lot on the left at the trailhead to Prettyboy Dam, and walk down to the river—a creek really—before you rig your rod. Look at the water, at the cold green pools wreathed with haze on the hottest days of the summer. The water temperature here is reasonably steady at 52 degrees F. Now, when you return to your car to rig your rod, you can think about the river and the browns and the rainbows that abide therein and how you'll try to fool them, and how they will end up fooling you.

From the dam, the first seven miles or so down to Blue Mount Road are restricted to catch-and-release fishing with artificial lures. Downstream, the river is managed for trophy trout; anglers may keep two fish over 16 inches per day. Anything smaller must be released. Once a warmwater river, the first fingerlings were stocked in 1983, and in 1986 efforts by the Maryland TU Council convinced the City of Baltimore to maintain steady flows in the river in amounts that are conducive to trout propagation. The last stocking of the upper river occurred in 1990.

BIG GUNPOWDER FALLS RIVER

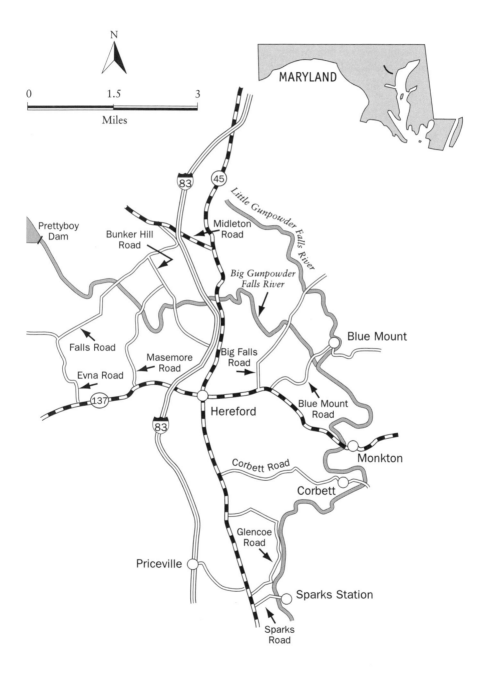

N

0   1.5   3

Miles

MARYLAND

83   45

Little Gunpowder Falls River

Prettyboy Dam

Midleton Road

Bunker Hill Road

Big Gunpowder Falls River

Blue Mount

Falls Road

Masemore Road

Big Falls Road

Evna Road

137

Hereford

Blue Mount Road

83

Monkton

Corbett Road

Corbett

Priceville

Glencoe Road

Sparks Station

Sparks Road

The river sees especially good hatches of sulfurs on afternoons and evenings starting in mid-May and running for a month. Below the interstate, the Gunpowder Valley
opens a bit and the river runs through small meadows. Terrestrials—hoppers, ants,
beetles—are very effective in late summer and early fall. But don't overlook reliable
hatches of little black stoneflies early in the year. Use Blue-Winged Olives,
Hendricksons, and March Browns in April and May; Light Cahills in addition to
the Sulfurs in May and June; and various caddis from mid-May through August.
When there's no action on the surface, particularly in the dog days of summer and
the dead of winter, fish streamers such as Clouser Minnows and the ubiquitous
Woolly Bugger. You'll be surprised. And the usual battery of nymphs—Hare's Ear,
Pheasant Tail, Prince—also produce.

A bit of an angling community has grown up around Big Gunpowder Falls. Wally
Vait (avoid the puns if you can) opened On the Fly, an excellent tackle shop in Hereford in 1992. And the indefatigable Ann McIntosh, author of "The Budget Angler"
column in *Trout* and of the book *The Mid-Atlantic Budget Angler*, owns the Gunpowder Bed and Breakfast in Monkton, just minutes from the river. As you'd suspect here, fishing is spoken fluently.

RESOURCES

Gearing up: On the Fly, 538 Monkton Rd., Monkton, MD 21111; 410-329-6821.
Fisherman's Edge, 1719 1/2 Edmondson Ave., Baltimore MD 21228; 410-719-7999.

Accommodations: Gunpowder Bed and Breakfast, 3810 Beatty Road, Monkton, MD 21111;
410-557-7594.

Books: *Mid-Atlantic Budget Angler*, Ann McIntosh, Stackpole, Mechanicsburg, PA, 1998.

23 POTOMAC RIVER, NORTH BRANCH

Location: West Virginia-Maryland border.
Short take: Destined to be one of the best tailwater fisheries in the country and less than three hours from Washington, D.C.
Type of stream: Freestone, tailwater.
Angling methods: Fly, spin.
Species: Brook, brown, cutthroat, rainbow.
Access: Easy to moderate.
Season: Year-round.
Nearest tourist services: Keyser, West Virginia.
Handicapped access: None.
Closest TU chapter: Nemacolin.

I KNEW I'D SEEN THIS RIVER BEFORE. It's faintly chalky lime green color matches the South Fork of the Snake, and here as well as there, you'll find cutthroat and browns. Both are tailwaters and superb fisheries, and floating them is the most effective way to get to the fish. But the canyons and cliffs of Swan Valley bear little resemblance to the deep, forested valley through which the North Branch courses. And at Pap's, a wonderful country store-cum-tackle shop at Barnum, the only sage you'll encounter is its octogenarian founder.

Acidified with coal mine seepage and heavily silted from run-off from clear-cut slopes and hardscrabble farms, the North Branch of the Potomac was as dead as a river could get for the middle half of the twentieth century. But in the mid-80s, the tall earth-fill dam impounding Jennings-Randolph Lake was closed and a new coldwater fishery was born. Trout were stocked in the last half of the decade and, above the lake, efforts to mitigate the low pH of the river were initiated. Dosers, Rube Goldbergesque contraptions that mix measured charges of powdered lime with a known quantity of water and then dump the slurry into the stream, were located on two feeder streams and at two sites on the main river. Alkalinity jumped into the 6.5 pH range, and aquatic life got an immediate boost.

The upper 18.5 miles of river above Jennings-Randolph is catch-and-keep water. The first 12 miles upstream of the impoundment, and the 952-acre lake itself, receive annual stockings of browns and rainbows. But the 6.5 miles of river that forms the southeastern boundary of Potomac-Garrett State Forest is managed under a delayed harvest concept. During the first half of the year—January to mid-June—this mileage is strictly artificials-only and catch-and-release. For the balance of the year, anglers are permitted to keep two fish per day on any bait or lure they prefer. In little feeder streams like Lost Land Run and Trout Creek, you may find a few wild brookies.

POTOMAC RIVER, NORTH BRANCH

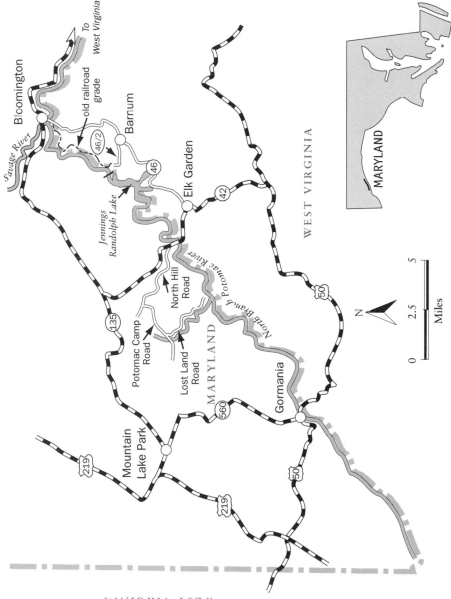

The main event, though, is below the dam. The first 0.38 miles is preserved as a breeding zone. Then there's a two-thirds of a mile stretch of catch-and-release. Below that, along the Mineral County picnic ground, you can keep what you catch. From Blue Hole to the junction of Piney Swamp Run the river again becomes catch-and-release water, and this is the section that attracts most of the attention. Seldom wider than 100 yards, flows are heavy between large blocky boulders and the stream runs much too deep to wade in places. In others, it runs fast and almost smooth, but under the surface you can see a troubled bottom of squarish rock. You'll find trout—browns, cutthroat, rainbows, and brookies—in this stretch, some up to 18 inches and more. In many places, you can wade the river casting either to pockets along banks overgrown with laurel and rhododendron or working the center flows, as is your choice.

The best way to fish the river, though, is to float it, launching at the picnic ground at Barnum and taking out in Bloomington. While the whitewater here is not up to *Deliverance* standards, there's enough of it to make you hold on tight as water heaves the raft through short class II and III rapids. Nymphs work best in this water—big stoneflies, particularly. Streamers like dark Woolly Buggers and Stremphys also produce. Hatches are not yet well developed on this section, but some mayflies, march browns and sulphurs, are starting to come off. While fishing is generally better during spring and fall, you'll find a full complement of terrestrials on the water from mid-summer onward.

Access to the stream is easy; an abandoned railroad grade runs the length of the West Virginia side and you can drive down from Barnum to the gate that marks (more or less) the start of the catch-and-release section of the tail water. Most TU members fish this stretch on foot from the railroad bed. Some even ride mountain bikes along the bed to their preferred holes. The north wall of the stream's valley is steeper and access is more limited. Wading across is tempting, but dicey. Should the flow increase while you're on the other side, your walk back will be, ah, memorable.

Accommodations are limited. The best bet is to hole up in the Econolodge in Keyser, about five miles downstream, and take home-cooked meals in the Royal Restaurant. Keyser is but a 15-minute drive from Barnum.

RESOURCES

Gearing up: Pap's Bait & Tackle, Rt. 4, Box 529A, Keyser, WV 26726; 304-355-2728.

Accommodations: Garrett Co. Chamber of Commerce, 200 S. Third St., Oakland, MD 21550; 301-334-1948.

Books: *Mid-Atlantic Budget Angler*, Ann McIntosh, Stackpole, Mechanicsburg, PA 1998.

24 SAVAGE RIVER

Location: Western Maryland.
Short take: A little tailwater that fishes big below the dam. Upstream you'll work for solitude and trout in a steep valley.
Type of stream: Freestone, tailwater.
Angling methods: Fly, spin.
Species: Brown, rainbow, brook.
Access: Easy down low, difficult above the lake.
Season: Year-round.
Nearest tourist services: Deep Creek.
Handicapped access: None.
Closest TU chapter: Nemacolin.

BLOOMINGTON, MARYLAND, is a company town set deeply amid high mountain ridges at the junction of two of the finest tailwater trout fisheries in the East. You won't find any quaint bed-and-breakfasts with the front room given over to a tier's bench and bins of local patterns for sale. There's no hardware store with cards of Mepps or Panther Martins or teeny rubber worms behind beaded tear-drop spinners. There's nothing here anywhere to tell you that Bloomington is a trout town. Nothing, that is, except special regulations posted on the Savage, and the cold, green rush of the North Fork of the Potomac which cools the air above and fairly breathes brown and rainbow trout.

At one time the Savage was aptly named. Before the earth-fill dam was built, heavy rains would turn the river into a rampaging torrent which gathered speed like an avalanche racing down its 25-mile valley before blasting into Bloomington below. Now danger from flooding is all but a memory. The lake's deep catchment detains run-off and meters it out into the lower river at a normal rate of 50 to 200 cfs. Surrounded by a 53,000-acre state forest, there's little barren land to give up silt. Except during the worst of storms, run-off will carry only the slightest tinge of suspended sediments.

The lake effectively divides the river into two sections. Of the 18.5 miles above the lake, only the lower third is really big enough to fish and that is only reached after a steep climb into the tight valley through which the stream flows. Early in the season, when lake-run rainbows are on the spawn and water levels are rising toward springtime highs, fishing with nymphs and streamer patterns can be good. But summer brings low flows, and the trout that don't drop back down into the lake with the receding waters tend to hole up beneath undercut banks or in the depths of coldwater seep-fed pools. Whether it's worth the effort to venture down to the waters of the upper Savage really depends on how desperate one is for solitude. That, and a few nice trout, is what you'll find there.

You'll find more trout, less solitude, and much easier access on the 5-mile-

SAVAGE RIVER

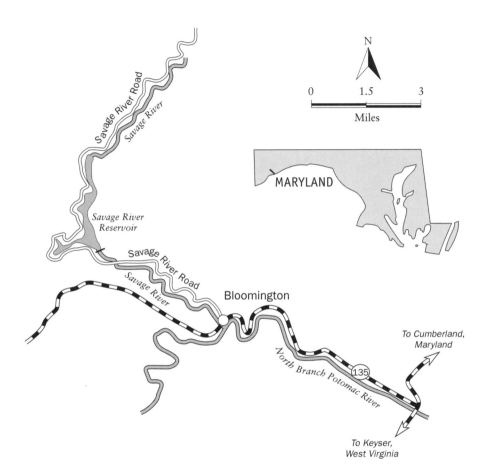

long lower section. When you turn from Route 135 onto Savage River Road, it's easy to be disappointed by the river. On your right, a big Westvaco maintenance yard dominates the far bank, and the intervening stream valley, while wooded, feels somehow industrial. Then, the road crosses the river and on the left, the river flows between backyards and Bloomington Hill. Not a bucolic setting.

But soon the road veers away from the river, and except for one more short patch of houses, it blooms into a marvelous little tailwater. Rhododendron spills over the banks and when laden with bloom, nearly brushes the smoky green flow. Large angular boulders pave the bottoms of pools deep enough to provide challenging wading at minimum flows. They've broken off of the ledges that cross the river, channeling its waters into foaming chutes. In between, the ledges are long glides and a few pocket-water riffles. Above Allegheny Bridge, 3.5 miles from the mouth of the Savage, runs a mile of fly-fishing-only water right to the base of the dam.

This is not a dry-fly stream. On cool, gray summer days, when beads of moisture coalesce into a mist too thick to be called fog, fishing standard nymph patterns can yield a dozen fish, mostly browns, in excess of a foot in length. You have to pick your spots, fishing each pocket carefully with a drag free drift. Patience and precision are the name of the game here. If the water's slightly off-color, so much the better. Dry-fly anglers will find more success on overcast days *sans* drizzle when the stream is running clear. Black stones come off first from February into April which also sees a blue quill hatch. Blue-winged olives, yellow and green stones, and caddis make up the menu for high summer. The late summer course features PMDs, terrestrials, and Slate Drakes grading into tiny BWOs and dark brown stones as first frosts turn streamside maples into flame.

Below Allegheny bridge, the uppermost of the two suspension foot bridges that cross the lower river, anglers can work gold, silver, and dark spinners through pocket water that's a bit deeper than that found upstream. Two- to four-pound test on an ultra-light is the ultimate rig for this area. Anglers who can flip a lure under the rhodas and flutter it through the pool have a decided advantage on this water. In summer, fishing is best early and late in the day. That's OK. If you've brought along a tent you can pitch it in the sylvan campground right across from the river.

RESOURCES

Gearing up: Pap's Bait & Tackle, Rt. 4, Box 529A, Keyser, WV 26726; 304-355-2728.

Accommodations: Garrett Co. Chamber of Commerce, 200 S. Third St., Oakland, MD 21550; 301-334-1948.

Books: *Mid-Atlantic Budget Angler*, Ann McIntosh, Stackpole, Mechanicsburg, PA, 1998.

25 Jackson River

Location: Southwestern Virginia.
Short take: The once-famed tail water is effectively closed pending future agreements on angler access. The middle section above Hidden Valley is wonderful and well worth fishing.
Type of stream: Tailwater below, freestone above.
Angling methods: Fly, spin.
Species: Brown, rainbow.
Access: Easy to moderate.
Season: Year-round.
Nearest tourist services: Hidden Valley.
Handicapped access: Yes.
Closest TU chapter: Charlottesville.

VIRGINIA'S HIGHLAND AND BATH COUNTIES are a compressed terrain. The mountains here have been crumpled upwards by thrusting of a continental plate from the southeast. In the valleys between the mountains run a number of rivers with some fishing—Bullpasture, Cowpasture, and Calfpasture—but the best trout river in this neck of the woods today is the Jackson, a river with good browns in its free-flowing middle reaches. It wasn't always so. Until the mid-90s the Jackson boasted an outstanding tailwater fishery below Garthwright Dam which impounds Lake Moomaw, ten miles or so north of Covington.

Plans to turn the tailwater fishery into catch-and-release trophy water ran afoul of local land owners, whose property deeds are based on grants from George and other English kings. While the grants allow navigation of the waterway, they reserve for landowners' dominion over fish in the river and birds in the air. In short, folks who own the land own the river's fish.

Residents of the narrow mountain valleys of southwest Virginia are a conservative lot. When the state told them they could no longer catch and keep fish from this stretch, the landowners went to court and had their property rights reaffirmed. Anyone caught fishing in a King's Grant section without permission is liable for prosecution. Some landowners post their property, others do not. Written permission is essential. There is some fishing in the mile immediately below the dam, but most fly shops in the region recommend that anglers try their luck farther upstream. Local TU chapters and the state department of game and fish are working hard to resolve this issue. Anglers who receive permission to fish can find themselves hooked onto nice browns in this year-round, easily waded fishery.

Above Lake Moomaw, the Jackson tumbles through two-mile long Richardson Gorge. A county road closely follows the path of the river, allowing instant access. Lake-run browns enter this section during the fall spawn, otherwise trout in this stretch are few. Above the gorge, the valley opens up into a wide pasture and row-

JACKSON RIVER

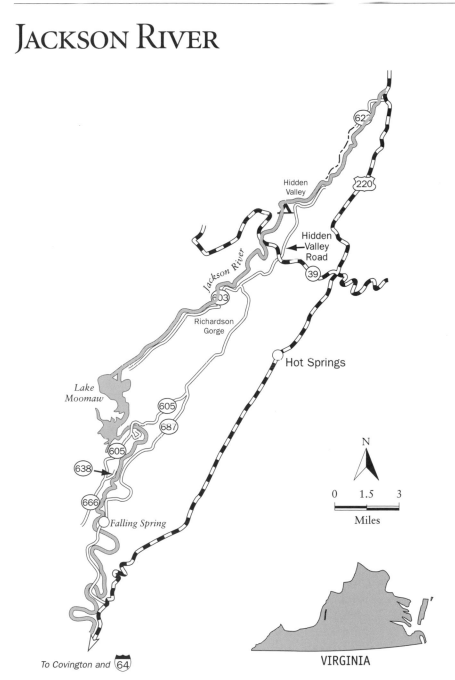

62

Hidden
Valley

220

Hidden
Valley
Road

39

Jackson River

603

Richardson
Gorge

Hot Springs

Lake
Moomaw

605

68

605

638

666

Falling Spring

N

0   1.5   3

Miles

VIRGINIA

To Covington and 64

GRANT MCCLINTOCK

Access can be tricky, but the Jackson River is well worth the effort it demands.

crop bottom. The river meanders with little shade. At the head of the valley, forest closes in and a pair of low mountains rise on either side. Here, in the Hidden Valley Recreation Area, is the best of the free-flowing Jackson.

Mayfly and caddis hatches are regular and trigger feeding by browns of 10 to 14 inches. Quill Gordons match the first hatches in March. They're followed by brown caddis, March Browns, Dark Hendricksons and Blue-Winged Olives. Light Cahills and Sulphurs continue from May into June which also sees some Green Drakes at the end of the month. Cloudy July days may trigger some action on BWOs, but in the main, the Jackson is too warm for good fishing in July and August. It picks up again in September and October with a very good tan caddis hatch and another run of Blue-Winged Olives. From August into the first frosts, small hoppers and ants are also productive. Along with dries, don't overlook stonefly nymphs, Woolly Buggers, and imitations of crayfish.

The river in the immediate neighborhood of the campground is stocked, catch-and-keep water, and heavily fished with bait and spinner in spring. But when stocking stops, the number of anglers declines and holdover trout reclaim the stream. Terrestrials can produce in this section during summer, and the water ought not be overlooked. The real action occurs about a mile and a half upstream from Warwickton (featured in *Sommersby*, a Civil War movie starring Richard Gere and Jodie Foster, this lovely brick ante-bellum mansion is now a comfortable bed-and-breakfast). A 30-minute walk up the streamside road, gated to bar vehicular traffic, brings anglers to the start of a few miles of trophy trout water—two fish per day over 16 inches taken on artificial lures with single barbless hooks. Long riffly runs and slow shady pools, the deeper ones studded with boulders and overhung by moss-draped outcrops, characterize most of the trophy trout section. Even in the dog days of August it's worth the walk, especially if you fish into dusk and return to your room at the bed-and-breakfast or camp in the recreation area across the stream.

Access to the trophy trout section is also provided by County Road 623 which breaks west off of U.S. Highway 220 at the base of Chestnut Ridge. Park at the gate and walk down the road. After half a mile or so, start fishing. US 220 follows the course of the Jackson all the way to its headwaters at Trimble Knob. Yet, like the section below Hidden Valley, the river flows through open, heavily grazed meadows with little habitat for trout. The best thing about this section of highway is that it leads right to the South Branch of the Potomac, another fine trout stream.

RESOURCES

Gearing up: The Outpost, 2 Cottage Row, Box 943, Hot Springs, VA 24445; 540-839-5442. The Bait Place, 707 E. Morris Hill Rd., Covington VA 24426; 540-965-0633.

Accommodations: Hidden Valley Bed & Breakfast, P.O. Box 53, Warm Springs, VA 24484; 540-839-3178.

Books: *Virginia Trout Streams*, Harry Slone, Countryman Press, Woodstock, VT, 1994.

Mid-Atlantic Budget Angler, Ann McIntosh, Stackpole, Mechanicsburg, PA, 1988.

26 RAPIDAN RIVER

Location: Central Virginia.
Short take: Heavily damaged by hurricanes in the mid-90s, Rapidan River is recovering. Good fishing for jewel-like native brook trout in upper reaches. Not a big fish river.
Type of stream: Freestone.
Angling method: Fly.
Species: Brook.
Access: Moderate.
Season: Year-round.
Nearest tourist services: Sperryville, Culpeper.
Handicapped access: None.
Closest TU chapter: Rapidan.

AMONG ANGLERS OF MID-ATLANTIC COUNTRY, the Rapidan is a favorite, as it was with presidents and, still, members of Congress. The allure is not big trout, but wild brookies found high on the flanks of the Blue Ridge within the Shenandoah National Park. You'll find your trout with a healthy dose of history for it's here that Herbert Hoover, a trout fisher, built a presidential retreat in the late 1920s. Camp Hoover is still maintained and occasionally used by members of Congress.

Above Camp Hoover is a short section where the Rapidan flows over ledges of granitic rock plunging into pools where five- to eight-inch brook trout hide. On this stretch, Big Rock Falls is a common destination for anglers. The upper reaches also contain fishable riffles. But the Rapidan is best described as a skinny stream. Fly fishing—all that's allowed—peaks in the spring when dainty patches of bluets brighten sunny spots along the trail.

These upper waters escaped the brunt of the devastation by two hurricanes that pillaged the stream in 1995 and 1996. Heavy oaks, uprooted by the raging torrent, were smashed to splinters by tumbling boulders loosened from the steep mountainside. Rock and log, coursing down the channel, blasted bridges off their iron beams and scoured the channel bare. Receding waters left the river littered with tree trunks and flotsam, providing shade and cover for the stocks of brook trout that somehow survived the deluge.

For a mile and a half, from Camp Hoover to the boundary of the Rapidan Wildlife Management Area, the stream picks its way through a series of tiny pools, fed by rushing sluices. If one were to fish it, dappling a #18 tan caddis at the end of a 6X leader on a 10-foot rod, would be the most successful technique. The angler who wears the muted colors of the woods and practices stealth will pick brookies painted as gaily as wildflowers. A big fish in this section will top seven inches.

A gravel road which crosses the gap between Chapman Mountain and Sag Top and becomes County Route 649 is open to vehicular traffic through the wildlife

RAPIDAN RIVER

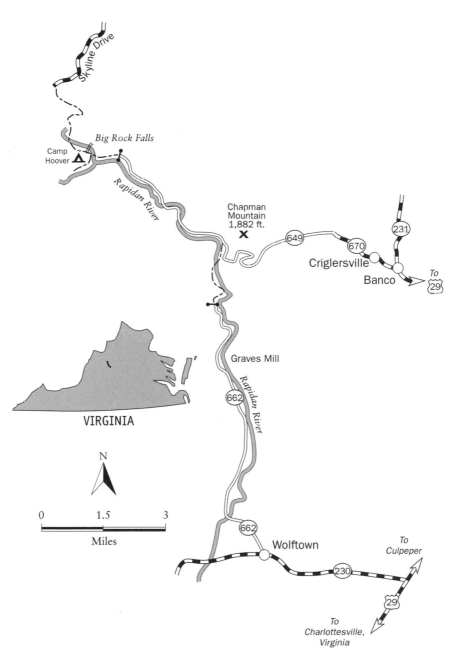

Skyline Drive

Big Rock Falls

Camp
Hoover

Rapidan River

Chapman
Mountain
1,882 ft.
X

649

670

231

Criglersville

Banco

To
29

VIRGINIA

N

0   1.5   3

Miles

Graves Mill

Rapidan River

662

662

Wolftown

To
Culpeper

230

29

To
Charlottesville,
Virginia

management area. The road terminates at a locked gate, about 1.5 miles downstream from Camp Hoover. The other way to reach the upper section is to hike down from Milam Gap on Skyline Drive.

Downstream from the gate, past Rapidan Camps, a collection of brown frame cabins built by the Marines as an annex to the presidential retreat in 1931, the stream gains in size and it's possible to make a cast. While no formal campsites exist per se, camping is permitted and the area fills up on summer weekends. Children splash in the brook where it's close to the road, but those places are fairly few. Generally, the river is far below the road. Dedicated anglers climb down and then fish their way upstream. Others drive into the lower section of the river at Graves Mill and fish the two miles or so up to the road over the mountains. In addition to brook trout, the lower mileage holds some browns that have migrated up from lower, stocked sections of the river.

Ant patterns and a local favorite, Mr. Rapidan, invented by Harry Murray, are generally successful in sizes of #16 and smaller. You'll also find the usual mayflies and caddis. Small nymphs also are effective, and they're best fished as droppers under a parachute-style dry.

RESOURCES

Gearing up: Murray's Fly Shop, P.O. Box 156, Edinburg, VA 22824; 540-984-4212; www.murraysflyshop.com; email: murrays@shentel.net. Thornton River Fly Shop, 12018C Lee Highway, P.O. Box 530, Sperryville, VA 22740-0530; 540-987-9499.

Accommodations: Culpeper County Chamber of Commerce, 133 West Davis Street, Culpeper, VA 22701; 540-825-8628.

Books: *Virginia's Trout Streams*, Harry Slone, The Countryman Press, Woodstock, VT, 1994.

Trout Fishing in Shenandoah National Park, Harry Murray, Shenandoah Publishing Company, Edinburg, VA,1989.

27 SMITH RIVER

Location: South-central Virginia.
Short take: Great tailwater, good hatches in trophy section.
Type of stream: Tailwater.
Angling methods: Fly, spin, bait.
Species: Brown, rainbow.
Access: Easy.
Season: Year-round.
Nearest tourist services: Martinsville.
Handicapped access: None.
Closest TU chapter: Smith River.

WITHIN VIRTUALLY A STONE'S THROW of each other, the Smith and the Dan Rivers rise on the east flank of New Brammer Ridge just below the Blue Ridge Parkway. The upper section of the Dan, from Pinnacles Powerplant past Townes Dam and up to Talbot Dam offers excellent brown and brookie fishing in small pool and pocket water for those willing to make the seven-mile trek. The Smith and its tributaries hold stocks of native brook trout in the upper mileage and you can reach the headwaters by hiking down from County Road 609.

But, while the little brook trout are indeed lovely, it's the tawny gold browns below Philpott Dam that have earned the Smith River a place on the nation's list of well-known tailwater fisheries. For 15 miles, the chill waters issuing from the base of this 200-foot dam nurture brown and rainbow trout, providing a year-round fishery. About two miles downstream from the dam, where Town Creek joins the river and provides needed nutrient, a three-mile stretch classified by the state as Trophy Trout water begins. Single, barbless, hooked lures or flies and only two trout, no less than 16 inches, are the rule. Roads for vehicles do not follow this section, but a gravel road, barred by a locked gate, provides easy walking access.

There's just one catch. While a call to 540-629-2432 will provide a schedule of releases from the dam, you'll want to have your ears open for the shrill blast of the siren warning on an impending discharge. Good fishing is found at 100 to 300 cfs. But when the horn sounds, water may rise three feet in just a few minutes. That caveat aside, the river is easily waded. A bottom of ledge rock or gravel underlies the riffles and runs that make up the trouty mileage. Vegetation overhangs the banks providing havens for hoglike browns that feed delicately during the day and more aggressively toward dusk. These fish are more wary than spooky, but fine tippets and small patterns are the order of the day. During a day's angling, you'll likely encounter at least a dozen fish, mostly browns, but possibly a rainbow or two, in the 10- to 12-inch range.

While the trophy section and the waters below the apron of the dam see most of the action, don't overlook the river from Bassett to the U.S. Highway 220 bridge.

SMITH RIVER

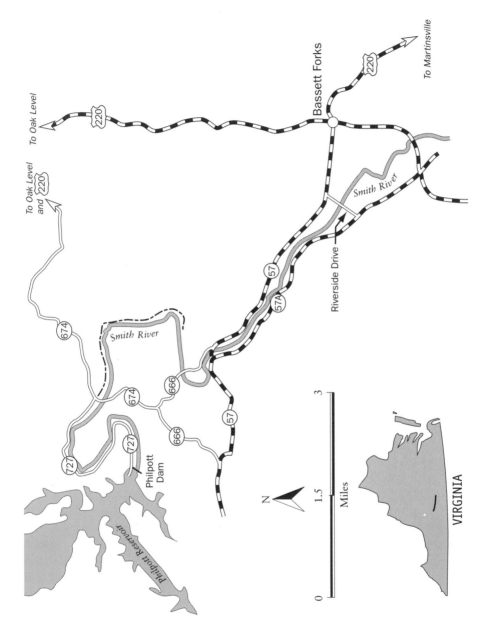

You'll find brown trout scattered throughout the long, smooth runs here. Terrestrials are particularly effective in this area late on a summer's day. And when winter's bitter chill grips the land, head for the water just below the dam. Browns will take small streamers and patiently fished nymphs. Otherwise, the Smith sees its share of March Browns and Hendrickson's and Blue-Winged Olives early in the season and caddis and BWOs in the fall. If there's one time to be on the river, it's late May and early June during the sulfur hatches. Action can be non-stop. Hardware hurlers will do well with Roostertails, Mepps, and Panther Martins in yellow or silver in the smallest sizes available. Anglers who fish minnow or crawdad imitations in the lower mileage just may find the fish of a lifetime ripping line from their reels.

To reach the tailwater section of the Smith, take Route 57 west from US 220 at Bassett Forks. It's also possible to pick your way down from the Blue Ridge Parkway from Cannaday Gap on county roads that will take you through Endicott and Mill Creek and eventually to the river. Motels and restaurants are found along US 220 and camp sites are available at Fairy Stone State Park on the western arm of Philpott Lake.

RESOURCES

Gearing up: Rakes Sporting Goods, 29 Philpott Dam Road, Bassett, VA 24055; 540-629-7220.

Accommodations: Martinsville Henry County Chamber of Commerce, P.O. Box 709, Martinsville, VA 24114; 540-632-6401.

Books: *Virginia Trout Streams*, Harry Slone, The Countryman Press, Woodstock, VT, 1994.

28 WHITETOP LAUREL CREEK

Location: Southwestern Virginia.
Short take: Premier trout river. Plunge pools, shaded runs, clear water, steep gradient. Two-mile walk into artificials-only section.
Type of stream: Freestone.
Angling methods: Fly, spin.
Species: Brown, rainbow.
Access: Easy.
Season: Year-round.
Nearest tourist services: Lodging in Damascus.
Handicapped access: None.
Closest TU chapter: Over Mountain.

WHEN YOU WALK THE CINDERED ROADBED along the best section of Whitetop Laurel, let your mind's eye see a chuffing narrow-gauge steam engine braking as much as the engineer dares to hold back its cargo of big-butted poplar and oak on the treacherous 4.5 percent grade. At night, if you listen carefully, you'll hear the shriek of the open whistle telling all that there's no stopping her now, not till she gets way down to Laureldale, a stone's throw east of Damascus. Folks would ride the train down and out of the narrow valleys to get groceries and to get doctored, and then they'd ride it back home again. A logging train was a primitive form of mass transit in this part of the country where today there's still not much mass.

The trains are gone, but in the shadows of eight trestles that carried the trains over Whitetop Laurel and its tributaries lie brown and rainbow trout, most of them stocked fish, but not all. If you are quiet and careful, you can see them in the oh-so-clear water of this mountainous freestone stream. (If you're not so careful, they can see you.) In the three-and-a-half mile, artificials-only section, the water flows from long pools through riffles and chutes, only to pool again. It is a classic stream, with reasonably easy access, but, as is the case with good streams, with a bit of a walk at either end into the best fishing. Such is the stream's gradient, that a frog-strangling gully washer which turns the river the color of lentil soup on Tuesday, will be clear enough to fish Thursday morning.

The run from Damascus to Konnarock is roughly 20 miles and the creek is fishable all the way. The lowest section from Damascus, through Laureldale to the point where the stream heads off to the south toward Taylor's Valley is hard by U.S. Highway 58, the main highway across southern Virginia. Traffic is sometimes heavy—trailer trucks during the week and tourists on summer weekends. Despite the constant pounding of passing vehicles, there are stocked rainbows to be caught along the highway and the two-and-a-half-mile stretch from US 58 southeast to Taylor's Valley. Normal regs apply.

WHITETOP LAUREL CREEK

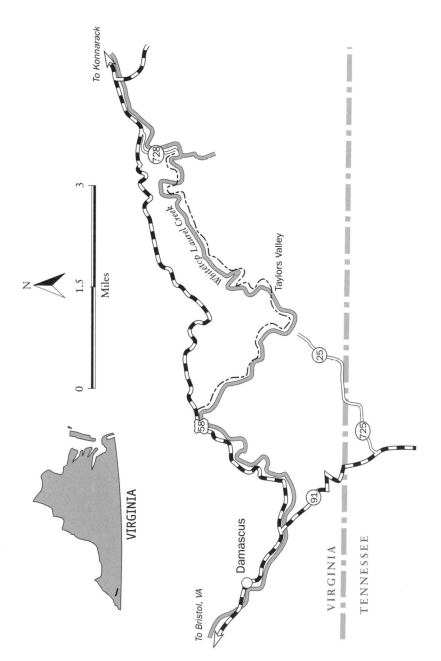

JOHN ROSS

The angler willing to walk a bit will be rewarded with wild trout on Whitetop Laurel Creek.

The best fishing is found in the 3.5 miles from Taylor's Valley to Creek Junction. Here in the shaded pools and runs, you'll find rainbows and browns up to about 16 inches, although 10- to 12-inchers are more usual fare. Artificial single-hooked lures are the rule here, regulations that the once active Abingdon, Virginia, chapter of TU helped establish. While at times, particularly summer weekends, angling pressure is heavy, it falls off during the week.

Trout aren't overly educated, though. Anglers fishing tiny spinners such as Roostertails or general patterns like a Parachute Adams or a tan caddis in #16 or #18 will catch fish. This stream is very clear and it's possible to sight-fish using nymphs. That's a real kick. Again, almost any small Hare's Ear, Prince, or Pheasant Tail will do the job. However, Green Drakes in early June provides four days of absolutely stunning sport, as do dark Blue-Winged Olives in May. Also try Yellow Sallies, Sulphurs, and Yellow Stones, all in sizes #14 to #16. Don't overlook ants, beetles, inchworms, and hoppers in late summer. The special regs section continues for a mile up Green Cove Creek at Creek Junction.

Above Creek Junction the stream takes on the name Little Whitetop Laurel, and normal rules apply. Here the river becomes smaller, but plunge pools are more frequent in the mileage up to US 58. Across the highway, the river fishes moderately well to the hamlet of Konnarock, but beyond that town, the water becomes quite small. You'll find some brookies in the upper headwaters, but they are few and far between and generally not worth a special trip. From Damascus to the headwaters, the Appalachian Trail follows the stream and as you fish, you're apt to be hailed by trekkers on their way from Maine to Georgia, but there's no camping along Whitetop Laurel. Parking is available on US 58 and, after a short excursion into neighboring Tennessee, in Taylor's Valley.

RESOURCES

Gearing up: Virginia Creeper Flyshop, 17172 Jeb Stewart Highway, Abingdon, VA 24211; 540-628-3826. Holston Angler, 110 Poplar Ridge Road, Piney Flats, TN 37686; 423-538-7412.

Accommodations: Washington County Chamber of Commerce, 179 East Main Street, Abingdon, VA 24210; 540-628-8141.

Books: *Virginia Trout Streams*, Harry Slone, The Countryman Press, Woodstock, VT, 1994.

29 CRANBERRY RIVER

Location: Central West Virginia.
Short take: A marvelous example of how a once-sterile stream can be restored to a prominent trout fishery.
Type of stream: Freestone.
Angling methods: Fly, spin.
Species: Brook, brown, rainbow.
Access: Moderate.
Season: Year-round.
Nearest tourist services: Tackle shops, accommodations in Richwood.
Handicapped access: Woodbine Recreation Area.
Closest TU chapter: Kanawha.

A DECADE AGO, THE CRANBERRY RIVER gained a sort of national renown as the case that proved the fact that acid rain could kill a river. For 41 miles, the river flows through wilderness as pristine as anywhere in the East. No towns, no industries, no mines, not even a house or farm, lie along its course. Famed as a wild trout fishery in the '40s and '50s, acidic precipitation eliminated the aquatic insects trout need to survive and decimated the trout themselves. Here and there, isolated pockets of brook trout were found, but in the main, the only fish were those stocked by West Virginia's Department of Natural Resources.

Today, the river is resurging. Hatches abound, particularly eastern green drakes in late May and June, and light cahills in June and July. Self-propagating populations of browns, rainbows, and brookies are reestablishing themselves throughout the river system and, according to Keith Comstock of Cranberry Wilderness Outfitters, "The river wouldn't exist without TU."

The West Virginia Council of TU supported the state's decision to install limestone grinders on two tributaries, the Dogway and North forks, and to establish special regulations including a pair of catch-and-release sections. Restoring the Cranberry "was not a matter of improving habitat," says Comstock. "The habitat was there. TU encouraged the state to adopt policies that are restoring the river."

And what a river it is. Rising in the Cranberry Glades between Black Mountain and Blue Knob, the river flows through a 35,864-acre wilderness area, the largest USDA Forest Service wilderness area in the state. The upper reaches of North, South, and Dogway Forks are brook trout country, those thin, dark, shady waters overhung by laurel and rhododendron where fishing is more a matter of dappling a fly on a long 7X tippet than making a cast. From the junction of the North and South forks down to the low water bridge where Dogway enters and all the way down Dogway, a combined distance of more than 6 miles is catch-and-release only.

You'll find rainbows in plunge pools and heavy pocket water in the middle section of the Cranberry. It's all wadeable, but the canyon section is quite difficult. To

CRANBERRY RIVER

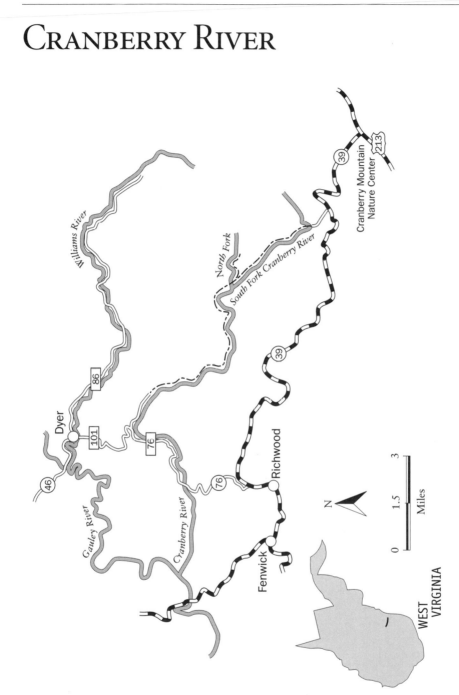

reach this mileage, you'll have to walk, ride a mountain bike, or—get this—take Comstock's mule cart, to reach this section. There's no vehicular access to the abandoned railroad grade that follows the river's course. The lower section from its mouth on the Gauley to Woodbine Picnic Area is slower with long gravel-bottomed runs reminiscent of stretches of the Beaverkill or Willowemoc. Fishing is a year-round proposition, but in September, Comstock urges folks not to fish. That's when the river is at its lowest and warmest, potentially a fatal combination for a good trout played on light gear. This is not big trout water, yet. A good-sized brookie will reach eight inches; big browns and rainbows are in the 12-inch class.

Accommodations are available in many of the towns in the area. But for those whose wallet permits, Comstock provides backcountry pack trips. He'll load up a wagon with 12- by 16-foot wall tents, stoves, tables, chairs, and vittles—quail, trout, steaks—and all the dunnage needed for a three-day wilderness trip up into the Cranberry. It's just like a pack trip into a remote river in Montana's Bob Marshall Wilderness, except you don't have to ride a horse. For the rest of us who labor under traditional economic constraints, there's parking at Cranberry Glades trailhead and along Forest Road 76. Like Seneca Creek in the northern part of the state, on the Cranberry, solitude and good fishing are not in short supply.

RESOURCES

Gearing up: Cranberry Wilderness Outfitters, 1 Park Place, Richwood, WV 26202; 800-848-8390; www.wvoutfitters.com.

Accommodations: Richwood Chamber of Commerce, 1 E. Main St., Richwood, VA 26261; 304-846-6790.

Books: *Mid-Atlantic Budget Angler*, Ann McIntosh, Stackpole, Mechanicsburg, PA, 1998.

30 SENECA CREEK

Location: Northeastern West Virginia.
Short take: A completely wild trout stream off the beaten path.
Type of stream: Freestone.
Angling method: Fly.
Species: Brook, rainbow.
Access: Long walk, but not difficult.
Season: Year-round.
Nearest tourist services: Seneca Rocks.
Handicapped access: None.
Closest TU chapter: Allegheny Highlands.

LIKE SO MANY OTHER PRODUCTIVE TROUT STREAMS, Seneca is somewhat Janused. Driving from Seneca Rocks, so named for a jagged bed of near vertical white Tuscarora sandstone that juts up above the surrounding mountains, west on U.S. Highway 33 you see a stream that looks trouty enough. Yet it flows through the backyards of houses and the old stores of the town of Onego and you know that its brookies and rainbows must succumb to relentless pressure. And when you turn south on Whites Run Road, a couple of miles beyond Onego, the presence of a campground does not bode well for Seneca's mileage.

But when you pull off Whites Run Road into the parking area for the Allegheny Mountain trailhead, you get an inkling of why Seneca is such a special stream. Parking is limited. A few well-placed rocks allow you to hop-scotch across Whites Run and a path leads to Seneca Creek. The water is generally skinny and very clear, except after storms of more than a day's duration. When it floods, Seneca browns a bit with humus flushed from the slopes of 3,800-foot Little Mountain and other peaks along its 10-mile course.

Flowing from southwest to northeast, Seneca makes a fairly straight run down a tight valley. In the lower reaches, it cuts through a narrow flood plain to rounded rock the size of paving stones. About two miles above the parking area is a low falls where a small stream enters from the east. The stream narrows above the falls, and its pockets are better shaded. The five miles from the falls to Judy Springs Campground—primitive is the operative term—is the best water in the stream. Most trout are tiny five- to seven-inch rainbows and brookies, but once in a while a 10- or 12-inch brook trout will surprise you. The ardent wild-trout angler will delight in exploring the three miles or so of fishable water that remain above Judy Springs. It's also possible to reach the campground by dropping down the trail from Forest Road 112 a couple miles east of the Spruce Knob Lake Campground.

During the spring, flows are heavier, of course, and it may then be possible to seduce larger trout with bead-headed nymphs—Hare's Ear with gold ribs or without, Prince, Pheasant Tail, or stonefly—or with small dark streamers such as the

SENECA CREEK

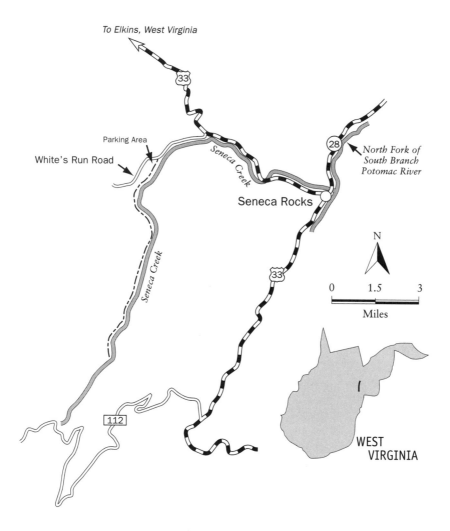

To Elkins, West Virginia

33

Parking Area

White's Run Road

Seneca Creek

28

North Fork of
South Branch
Potomac River

Seneca Rocks

Seneca Creek

33

N

0   1.5   3
Miles

112

WEST
VIRGINIA

ubiquitous Woolly Bugger and Muddlers. Try attractors as well. For dries, carry Hendricksons, Blue-Winged Olives, Quill Gordons and green caddis, all small. As summer comes on, Sulphurs, Light Cahills and terrestrials all make their appearances. Ants, inchworms, beetles, and small hoppers will take trout from July into September. Small tan caddis are also good. Parr-marked rainbows and brook trout are not too choosy, but larger fish are. Tippets need to be fine, but drifts are short. It's always a toss-up between using a rod long enough to dapple a fly (assuming you're dressed in earthy colors and moving with the stealth of a deer) or one short enough to cast in the tight, shaded quarters. A little two- or three-weight is dandy.

Because access is limited to anglers willing to hoof it, you'll seldom see anyone other than your partner when fishing Seneca Creek. The length of the stream (and the Forest Service's liberal camping policy) makes this an ideal spot to pack in a mountain tent and a few days' provisions to create a wilderness fishing camp of the style so popular a century ago. Here's a place where Nessmuk would be right at home.

RESOURCES

Gearing up: Harper's Old Country Store, P.O. Box 9, Seneca Rocks WV 26884; 304-567-2586.

Accommodations: Seneca Rocks Visitors Center. Hedrick's 4-U Motel, HC 73 Box 10 A, Seneca Rocks WV 26884; 304-567-2111. Yokum's Vacationland, HC 59, Box 3, Seneca Rocks WV 26884; 304-567-2351.

Books: *Mid-Atlantic Budget Angler*, Ann McIntosh, Stackpole, Mechanicsburg, PA, 1998.

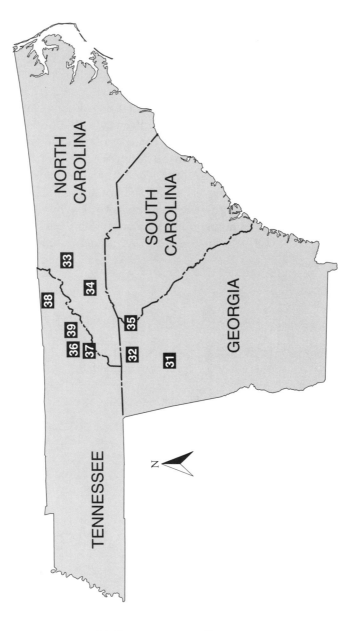

31. CHATTAHOOCHEE RIVER
32. DUKES CREEK
33. DAVIDSON RIVER
34. NANTAHALA RIVER
35. CHATTOOGA RIVER
36. CLINCH RIVER
37. HIWASSEE RIVER
38. HOLSTON RIVER, SOUTH FORK
39. LITTLE RIVER

SOUTHEAST

GEORGIA

NORTH CAROLINA

SOUTH CAROLINA

TENNESSEE

31 CHATTAHOOCHEE RIVER

Location: Northern Georgia.
Short take: Two sections are worthy of note. The lower river upstream from Atlanta is an outstanding tailwater fishery. Don't overlook the upper river in the mountains near Helen.
Type of stream: Freestone, tailwater.
Angling methods: Fly, spin, bait.
Species: Brown, rainbow, few brook.
Access: Easy to moderate.
Season: Year-round.
Nearest tourist services: Atlanta, Helen.
Handicapped access: Chattahoochee National Recreation Area.
Closest TU Chapters: Chattahoochee, Tailwater, Upper Chattahoochee.

YOU CAN COUNT ON THE THUMB of your left hand the number of major cities in the South or anywhere else in the nation, for that matter, that have a great trout stream running through their centers. But that's just what the Chattahoochee brings to Atlanta, thanks to the frigid outflow from the base of Buford Dam about 45 miles north. The suburban 'Hooch is the section of river that gets all the glory, but high in its headwaters in the mountains above Helen, the river is quite good for both wild and stocked browns and rainbows.

Rising between Coon Den Ridge and Spaniards Knob where the southern Appalachians brush 4,000 feet, the Chattahoochee gathers its waters from beneath hemlocks, rhododendron, and azalea, and tumbling over granite boulders, runs thin and cold. This is native brook trout country. You can catch tiny trout of six inches or so, as gaily colored as the wildflowers that bloom in the spring woods. A 30-foot waterfall at Henson Creek protects the brookies from browns and rainbows lower down. The falls are a short hike from the Wilks Road, which branches off the Poplar Stump Road at Vandiver Branch, about a mile to the west. At that point the Poplar Stump Road is fairly high above the Chattahoochee, which is flowing in a gorge. There's less fishing pressure there, yet the fishing is very good, probably because the river is not easy to reach. Below the gorge to State Route 75, the river runs right along the road. On weekends, campers abound.

Between Helen and Gainesville the river warms as it flows out of the foothills and across the piedmont into 38,000-acre Lake Sidney Lanier, the most heavily used of the Corps of Engineers reservoirs. When Buford Dam was closed in 1957 and the lake began to fill, no one had given any thought to creating a tailwater trout fishery. A couple of years later, the Izaak Walton League stocked a few thousand trout fingerlings into the chill waters below the dam and thus was born Georgia's premier trout fishery.

UPPER CHATTAHOOCHEE RIVER AND DUKE'S CREEK

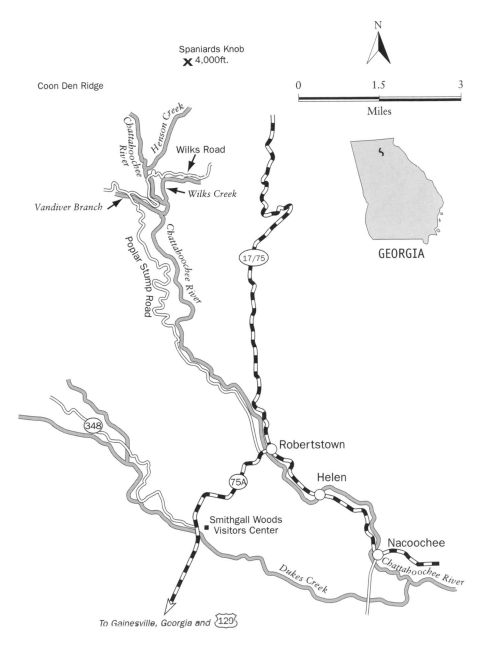

Spaniards Knob
✗ 4,000ft.

Coon Den Ridge

N

0   1.5   3

Miles

Henson Creek

Chattahoochee River

Wilks Road

Wilks Creek

Vandiver Branch

Poplar Stump Road

Chattahoochee River

17/75

GEORGIA

348

Robertstown

75A

Helen

Smithgall Woods
Visitors Center

Nacoochee

Dukes Creek

Chattahoochee River

To Gainesville, Georgia and 129

115

CHATTAHOOCHEE TAILWATER

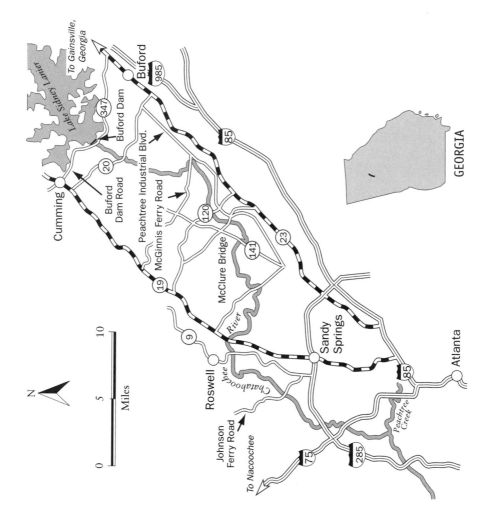

The river may see some natural propagation, but it is heavily stocked with browns and rainbows. They thrive and provide anglers with exciting fishing. Public access is assured. The first two-and-a-half miles below the dam is a cold, sterile stretch, best suited to bait and spinner fishing. Because of sudden and rapid releases from the dam, all who fish this uppermost section are required to wear life vests. The next 14 miles are best floated in canoe or johnboat. You'll find some holdovers here, but in the main you'll catch 10- to 12-inch stocked fish by casting to brush along the banks. Rapalas and similar lures take the bigger fish. Fly fishers have fun with terrestrials.

Decent fly fishing begins to pick up at Jones Bridge shoals, about a mile downstream from the Medlock Bridge on SR 141, where caddis hatch. Another shoal in this section, at Island Ford, is also worthy of attention. Browns to 16 pounds and rainbows of 14 pounds have been taken from this section. Morgan Falls Dam slows the Chattahoochee and evens out the remaining tailwater surges. And the flow below the dam crosses a number of riffles—Cochran and Thornton Shoals and Devil's Race Course—of interest to trouters. Most of the public access to the river from Buford Dam to Atlanta is contained in the Chattahoochee National Recreation Area, a series of about 13 parcels of land totaling about 4,000 acres, administered by the National Park Service.

RESOURCES

Gearing up: Fish Hawk, 279 Buckhead Ave., Atlanta, GA 30305; 404-237-3473 Unicoi Outfitters, 7082 S, Main St., Helen GA 30545; 706-878-3083.

Information: Chattahoochee National Recreation Area, 1978 Island Ford Parkway, Atlanta, GA 30350; 770-399-8070. Chattahoochee Wildlife Management Area, Helen, GA 30545; 770-535-5700.

Accommodations: Helen Chamber of Commerce, P.O. Box 192, Helen, GA 30545; 800-858-8027. Atlanta Convention and Visitors Bureau, 233 Peachtree St. NE Ste 100, Atlanta, GA 30303; 800-285-2682; www.acvb.com.

Books: *Tailwater Trout in the South*, Jimmy Jacobs, Backcountry Publications, Woodstock, VT, 1996.

Trout Streams of Southern Appalachia, Jimmy Jacobs, Backcountry Publications, Woodstock, VT, 1994.

32 DUKES CREEK

(See map on page 115)

Location: Northern Georgia.
Short take: Wild conditions for almost wild trout.
Type of stream: Freestone.
Angling methods: Fly, spin.
Species: Brown, rainbow.
Access: Moderate.
Season: Year-round.
Nearest tourist services: Helen.
Handicapped access: None.
Closest TU chapter: Foothills.

CHARLES SMITHGALL WAS A NEWSMAN with a vision. He began buying up parcels in the north Georgia mountains. His dream was to create a retreat where he and his guests could enjoy some of the finest trout fishing in the Southeast. He set about building a lodge, ancillary cabins for staff, and restoring all but the upper-most reaches of Dukes Creek, one of the major tributaries to the Chattahoochee. About five years ago, he sold the holdings, including about five miles of the creek (at about 50 percent of their appraised value) to the state which then established the Smithgall Woods-Dukes Creek Conservation Area. This was no Dutch uncle!

Fishing here is like visiting your rich uncle's estate. You'll call the conservation area at 706-878-3087 and tell the receptionist who answers that you'd like to visit. She or he will ask you which Wednesday, Saturday, or Sunday you'd prefer. You'll offer a couple of ideas, two or three weeks away, and more than likely you will be given a reservation. You'll be sure to attend. Only 15 anglers are permitted on the stream during each of the two six-hour fishing sessions daily. Once there, you'll either walk or be driven, to the mileage you wish to fish. And, on the stream, you'll cast nymphs to some of the largest trout in the mountains. Jim Harris who runs Unicoi Outfitters in nearby Helen talks of a 28-inch rainbow that he had to return to the stream. All fish are returned, and rules call for barbless hooks on artificial lures. The fee for all this hospitality—a mere $2 for a parking permit.

The fishery is divided into four sections of approximately equal length. The upper mileage runs through a bit of a gorge with lots of cascades and plunge pools. Hemlock, laurel, and pine overhang the waters, clutching at backcast lures and flies. On the middle two sections, the gradient lessens and the stream flows past abandoned farm land. The bed contains some gravel and limited hatches of caddis and sulfurs occur. In the lower section, the river again enters a tight gorge that's difficult to fish. Spinners and nymphs are on the menu here. Woolly Buggers, Prince, Tellico, Pheasant Tail, Hare's Ear, Beadheads—they'll all do the job. You may provoke strikes with Parachute Adams and Wulffs.

Ordinarily, these waters would contain populations of native brook trout, and occasionally you'll catch one. But stocking over the last 30 years or so has pretty well destroyed the indigenous char. And there's little natural food to support trophy-sized browns and rainbows. How's it done? Well, here's the secret: these trout are being fed a supplemental diet. You'll seldom see it, but staffers spread pellets on the water. That keeps them healthy and in the stream. Is this fishery too artificial for you? If it is, try your luck in the Dukes Creek Wildlife Management above the conservation area. You can catch stocked trout there too, on lures, flies, or bait.

Mr. Smithgall's lodge and cabins, by the way, are operated as a luxury retreat for a fee of about $300 per couple per night. It's a favorite getaway for southern corporations. Catering and accommodations are absolutely first class, and the proceeds help support the fishery.

RESOURCES

Gearing up: Unicoi Outfitters, 7082 S. Main St., Helen, GA 30545; 706-878-3083.

Information: Smithgall Woods-Dukes Creek Conservation Area, Helen, GA 30545; 706-878-3087.

Accommodations: Helen Chamber of Commerce, P.O. Box 192, Helen, GA 30540; 800-858-8027.

Books: *Angler's Guide to Dukes Creek*, Mitchel Barrett, Smithgall Woods–Dukes Creek Conservation Area, Helen, GA, 1997.

33 Davidson River

Location: Western North Carolina.
Short take: Easy access, big wild trout, but they're wise.
Type of stream: Freestone.
Angling methods: Fly, spin
Species: Brown, rainbow, brook.
Access: Easy.
Season: Year-round.
Nearest tourist services: Asheville, Brevard.
Handicapped access: None.
Closest TU chapter: Pisgah.

No one is quite sure about the origins of the big grassy balds that top some of the mountains in the southern Appalachians; perhaps they were old burns where new growth was kept down by more than two centuries of grazing by livestock of those hearty pioneers who lived in this land where contours are close and people are not. You'll cross a pair of these balds—Silvermine and Fork River—if you drive east along the Blue Ridge Parkway from State Route 215 to U.S. Highway 276, the twisting mountain highway that drops down along Looking Glass Creek to its union with the Davidson River where Forest Road 475 comes in from the right.

The Davidson is justly famed as one of North Carolina's premier trout fisheries. From its headwaters to Avery Creek, about 14 miles, the river is managed for wild trout. There's no stocking. Angling is strictly catch-and-release and open to fly fishers only. Below Avery Creek, general regulations apply and the river is heavily stocked. From Avery downstream to the boundary of Pisgah National Forest, access is easy. But outside the forest, the land becomes private and access is more restricted.

Most anglers head for the main stem from the confluence of Looking Glass Creek down. They find a few deep pools under the shade of hemlock and poplar, much good pocket water and a few riffles and runs. The river is wide enough and the tree canopy high enough for reasonable casting. The river's proximity to Asheville and the Interstate, about 40 minutes away, make this stretch very popular. At times it seems that all its trout have master's degrees, so familiar are they with variations of the common patterns which work here: caddis, little stones, Adams, and others. Green Drakes of late May and early June are the signature hatch on this stream. Anglers arrive at noon to stake out the pools that they'll fish in the frantic half-hour before dark. At other times, the usual run of nymphs is successful. If the lower reaches are overcrowded, try the miles between Looking Glass Creek and the Pisgah Fish Hatchery below FR 475. There's even less pressure on the three miles or so above the hatchery. The upper reaches hold very nice trout.

If you've come to fish the Davidson, don't pass up Looking Glass below the falls. These waters abound with not-so-small rainbows thanks to TU's feeding program.

DAVIDSON RIVER

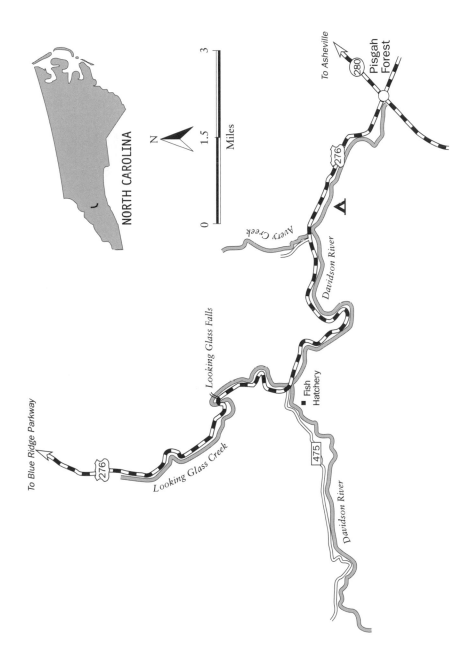

NORTH CAROLINA

Off and on, the size of one will surprise you as will the occasional brown. The water is much thinner than the Davidson itself. Carefully work single-hooked flies or spinners through the deeper runs and pools. Beneath 100-foot Looking Glass Falls is a deep plunge pool that's usually filled with swimmers in warm months as is the pool below Sliding Rock. But the best swimming in these waters generally does not include March and April, or late September and October, prime months on southern Appalachian waters.

Also worthy of note is Avery Creek, which enters the Davidson from the north a mile upstream of the Davidson River campground. Though offering something less than two miles of river, Avery offers respite from crowds on the main river. Most of Avery's fish run in the 7- to 10-inch range, but occasionally a 13- or 14-inch rainbow shows up.

As is the case with all freestone streams in the Southern Appalachians, the Davidson is prone to low flows in late summer and early fall. Yet, because of its deeply shaded course, the river seems to resist the warming that plagues other similar waters in the region. Its trout move into holes where there's oxygenated current. Check with local flyshops for the latest information on the river.

RESOURCES

Gearing up: Davidson River Outfitters, 4 Pisgah Highway, Pisgah Forest, NC 28768; 888-861-0111; www.DavidsonFlyFishing.com. Hunter Banks Co., 29 Montford Ave., Asheville NC 28801; 828-252-3005; www.hunterbanks.com.

Accommodations: Brevard Transylvania Chamber of Commerce, 35 W. Main St., Brevard, NC 28712; 800-648-4523; www.visitwaterfalls.com.

Books: *Trout Streams of Southern Appalachia*, Jimmy Jacobs, Backcountry Press, Woodstock, VT, 1995.

34 NANTAHALA RIVER

Location: Southwestern North Carolina.
Short take: Kayaks and rafts own the river, but not until the sun's well on the water.
Type of stream: Tailwater.
Angling methods: Fly, spin.
Species: Rainbow, brown.
Access: Easy.
Season: Year-round.
Nearest tourist services: Cherokee, Bryson City, Sylva.
Handicapped access: None.
Closest TU chapter: Tuckaseigee.

REACH THIS STUNNING NORTH CAROLINA TAILWATER after 10 A.M. on a summer's day, and you'll see scores of lavender and yellow kayaks and dozens of fat rubber rafts bobbing through the rapids. The kayakers are serious on this championship water. They ride the reverse eddies to have another run through the chutes. Rafters are the opposite. They shriek as their elongated donuts tip precariously over roostertails and splash each other where the water is dull and flat. It's enough to send a dedicated trouter to the relative sanity of a fish-for-fee pond, but don't let yourself be turned off. The trout aren't; why should you be?

The 'bows and browns of the lower eight miles of this 20-mile tailwater have seen it all and on every summer day. They're used to people. And that's the first of the Nantahala's big secrets. When the river is "on" it flows bank full. Trout look for refuges, those little lies in eddies behind logs and boulders and along the bank. Anglers who work the edges and cast flies, spinners, or bait upstream will be rewarded by some very nice fish—20-inch browns and 'bows are not at all unusual. And every once in a while, some lucky fisher hauls out a four- or five-pounder. If you don't mind the clamor of the rafters, fishing through the day can be productive. But angling is really better morning and evenings, before and after flotillas of happy vacationers have passed.

The Nan is one of the few, if not the only, state-approved trout water that's fishable at night. Local anglers fire up lanterns and fish baits in deep pockets and pools. Fly fishers roll cast big dries to likely looking pockets or work streamers deep through glassy runs. Fishing the river at night may offer the best opportunity for a true trophy trout. But the course is littered with huge blocks of rock, the product of construction of rail and auto roads along most of its course. Wading can be dicey. Spend an hour or two before nightfall thoroughly scouting the area you plan to fish.

Near Beechertown on U.S. Highway 19/74, the Nantahala takes a sharp turn to the south and a few hundred yards upstream is the powerhouse that releases cold water into the river. Above the powerhouse, the Nantahala dons a completely different costume. Fed only by run-off from countless tributaries and coldwater

NANTAHALA RIVER

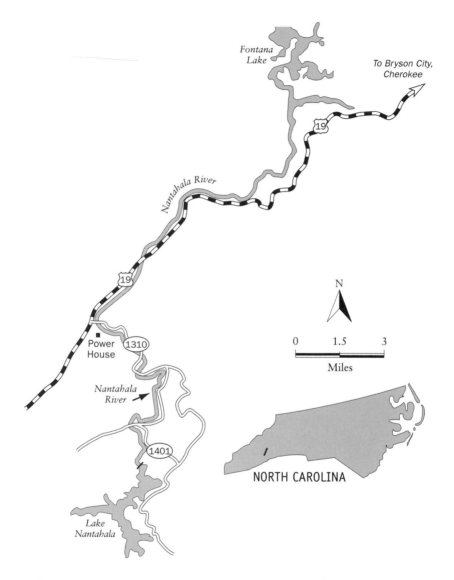

seeps, this upper mileage is small but lovely trout water. Runs slide around boulders and plunge, under overhanging rhododendron and laurel, into dark pools. Here and there the stream scampers across beds of uneven cobbles before calming into short-lived glassy flats. For four miles upstream from the powerhouse, the Nantahala is designated as "Delayed Harvest Water" meaning that bait fishers can have a go at it from June through September and keep what they catch, but for the rest of the year, the mileage is strictly catch-and-release and only single-hooked, artificial lures are

JOHN ROSS

As one of the most popular whitewater runs in the southeastern United States, the Nantahala River demands that anglers get an early start, before the paddlers take over the river.

allowed. Effective patterns include Elk Hair Caddis, Adams, and the Borcher Special, all in #12 or #14.

Most of the tourists leave these parts in November after autumn's gaily colored leaves have fallen from the trees. Fishing in the Nantahala holds up then, and it can be good even in the dead of winter. If sun warms the water temperature a degree or two from, say 9:30 A.M. to noon, you may be assured that trout will feed for an hour or two.

Flowing through the Nantahala National Forest and with good highway and secondary roads following most of its route, the river is quite accessible. Pull-offs and parking places are ample, and if you arrive early or late in the day, you'll avoid the floaters. Accommodations are available in nearby Bryson City or Cherokee. One could spend a week on the Nan alone, but it would be hard to ignore the other great trout streams in the neighborhood: Deep, Forney, and Hazel Creeks that flow into Fontana Reservoir from the Great Smoky Mountain National Park and the Oconaluftee at Cherokee.

RESOURCES

Gearing up: One Feather Fly and Tackle Shop, P.O. Box 553, Cherokee, NC 28719; 828-488-8943. Kingfishers Angling Shop, P.O. Box 449, Bryson City, NC 28713; 828-488-4848.

Accommodations: Swain County Chamber of Commerce, P.O. Box 509, Bryson City, NC 28713; 800-867-9246; www.greatsmokies.com.

Books: *Tailwater Trout in the South*, Jimmy Jacobs, Backcountry Publications, Woodstock, VT, 1996.

35 CHATTOOGA RIVER

Location: Northern Georgia–South Carolina border.
Short take: Big, brawling trout water.
Type of stream: Freestone.
Angling methods: Fly, spin.
Species: Rainbow, brown.
Access: Moderate.
Season: Year-round.
Nearest tourist services: Clayton, Georgia, Cashiers, North Carolina.
Handicapped access: None.
Closest TU chapter: Chattooga (SC), Rabun (GA).

TRIVIA QUESTION: Who played the sheriff in the movie *Deliverance*? Answer: the novel's author, James Dickey. Letting sleeping dogs lie department: It's probably best not to mention this 1970s classic if you're up in that neck of the woods. Local folks weren't given a square shake in their portrayal and they're still aggravated. Do, however, listen to "Dueling Banjos," the movie's theme. It'll put you in the mood to fish this isolated and rugged mountain country. Rising in Cashiers Lake in North Carolina, the stream gathers force from a score of tributaries before crossing the state line at Ellicott Rock. The rock was placed there in 1813 to mark the point where the boundaries of North Carolina, South Carolina, and Georgia intersect. From the marker south, the Chattooga follows the line separating South Carolina and Georgia. A license from either state can be used on this water, but if you turn to fish a tributary, you'll need a ticket from that state.

When anglers think of the Chattooga, they think of the mileage along the border. It's as wild and woolly a trout fishery as any found in the eastern United States roads cross the river at Burrells Ford and again at Route 28, about 14 miles downstream from the North Carolina line. Trails run pretty much the length of this section. The lower mileage is characterized by large deep pools, broken by riffly flats, but upstream from Burrells, the river gains more pocket water, runs and chutes, and plunge pools. A typical trout will run in the vicinity of a foot. But browns have been taken that exceed 10 pounds. Because of the river's popularity—not only from anglers, but from kayakers—you'll need to pack your waders and hike in at least a mile from either of the two bridges. While the months of spring produce the best hatches of March browns, light cahills, and caddis, the river comes into its own with green drakes that begin about Mother's Day and continue for a week or so. Hatches, however are rarely consistent, even from day to day.

The Chattooga, as Jimmy Jacobs says in his book *Trout Streams of Southern Appalachia*, is already a well developed stream. Above the state line, the river continues to be difficult to access. The terrain is difficult, distances from even gravel roads (try the bridges on Bull Penn and Whiteside Cove Roads) are significant, campsites are

CHATTOOGA RIVER

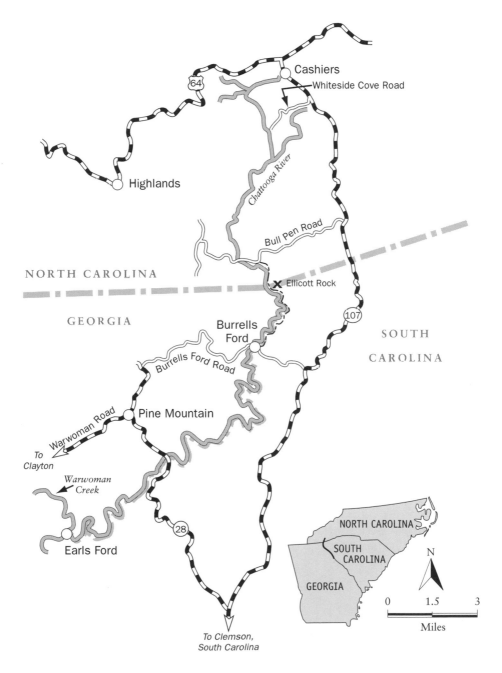

Cashiers

64

Whiteside Cove Road

Highlands

Chattooga River

Bull Pen Road

NORTH CAROLINA

X Ellicott Rock

GEORGIA

Burrells
Ford

107

SOUTH

CAROLINA

Burrells Ford Road

Warwoman Road

Pine Mountain

To
Clayton

Warwoman
Creek

28

Earls Ford

To Clemson,
South Carolina

NORTH CAROLINA

SOUTH
CAROLINA

N

GEORGIA

0   1.5   3

Miles

quite limited, and some of the land is held privately. Still, the trek in can be very worthwhile. From April to June, the river is in its prime. So too are the myriad wildflowers blooming along its banks. Larger browns (and there are many) will fall for attractor patterns more readily than for the smaller flies that match sporadic hatches. A bug that comes off one day may or may not hatch the next. Nymphs are very effective, particularly big black or brown stones early in the season. Streamers like the Woolly Bugger also produce.

On the Georgia side, Clayton is the closest town with facilities for anglers. In North Carolina, there are Highlands and Cashiers, old resort communities with first-class accommodations.

RESOURCES

Gearing up: Brookings, Old Schoolhouse Road, Box 1069, Cashier, NC 28717; 704-743-3768. Reeves Ace Hardware, P.O. Box 345, Clayton, GA 30525; 706-782-4253.

Accommodations: Cashiers Area Chamber of Commerce, P.O. Box 238, Cashiers, NC 28717; 704-743-5941. Rabun County Chamber of Commerce, P.O. Box 750, Clayton, GA 30525; 706-782-4812; www.gamountains.com/rabun.

Books: *Trout Streams of Southern Appalachia*, Jimmy Jacobs, Backcountry Publications, Woodstock, VT, 1994.

36 CLINCH RIVER

Location: Eastern Tennessee.
Short take: The oldest of Tennessee's TVA tailwaters is arguably its best.
Type of stream: Tailwater.
Angling methods: Fly, spin.
Species: Brown, rainbow.
Access: Moderate.
Season: Year-round.
Nearest tourist services: Knoxville.
Handicapped access: Yes.
Closest TU chapter: Clinch River.

IN ITS EARLY DAYS, the Tennessee Valley Authority was hailed as a savior. Its high tributary dams and wide main-river structures withheld flood waters, generated power, and provided jobs for the poverty stricken. But with the construction of Tellico Dam in the late '60s and early '70s, which removed the Little Tennessee River from the list of fine tailwaters of the east, TVA lost much favor with the coldwater angling community. In the last two decades, however, the authority has undergone a significant metamorphosis, and is working hard and successfully with TU and others to mitigate the adverse affects of dam releases on the river's tailwaters. The results have been consistently positive and occasionally dramatic.

Nowhere is this story better told than on the 14 miles of Clinch River that flows from Norris Dam, the oldest in the TVA system. Closed in 1933, the dam backed up the Clinch and Powell Rivers forming a lake noted for its walleye fishery. The river below the dam was stocked with browns and rainbows from the mid-40s on, but erratic releases would scour the river with near flood levels one day and leave it almost parched the next. Trout fishing was strictly a put-and-take effort, and not a very good one at that.

In the early '80s, things began to change. A fisheries team, with input from TU members, recommended creation of a low overflow weir two miles below the dam to alleviate the problem of low flows when generators were not in use. Baffles were added to the turbines to suck air into the water, adding dissolved oxygen so vital to a healthy trout population. Volunteers worked to establish communities of aquatic insects in areas where heretofore rampaging waters had stripped the riverbed clean. As a result, the Clinch River has come into its own. Just ask Greg Ensor about his 28-pound-plus state record brown, pulled from the Clinch near the weir two miles below the dam. The river regularly yields browns in the 8- to 15-pound range and rainbows of five pounds or more. While there are big fish here, the river is still heavily stocked and rainbows and browns of 10- to 12-inches are the most frequently caught.

From the dam down to Miller Hollow, a distance of three miles or so, the river runs through a tight and wooded valley. In periods of low flow, there is some fishing above the weir, but in the main the best action is found downstream. When the water

CLINCH RIVER

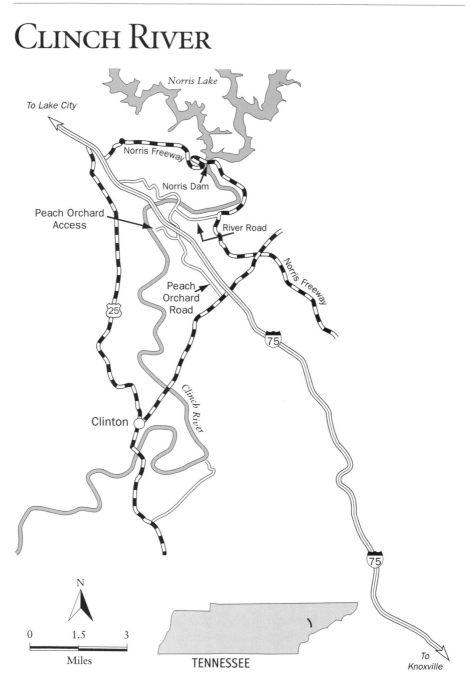

To Lake City

Norris Lake

Norris Freeway

Norris Dam

Peach Orchard
Access

River Road

Norris Freeway

Peach
Orchard
Road

25

75

Clinch River

Clinton

N

0   1.5   3

Miles

TENNESSEE

75

To
Knoxville

is off, the river divides into a number of small channels. Large trout, which forage freely when the water is up, tend to hide under any available structure. They're quite spooky and flee at the slightest danger sign. Below Miller Hollow, the valley begins to open up into a quilt of farm land and parcels occupied by vacation homes. As

JOHN ROSS

This is a trophy tailwater fishery—the 28-pound Tennessee record brown came from the Clinch.

with the South Holston, the best access is found at bridges and a number of anglers float and fish along the way.

Any legal lure or bait can be used on the Clinch River. Ultra-light spin fishers do very well with small spinners when the water is low and with Rapalla lures (shades of the old Little Tennessee) when the water is booming. Dry-fly fishing in the reaches from the dam down past Interstate 75 to Peach Orchard Access is left to those who enjoy midging or working scuds. From I-75 down past Peach Orchard to the Clinton Bridge, the Sulphur hatch (June and July) is sustained and productive. Bringing a half-dozen browns from 15 to 18 inches in a day's fishing is not uncommon. Little Black Caddis come off early in the spring holding up into May. They appear again in November and December.

The Clinch is an easy half-hour auto ride north of Knoxville. And the Great Smoky Mountains National Park is about an hour to the South. Thus, the angler visiting one can easily plan to spend a day in the other.

RESOURCES

Gearing up: The Creel, 6907 Kingston Pike, Knoxville, TN 37919; 423-588-6159.

Accommodations: Knox County Tourist Commission, 601 W. Summit Hill Dr., Suite 200B, Knoxville, TN 37902-2011; 800-727-8045.   Anderson County Tourist Council, P.O. Box 147, Clinton, TN 37717; 800-524-3602.

Books: *Tailwater Trout in the South*, Jimmy Jacobs, Backcountry Publications, Woodstock, VT, 1996.

Tailwaters of the Southern Appalachians, C. Richards and J. Krause, Antekeier & Krause Publications, Kentwood, MI, 1996.

37 HIWASSEE RIVER

Location: Southeast Tennessee.
Short take: Big fish, great wading, and lots of bugs.
Type of stream: Tailwater.
Angling methods: Fly, spin.
Species: Brown, brook, rainbow.
Access: Easy.
Season: Year-round.
Nearest tourist services: Reliance, Chattanooga.
Handicapped access: None.
Closest TU chapter: Hiwassee.

THE SECRET TO THE HIWASSEE'S REPUTATION as Tennessee's premier trout tailwater may be found in the fact that its flows are slightly warmer than those of the Clinch, South Holston, or Watauga. That means prolific hatches of mayflies, caddis, and stoneflies. Rising in the mountains of Northeastern Georgia, the Hiwassee flows through four impoundments before slipping into the tunnel at Appalachia Dam and emerging about 10 miles downstream to reclaim its channel. Spreading into a wide run of riffles with some pocket water, the river is open to all lures and baits before entering a Trophy Trout section which begins at the Forest Service Big Bend Parking lot and extends for three miles downstream to the L&N railroad bridge. In this mileage, artificial lures are the order of the day and anglers are permitted no more than two fish of 14 inches or greater in length. At the bridge, the river returns to general trout regulations and trout fishing is good for about five miles. Below the U.S. Highway 411 bridge, the river becomes difficult to access, and its appeal is largely enjoyed by lure and bait anglers in search of big fish.

While you can't set your watch by it, the run of the river in the Trophy Trout area above Reliance is reasonably regular. Blue-Winged Olives *(Baetis tricaudatus)* come off first in March with the heaviest hatches extending from April into May. Tiny (#24) *Psuedocloeons* emerge from July through August. April and May see Quill Gordons and Hendricksons. Sulphurs, Slate Olive Duns, and Light Cahills also progress through the spring months. Slate drakes of #12 to #14 put in appearances in June and early July and again in late October and November. Caddis are represented as well—little blacks on March and April mornings, cinnamon sedges in April and May, tans and little olives in May, grading into June. In October you're liable to encounter a hatch of little dot-wing sedges. Richards and Krause, in their book *Tailwaters of the Southern Appalachians,* also suggest trying Big Golden Stones (#4 to #8) and Giant Blacks (#2) in spring.

Like most of Tennessee's tailwaters, the biggest trout are caught when the river is running heavily, if not bank-full. The bed from the powerhouse at the mouth of Appalachia Tunnel to Reliance becomes a series of Class II rapids, a favorite of rafters

HIWASSEE RIVER

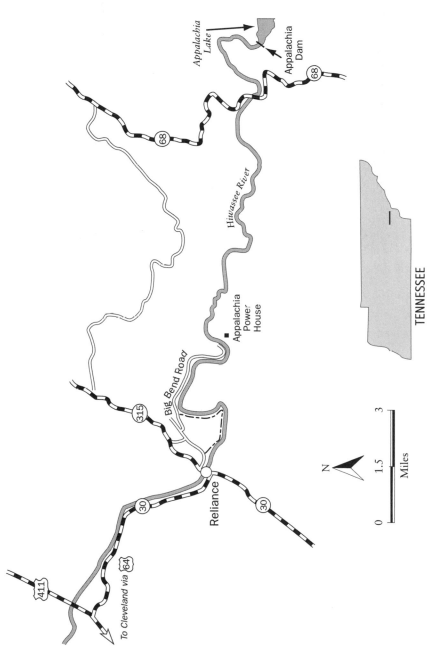

Appalachia Lake

Appalachia Dam

Hiwassee River

Appalachia Power House

Big Bend Road

Reliance

To Cleveland via 64

TENNESSEE

N

Miles

and kayakers, when both generators are running (call 800-238-2264 and press 4, then 22 for water release schedules). If heavy discharges are anticipated, plan to fish the lower reaches of the river. TVA does pulse its generators; normally there's a window of an hour or two between heavy releases. Currently TVA and TU are working to monitor the impact of the release program on the fishery and its supporting aquatic insect populations. And, using radio telemetry, TU recently completed a study of the migration patterns of rainbows and browns in the river. Preliminary results suggest that the fish are more territorial than once thought and tend to range through less of the river.

From Appalachia Dam down to the US 411 bridge, the Hiwassee flows through the Cherokee National Forest and access is excellent. State Route 30 runs up along the south side of the river from the campground at Quinn Springs to Reliance. Forest Road 108 follows the north side of the river for much of its course. Only an hour or so from Chattanooga and three hours from Atlanta, the Hiwassee sees its share of fishing pressure, but the river is big enough and access is ample enough so that you'll never feel too crowded. Accommodations are available in Cleveland, a small city some 25 miles west of the river on Interstate 75.

RESOURCES

Gearing up: Adam's Fly Shop, Rt. 2, Box 122, Reliance, TN 37369; 423-338-2162.

Hiwassee Outfitters, P.O. Box 62, Reliance, TN 37369; 800-338-8133.

Accommodations: Greater Cleveland Area Chamber of Commerce, P.O. Box 2275, Cleveland, TN 37320; 423-472-6587; www.clevelandchamber.com.

Books: *Tailwater Trout in the South*, Jimmy Jacobs, Backcountry Publications, Woodstock, VT, 1996.

Tailwaters of the Southern Appalachians, C. Richards and J. Krause, Antekeier & Krause Publications, Kentwood, MI, 1996.

38 HOLSTON RIVER, SOUTH FORK

Location: Northeastern Tennessee.
Short take: Weir adds life-giving oxygen to this superb tailwater.
Type of stream: Tailwater.
Angling methods: Fly, spin.
Species: Brown, rainbow.
Access: Easy.
Season: Year-round.
Nearest tourist services: Bluff City.
Handicapped access: Yes.
Closest TU chapter: Overmountain.

WHEN THE TENNESSEE VALLEY Authority's 285-foot-high South Holston Dam plugged the river's course through a low ridge in 1947 and backed water far upstream into Virginia, it created a fine tailwater fishery downstream in Tennessee. But the fishery struggled. Sure, plenty of cold water ran in the channel for more than a dozen miles down past Bluff City. It was stocked with trout, but mortality was very high and holdovers were few. The problem: Cold releases from the dam contain too little dissolved oxygen to sustain trout. In 1991, a cooperative project involving TU, TVA, the Tennessee Wildlife Resources Agency, and others led to installation of reregulation weirs on the South Fork of the Holston, the Clinch, and the Hiwassee Rivers. The weirs are, essentially, low dams designed to retain a low reservoir of water that both maintains a stable minimum flow at times when the dams are not generating and adds oxygen via artificial plunge pool or rapids. Thanks to the weirs, these tailwaters are, indeed, year-round fisheries. The number of holdovers is increasing. And some natural propagation may be taking place.

After leaving the dam, the South Holston twists and turns through a bucolic farm valley. In places, the valley curves against hardwood ridges with boulders or rock outcrop at their bases. In others, the river spreads across flats with banks defined by meadow or cornfield and edged with sycamore trees. Here and there are blunt-nosed islands with tails that taper sharply and point down stream. The bottom is generally ledge or cobble, but prolific grasses and moss do make felt-soled wading shoes a must. The first mile below the dam is impounded by the river's weir, located in Osceola Park. When flows are down, the park is a great place to enter the river. Fly fishers look for rising trout and cast Sulphurs or Elk Hair Caddis. Spin fishers chuck hardware—Panther Martins or Mepps are popular—or fish night crawlers along sunken logs. As long as anglers yield space to each other, the mileage seems to accommodate both quite well. When the water is "off," as they say, the river's upper reaches are easily waded. Minimum flow is about 200 cfs. But when TVA is generating (call 800-238-2264, press 4, and use river code #01 to find out), flows can reach 2,800 cfs and the bottom becomes utterly impossible to negotiate. That's

HOLSTON RIVER, SOUTH FORK

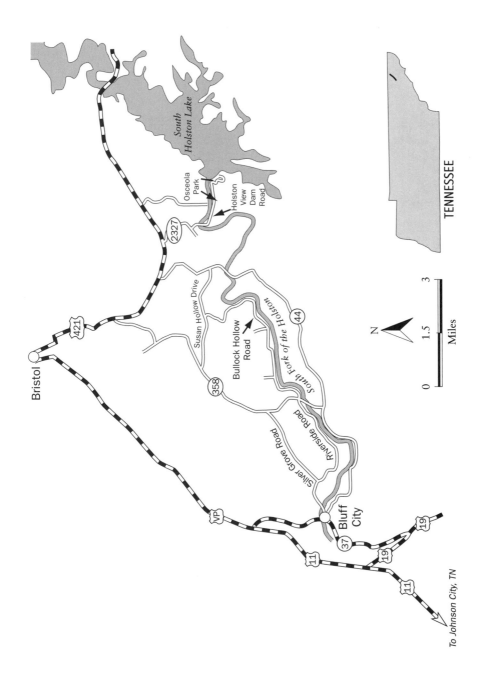

when the river is best floated by raft or canoe. Cast spinners or spoons or crawlers weighted with non-toxic shot. Fly fishers willing to leave sinking lines with large weighted streamers and nymphs also find success. Bigger fish generally become more active during periods of high flow.

The river is most charming in spring when redbud and dogwood bloom along its banks. Flows are often low, and waders work pocket water and riffles at the tails of long, slick pools. The Sulphur hatch begins in April following a good run of black caddis that begins in March. Try Blue-Winged Olives and Hendricksons in April and again in August. Aside from the little black caddis, the cinnamon sedge, olive and big green caddis are also productive. Attractor flies, Adams and Wulffs, sometimes work.

While the river is well served by a number of secondary roads, both gravel and paved, along the 14 miles of its best fishing water, public access is limited. Routes 44, 358, and 37 bridge the stream at sites progressively farther downstream from the dam. A maze of farm roads and lanes lead toward the stream, so all you need do is follow your nose. Yet, the bulk of land is held privately. Some owners will grant permission to fish when asked. Others charge a small fee for parking and access.

Upper East Tennessee includes a number of fine trout waters, particularly the Watauga River tailwater, the Doe River, and Beaver Dam and Stony Creeks, making the region a good destination for traveling anglers. Each of these waters offers something a little different. As a whole, the region has yet to be plagued by the commercialism which surrounds the Great Smoky Mountains, and accommodations are fairly inexpensive. Fly into Tri-Cities Airport or drive via Interstate 81 to Bristol.

RESOURCES

Gearing up: The Holston Angler, 110 Poplar Ridge Road, Piney Flats, TN 37686; 423-538-7412. Mahoney's, 830 Sunset Drive, Johnson City, TN 37604; 423-282-5413.

Accommodations: Bristol Chamber of Commerce, P.O. Box 519, Bristol, VA/TN 24203; 423-989-4850; www.bristolchamber.org.

Books: *Tailwater Trout in the South*, Jimmy Jacobs, Backcountry Publications, Woodstock, VT, 1996.

Tailwaters of the Southern Appalachians, C. Richards and J. Krause, Antekeier & Krause Publications, Kentwood, MI 49508.

39 LITTLE RIVER

Location: Southeastern Tennessee near the North Carolina border.
Short take: Followed by highway for much of its length, this is nonetheless one fine trout stream.
Type of stream: Freestone.
Angling methods: Fly, spin.
Species: Brown, rainbow.
Access: Easy.
Season: Year-round.
Nearest tourist services: Gatlinburg, Townsend.
Handicapped access: in Townsend.
Closest TU chapter: Little River, Great Smoky.

THE LITTLE RIVER IS, PERHAPS, the quintessential Smoky Mountain trout stream. But it is more than a single river. The largest fork, or "prong" in mountain parlance, is the East which draws its waters from the flanks of a quartet of 6,000-foot-plus mountains along the Old Smoky's backbone. But so too does the Middle Prong which passes through the environmental center at Tremont, and the West Prong which rises on ridges named "Defeat" and "Doghobble" on the slopes of Thunderhead. Yet, when most Tennessee and Tar Heel anglers talk about the Little River, they mean the East Prong, and that's the one that gets most of the attention.

In its upper reaches, the East Prong bounces from pool through chute to pool working through a maze of mammoth boulders left from an earlier geologic age. Fish Camp Prong joins the East Prong about four miles by trail upstream from Elkmont, and at this junction, the river becomes a consistently good fishery. You'll find dainty rainbows of seven to ten inches willing to take Adams or caddis or little Gray Hare's Ears. Tiny Mepps or Rooster Tails also get results, but they are better fished in the larger waters below.

Jakes Creek adds its waters to the East Prong at Elkmont, once the site of massive logging operations during the early years of the century and of a wonderful old clapboard hotel. Today, the area provides camping and picnicking facilities for anglers and other tourists. But the roadbed of the narrow gauge railroads that hauled massive butts of poplar and hemlock down out of the mountains provide an easily graded trail up the East Prong. The lower section of the river is matched with paved road all the way to the entrance of Great Smoky Mountains National Park at Townsend.

At times this water seems to be very thin, particularly during periods of drought which plague the mountains every few years. Yet plunge pools associated with the Sinks (a favorite spot for swimmers in summer), undercut ledges, and deep channels around house-sized boulders provide cover for big trout in the driest of times.

LITTLE RIVER

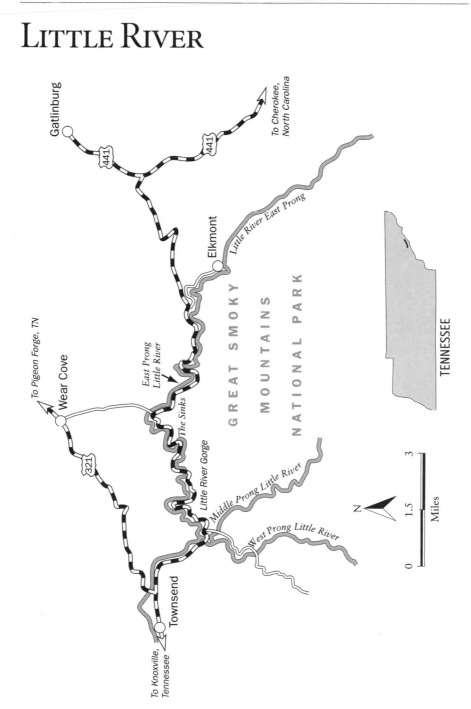

JOHN ROSS

Despite easy highway access, the Little River still produces quality rainbows and browns.

Browns upwards of five pounds are caught each season as are rainbows of two to four pounds. In the main, however, fish run in the seven-to-ten-inch range. The percentage of browns is higher in the lower, warmer reaches of the river, and you'll find more rainbows on the upstream mileage. The river system is subject to intense flooding and drought which can cause the trout population to fluctuate as much as 50 to 200 percent.

Because the river is so accessible from SR 73 (the main east-west highway through the national park)—you can see rising trout from your car window if you dare take your eyes from the winding road—the East Prong fills with swimmers and, when water is high, kayakers, in summer. It's a curse, but it comes with a silver lining. The fishing is lousy when folks play in the river, but the trout do become somewhat acclimated to the presence of people. If you want solitude, head for the backcountry section of the West Prong, a small stream that's followed by the road into Cades Cove but veers sharply south.

In 1997, Trout Unlimited and the Great Smoky Mountain National Park initiated an historic agreement to intensively monitor the watershed. In cooperation with the fisheries staff in the park, TU's Great Smoky Mountain and Little River Chapters are heavily involved in gathering data on acid deposition in high-altitude creeks, restoration projects funded with Embrace-A-Stream grants, bank and stream clean-up, and ongoing monitoring of various species in the river. Without the countless hours donated by TU volunteers, and outstanding leadership and cooperation from the National Park Service, the Tennessee Wildlife Resources Agency and the University of Tennessee, the future of the fisheries in Great Smoky Mountains National Park would be in severe jeopardy.

RESOURCES

Gearing up: Little River Outfitters, 7807 E. Lamar Alexander Pkwy., P.O. Box 505, Townsend, TN 37882; 423-448-9459. Smoky Mountain Anglers, Brookside Village, Hwy 321 N., P.O. Box 241, Gatlinburg, TN 37738; 423-436-8746.

Accommodations: Townsend Area Visitor's Bureau, 7906 E. Lamar Alexander Pkwy, Townsend, TN 37882; 800-525-6834; www.smokymountains.org. Gatlinburg Department of Tourism, 234 Airport Road, Gatlinburg, TN 37738; 800-267-7088; www.gatlinburgtennessee.com.

Books: *Fly-Fishing Guide to the Great Smoky Mountains*, Don Kirk, Menasha Ridge Press, Birmingham, AL, 1996.

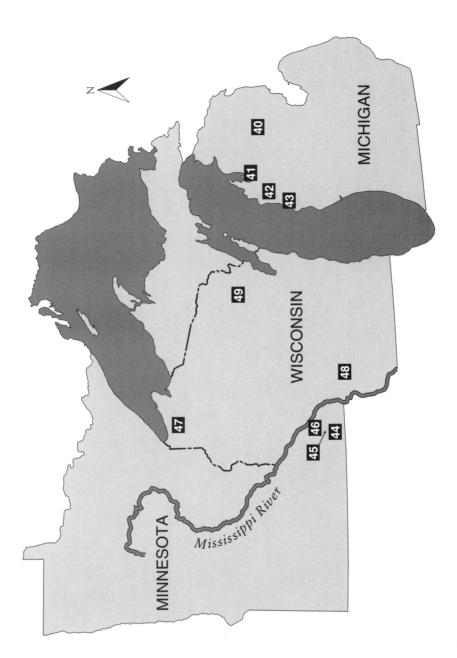

40. Au Sable River
41. Boardman River
42. Little Manistee River
43. Pere Marquette River
44. Root River, South Fork

45. Trout Run Creek
46. Whitewater River
47. Bois Brule River
48. Kickapoo River, West Fork
49. Wolf River

GREAT LAKES

MICHIGAN

MINNESOTA

WISCONSIN

40 AU SABLE RIVER

Location: Northeastern Michigan.
Short take: TU's home waters. Ride a narrow riverboat or wade for big browns.
Type of stream: Freestone.
Angling methods: Fly, spin.
Species: Brown, rainbow, brook.
Access: Easy.
Season: Year-round.
Nearest tourist services: Grayling, Mio.
Handicapped access: Yes.
Closest TU chapter: Challenge Chapter.

THE AU SABLE RIVER might be called TU's home waters, for on its banks the organization was founded in 1959. The driving force behind TU was George Griffith, a passionate angler and conservationist whose residence was known as "Barbless Hook." There, on a July afternoon, he and 15 other influential anglers fashioned an organization that would do for coldwater fisheries what Ducks Unlimited, begun 25 years earlier, was accomplishing for waterfowl and wetlands. Early efforts focused on reforming state policy, which then favored stocked over wild trout, and the rehabilitation of the Au Sable, long threatened by logging, pollution, and development. President of TU from 1961 to 1964, Griffith saw TU expand to play a leading role in the protection and enhancement of trout and salmon fisheries. He was an ardent TU leader until his death in 1998.

Were Griffith fishing the river today, he would like much of what he sees. Local TU chapters are continuing the effort to stabilize sand banks that threaten to erode and dump suffocating sediments into the river. He would admire the growing brown trout fishery, particularly in the mileage from Burton's Landing to Wakely Bridge, known as the "Holy Water," and the section from Mio Dam down to McKinley which is managed by Michigan Department of Natural Resources as Trophy Water. He would especially enjoy other reaches, those with no name and no special regulations which day in and day out provide everyday anglers with opportunities for excellent brown trout fishing. You might find him in late fall and spring, on the lowest section of the river, from Foote Dam to the town of Au Sable on the Huron shore. That's where steelhead and salmon run.

The main stem of the Au Sable rises just west of Interstate 75 north and west of the town of Grayling. Wild brookies, browns, and rainbows are found in the headwaters. After cutting through the town, gathering water from the confluence with its East Branch and ducking under the highway, the river takes the shape that will sustain it through the Holy Water, eight miles of fly-fishing-only, no-kill angling. Riffling a gravel and sand bottom, tufted here and there with waving strands of aquatic grasses, this stretch is quite wadeable and fish hold in easily seen lies. Seducing

Au Sable River

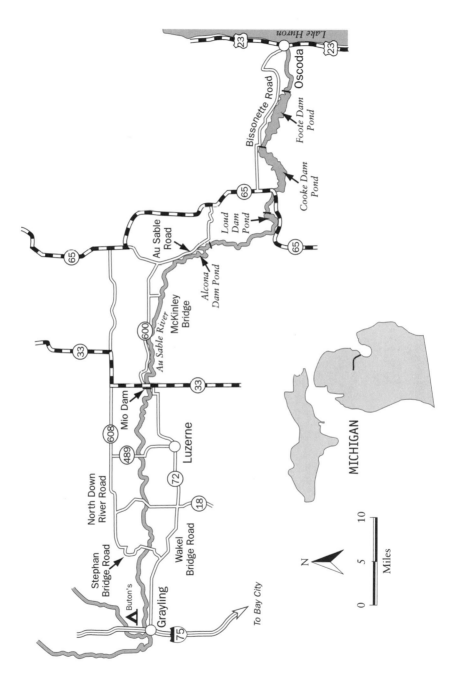

them to strike is another matter. Early in the year, Hendricksons garner the most interest from anglers. Later, in May, come the Sulphurs. Near the middle of this section is Rusty Gate's famed Au Sable Lodge. Bridges provide good access for waders. And there are ample launching points for those who choose to fish this section from those wonderful narrow wooden three-man boats named for the river.

Hexigenia limbata, also called the Michigan Caddis, is the signature hatch of the river's next run from Wakely Bridge to Mio Pond. From late May into mid-June, nymphal forms will prove successful if fished late in the day and into the evening. Duns emerge in June and early July, and fishing for hoggish browns in the dark of night is as challenging as it is exciting. The famed Au Sable Brown Drake hatch is a precursor to the Hex. Then the river is in its prime. Below Mio Pond Dam to McKinley Bridge, anglers are permitted only two trout and each must exceed 15 inches. They may be taken only by artificial means. Here the river is generally too big to wade safely, though McKinley Road leads to many access points that allow some wading and bank fishing.

Along with the main stem of the Au Sable, don't overlook the South Branch, which enters the river about two miles east of Wakely Bridge, or the North Branch which comes about a mile down stream from McMaster's Bridge. Both provide excellent angling and may be a good bet when aluminum flotillas crowd the big water on sunny weekend afternoons.

RESOURCES

Gearing up: Gates Au Sable Lodge and Flyshop, 471 Stephan Bridge Road, Grayling, MI 49738; 517-348-8462. The Fly Factory, P.O. Box 709, Grayling, MI 49738; 517-348-5844.

Accommodations: Grayling Regional Chamber of Commerce, P.O. Box 406, Grayling, MI 49738; 800-937-8837; www.grayling-mi.com.

Books: *Au Sable River Guide*, John J.P. Long, ed., Challenge Chapter TU, 1988.

Au Sable River, Bob Linsenman, River Journal Series, Frank Amato Publications, Portland, OR, 1998.

Michigan Trout Streams, Bob Linsenman and Steve Nevala, Backcountry Publications, Woodstock, VT, 1993.

41 BOARDMAN RIVER

Location: Northwestern Michigan.
Short take: Perhaps the finest wild trout stream in Michigan.
Type of stream: Freestone.
Angling methods: Fly, spin.
Species: Brown, brook.
Access: Moderate.
Season: Late April through September.
Nearest tourist services: Traverse City.
Handicapped access: None.
Closest TU chapter: Adams.

COLD AND CLEAR AND RISING in a swamp of mixed cedar, pine, and hardwood, the Boardman has earned a reputation as a small, fine trout stream. Like most of the streams that drain the state's great thumb westward into Lake Michigan, this river picks up speed as it cuts through moraines before flattening out in the ancient beaches somewhat inland from the shore. Nowhere is this river really wide enough to fish from a drift boat, though armies of canoeists ease their way along its bucolic course on the hot weekends of summer. But, for the large part, they leave the river alone during the week, and in fall, when fishing can be spectacular, they are all but gone.

On the lower end of the river, fine access is provided at a picnic area at the Beitner Road a few miles due south of Traverse City. Often congested with tubers and canoers, anglers have their shot at the water early and late in the day. Those willing to work their way upstream may find a measure of quiet. About two miles upstream, Shumsky Road leads to the river, and here too, the angler who heads upriver will not be disappointed.

The only dam on the river, at Brown Bridge Pond east of Mayfield, is a very low overflow structure. The lake is about a mile in length, and it is not large enough to warm the water significantly. Some of the river's best water is found in the vicinity of Scheck's campground. Flow is swift, the bottom rocky, and wading during periods of high water, more than a little dicey. A mile to the east is Ranch Rudolph, a motel-cum-campground and bar/restaurant, where anglers often overnight. Here, too, dusk and dawn are the best times to be on the river. Upstream from the ranch, near the Forks Campground, Supply Road (CR 660) crosses the Boardman, marking the end of the river's most popular section.

The Boardman is open to all legal sport fishing gear. It's ideally suited to ultra-light spinning with little lures. Try also those small minnow- or crayfish-imitating plugs. (Replace treble hooks with a single barbless hook. You'll catch as many fish and have an easier time releasing them.) Fly fishers will find the Royal Wulff, Lime Trude, Elk-hair Caddis and Adams (from which the local TU chapter allegedly took its name) quite productive. If this river were to have a signature hatch, it would have

BOARDMAN RIVER

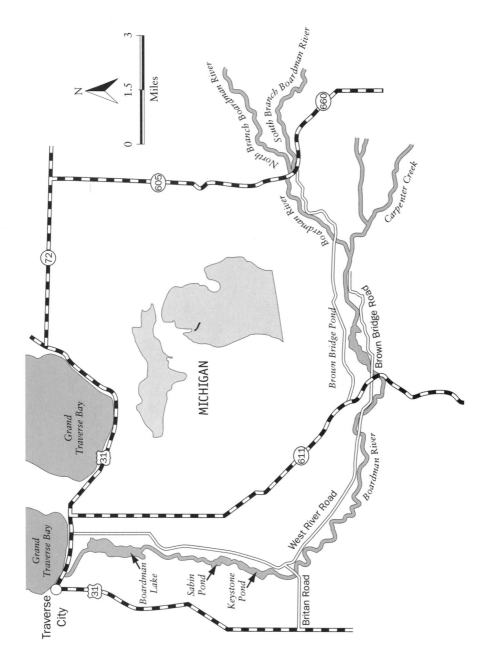

N

Miles

0   1.5   3

North Branch Boardman River

South Branch Boardman River

660

605

Carpenter Creek

Boardman River

72

Brown Bridge Pond

Brown Bridge Road

Grand Traverse Bay

MICHIGAN

611

West River Road

Boardman River

31

Grand Traverse Bay

Boardman Lake

Sabin Pond

Keystone Pond

Britan Road

Traverse City

31

to be *Hexigenia limbata*, which begin coming off during the last week of June and continues into the second week of July. In August, anglers fish tricos in the morning, terrestrials during midday and Blue-Winged Olives in the evening. A wide variety of nymphs and streamers, including the Light Spruce, are also very effective.

The upper section of the Boardman, above the Forks, offers fine angling as well. Here the South Branch and the North Branch come together. They drain a large section of the Pere Marquette State Forest of marginal jack pine, popple, and hardwoods. Seldom wider than 20 feet, overhung by trees, impounded by beaver dams, this is lovely water for wild brook trout and a few browns. Small nymphs and streamers, roll-cast under branches, often connect with fish that will test delicate #2 or #3 weight systems.

RESOURCES

Gearing up: Troutsman, 4386A. US 31N, Traverse City, MI 49686; 616-938-3474. Streamside Orvis, 4400 Grand Traverse Village Blvd. E-4, Williamsburg, MI 49690; 616,938-5337.

Accommodations: Traverse City Area Chamber of Commerce, 202 E. Grandview Parkway, P.O. Box 387, Traverse City, MI 49685-0387; 616-947-5075.

Books: *Michigan Trout Streams*, Bob Linsenman and Steve Nevala, Backcountry Publications, Woodstock, VT, 1993.

Boardman River Guide, John J. P. Long, Challenge Chapter TU, 1994.

42 Little Manistee River

Location: Central western Michigan.
Short take: Best known for steelhead and salmon, its browns sometimes get overlooked.
Type of stream: Freestone.
Angling methods: Fly, spin.
Species: Steelhead, Chinook, rainbow, brown.
Access: Moderate.
Season: April through December.
Nearest tourist services: Wellston and Irons.
Handicapped access: None.
Closest TU chapter: Pine River.

So, you pays your money and you takes your choice: is it steelhead of early winter when lake-spawned snow squalls clog the guides of your rod or is it those big Chinook that burst into the river like fireworks on the Fourth of July? What about rainbows, foolishly slashing at almost any pattern or secretive and sizeable browns that feed gently in the gathering dusk of evening in the upper river? The Little Manistee may not be the best trout river in the area, but few streams offer more variety and fish as well.

The upper river rises in blackwater swamps near Luther, east of Route 37, and glides over a sandy bottom through alders so thick they sometimes form a tight canopy over the stream. Brookies lurk in the little pools and you'll find a few browns. Below the Route 37 bridge, the river becomes easier to fish. Many park at the Old Grade Campground, but if you want to escape other anglers, take a hike for a mile or two down the river. Amazing, isn't it, how distance thins the crowds? From Spencer Bridge to Johnson's Bridge marks seven miles of fly-fishing-only water, and most of it is private, controlled by the Indian Club. The Michigan Department of Natural Resources provides access below the bridge and if you stay in the river, you won't trespass. The river continues to follow a northwesterly course past woods, fields, bits of bog, and a few cabins. Dozens of roads, some of them gravel, most little more than two-lane dirt tracks, intersect the river's channel. Pull-offs provide clues to public access.

In the area of the Udell Hills, moraines left by retreating continental glaciers 12,000 years ago, the river's pace quickens as it cuts down through the low hills. Bob Linsenman, author and angler extraordinare, loves to fish the frisky runs that slam into right-angle turns where the dark water swirls under a head of frothy foam. Weighted streamers often pick up steelhead or browns that lie here in the dark choosing their fare *a la carte*. The best of this water flows between Nine Mile and Sixmile Bridges. Below, the river slows and at Old Stronach Bridge, Michigan DNR runs a fish weir where eggs from migrating steelhead and salmon are collected for incubation.

LITTLE MANISTEE RIVER

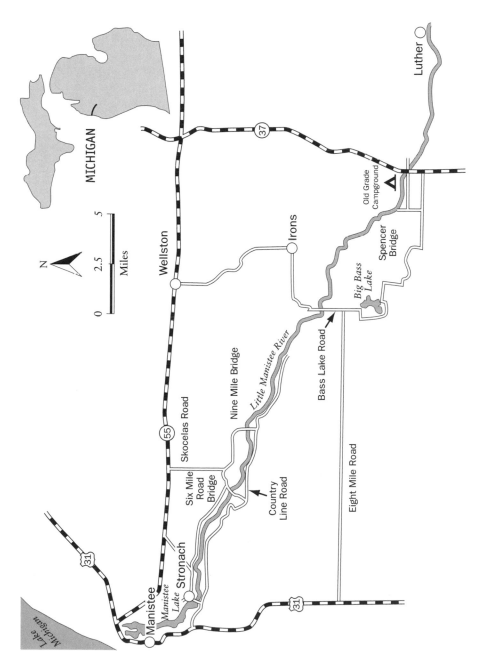

There are those, Ray Schmidt among them, who will tell you that as a trout stream, the Little Manistee is not nearly the stream it once was, thanks to the tens of thousands of steelhead and salmon that enter the system to breed. But he will also let you know that each pool in the upper 15 miles of main river, below the Route 37 bridge, holds at least one heavy brown and maybe two. The best times to fish the river vary, of course. For salmon, come in July and early August; for steelhead, fish in April or November and December; for trout, work the Hex hatch during late June. In between, chase those wise old browns the same way you'd hunt a trophy buck— hike a mile down to a likely pool, set yourself down with back against a tree, and watch the water as afternoon fades into dusk.

RESOURCES

Gearing up: Schmidt Outfitters, 918 Seaman Road, Wellston, MI 49689; 616-848-4191. Pappy's Bait & Tackle, 17092 Hwy. M55, Wellston MI 49689; 616-848-4142.

Accommodations: Manistee Area Chamber of Commerce, 50 Filer St., Suite 224, Manistee, MI 49660; 800-288-2286; www.manistee.com/~edo/chamber/.

Books: *Michigan Trout Streams*, Bob Linsenman and Steve Nevala, Backcountry Publications, Woodstock, VT, 1993.

43 Pere Marquette River

Location: Central western Michigan.
Short take: Famous steelhead, salmon, and brown trout river.
Type of stream: Freestone.
Angling methods: Fly, spin.
Species: Brown, rainbow, steelhead, salmon.
Access: Moderate.
Season: Year-round.
Nearest tourist services: Tackle shops, guides, accommodations.
Handicapped access: Yes.
Closest TU chapter: Grand Rapids.

DRAINING A NATIONAL FOREST of the same name, the Pere Marquette wears three faces. From September to March, steelhead run up into the river from its mouth at Ludington, a small town a little more than halfway up Lake Michigan's eastern shore. Chinook enter the system in August and continue into October. Browns and rainbows, with the former predominating, are the mainstays of the river which author Bob Linsenman divides into three sections.

The upper river, east of Route 37 and south of Baldwin, offers fine angling for browns for about nine miles up to Rosa Road where it becomes a bit small to fish comfortably. In this section the river is narrow, averaging about 20 feet, and shallow—seldom more than three feet deep. Water chatters happily down gravel riffles in places. In others, it flows like glass over sandy bottoms. Overhanging brush provides shade and shelter, as do a number of undercut banks, for surprisingly nice browns. Mayfly and caddis hatches are reasonably reliable with the sulphurs, caddis and gray drakes of June doing the most to turn on the fish. Terrestrials work very well in late summer.

When it reaches the beginning of the fly-fishing-only section, where you'll find the greatest pressure, the river has widened to 50 feet, and the bottom is of clay, sand, or gravel depending on gradient. Here too, the river begins those tight, squiggly meanders, almost but not quite looping back on itself, that characterize the channel all the way down to the mileage south of Walhalla. Generations of anglers have trod paths into the soil along the banks through the eight-mile fly-fishing-only section. Though it is fished heavily, the trout don't seem to mind. From the bridge down to Green Cabin, about half-way down the fly-only stretch, the river is wadeable, but below you'll want to use caution or engage a guide (or friend) with a boat. This lower section of the fly-fishing-only water has a distinct western feel—deep pools, wide flats, sharply powerful runs—about it. Nymphs and streamers are the order of the day here. Fish black stonefly nymphs, Woolly Buggers, almost black Hare's Ears, dark Clousers, yellow and black Marabou Muddlers. Large dries also payoff in June: *Hexigenia limbata*, Brown and Gray Drakes. Fly boxes should also contain Adams, Elk Hair Caddis, Boercher's Drake, and Lime Trude.

PERE MARQUETTE RIVER

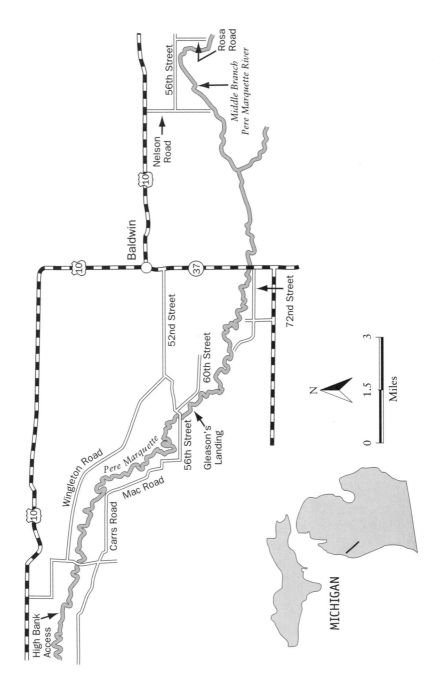

The Pere Marquette reaches maturity below Gleason's Landing, the western limit of the special regulations water. Just before snow begins to melt in March, the runs near Gleason's are at their lowest and clearest and seem to attract numbers of steelhead. Egg patterns, wiggler flies, and stonefly nymphs are successful then. You can wade the river if you're careful. But farther down, most anglers use boats, and cast to trout holding in structure created by the scores of sunken logs along the banks.

It is just the instability of these banks that led the Michigan Council of Trout Unlimited, in cooperation with Michigan's Department of Natural Resources, the Forest Service, Pere Marquette Watershed Council, Federation of Fly Fishers, county governments, and conservation agencies to undertake the largest stream-bank restoration project in the United States, says Bill Walker, editor of *Michigan Trout*. Over a decade, and at a cost of $1.5 million, 24,000 cubic yards of fieldstone riprap were used to repair 172 eroding sandbanks along the 41-mile stretch of the main stem. Under the riprap, lunker structures were placed, creating cover where erosion had filled it in. Early studies on the river showed that the amount of suspended sediment in the river was inhibiting the ability of trout to reproduce. New studies conducted by Michigan DNR show that the amount of sand carried by the stream is beginning to decline.

RESOURCES

Gearing up: Johnson's Outdoors and Pere Marquette Lodge, Rt. 1, Box 1290, Baldwin, MI 49304; 616-745-3972. Baldwin Bait & Tackle, Rt. 3 Box 3223, South M-37, Baldwin, MI 49304; 877-422-5394.

Accommodations: Lake County Chamber of Commerce, 911 Michigan Ave., P.O. Box 130, Baldwin, MI 49304; 616-745-4331.

Books: *Michigan Trout Streams*, Bob Linsenman and Steve Nevala, Backcountry Publications, Woodstock, VT, 1993.

Pere Marquette River Guide, John J. P. Long, Ed., Challenge Chapter TU, 1992.

Pere Marquette River, Matt Supinski, River Journal Series, Frank Amato Publications, Portland, OR, 1995.

44 ROOT RIVER, SOUTH FORK

Location: Southeastern Minnesota.
Short take: Limestone springs, consistent stocking, and a little help from Mother Nature make the upper Root a premier stream.
Type of stream: Freestone.
Angling methods: Fly, spin.
Species: Brown, rainbow, brook.
Access: Easy.
Season: Mid-April through September.
Nearest tourist services: Lanesboro, Preston, Rochester.
Handicapped access: None.
Closest TU chapter: Hiawatha, Win Cres.

SOUTHEASTERN MINNESOTA MAY BE the least well-known fly fishing mecca in the United States. During the four major glacial epochs, the vast sheets of continental ice that spread southward from Canada seemed to run out of gas as they approached a topographic highland where Iowa, Minnesota and Wisconsin now come together. The Mississippi River flows through the center of the region, creating bluffs of 600 feet that rise from the narrow floodplain to the flat prairie above. Meltwater from the glaciers streamed through existing creek valleys, deepening and steepening them until they reached the level of the river. Where gradient was steepest, they ate away the land, drawing the heads of the valleys back away from the river for scores of miles. In addition, much of the prairie is underlain by horizontal beds of limestone. Waters from rain and snow dissolve their way through the soluble rock, and issue forth as springs when they encounter impervious beds. Geology and hydrology created the tableau for this marvelous fishery.

But there are other factors as well. Brook trout were the native fish of this region, but they were caught out long ago. Successive waves of browns and rainbows were stocked with varying degrees of success. Intensive farming and logging, insensitive to the fragility of these watersheds, resulted in continuous flows of silt-laden run-off and disastrous floods that choked the coldwater fish from the rivers. But beginning in the late 1950s, partnerships between the Minnesota Department of Natural Resources, Trout Unlimited, and agricultural interests have reformed farming practices, secured easements along many of the best streams, rehabilitated the stream beds, and reintroduced trout, particularly browns and brook trout, but also rainbows.

The South Branch of the Root River is one of the larger streams in Southeastern Minnesota. Above its junction with the North Branch at Lanesboro, the South Branch meanders through a modest flood plain once devoted to row crops, but now generally pastured. In Lanesboro, a tiny tourist town with excellent bed and breakfasts and a good restaurant or two, you can take stocked rainbows and browns below

Root River, South Fork

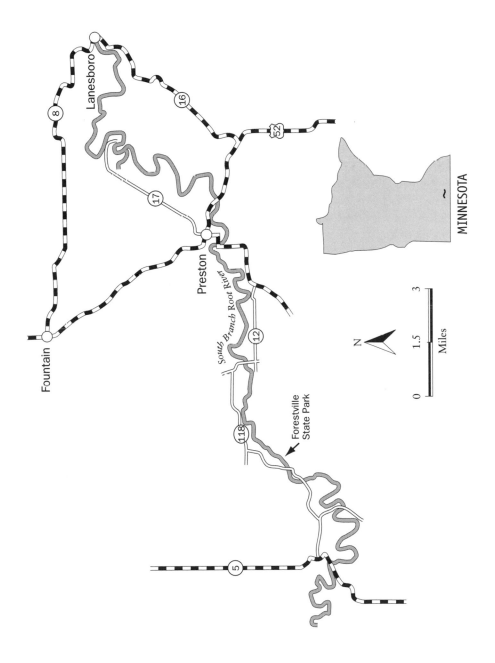

MINNESOTA

Lanesboro

8

16

52

17

Preston

Fountain

12

South Branch Root River

118

Forestville State Park

5

N

0   1.5   3

Miles

the dam and through the village. The river above Lanesboro holds some nice browns, but the better fishing begins at Preston, roughly a dozen miles to the west.

Here the river is smaller and gradient begins to increase. Just west of Preston, River Road turns west from County Road 12 and crosses the river twice. Near the first bridge is a picnic area with good access, but the water above the second bridge is better and less apt to be crowded. CR 12 runs straight up the valley while the river meanders through the meadows to the north. Often, all that's needed to fish this stretch is a polite request to the farmer who owns the land. At Carimora, the road turns north and crosses the river, providing additional access, and a couple of hundred yards further, County Road 118 turns west toward Forestville State Park. You'll find pulls, stiles, and access to the river along the road, but it's the three miles in the state park that attract most attention from fly fishers. Tricos in August are the signature hatch on this water, but Hendricksons in May and June, caddis from June on, Blue-Winged Olives and midges throughout the season are all very productive. Nymphs, particularly the Prince and Pheasant Tail, also bring good fish to net. These waters are not restricted to fly fishing or catch-and-release. Spin anglers who work the tiniest of Rooster Tails, Mepps, and Panther Martins, will also do very well.

RESOURCES

Gearing up: Gander Mountain, 1201 S. Broadway, Rochester, MN 55902; 507-285-7427.

Accommodations: Lanesboro Visitor Center, P.O. Box 348, Lanesboro, MN 55949; 800-944-2670.

Books: *Wisconsin and Minnesota Trout Streams,* Jim Humphrey and Bill Shogren, Backcountry Publications, Woodstock, VT, 1995.

45 Trout Run Creek

Location: Southeastern Minnesota.
Short take: 12 miles of small spring-fed creek with consistent flows, good pools and pockets, and surprising browns.
Type of stream: Freestone.
Angling methods: Fly, spin.
Species: Brown, brook.
Access: Easy.
Season: April through September.
Nearest tourist services: Lanesboro, Rochester.
Handicapped access: None.
Closest TU chapters: Hiawatha, Win Cres.

IN THIS LAND OF TROUT STREAMS, two carry the name Trout Run Creek. One however, is a tiny tributary of the Middle Branch of the Whitewater. The other and larger flows into the North Branch of the Root River not far from Lanesboro. This is one of the prettiest of trout streams anywhere and paths along the bank, stiles over fences, and general freedom from litter show that, while heavily fished, it's fished by anglers who care.

The river rises on the prairie south of Saint Charles and it flows almost due south to the Root. Access is easy and ample. Take the Saint Charles exit from Interstate 90 and turn south on State Route 74. The first stream crossed by this road is the headwaters of Trout Run, but the stream does not reach really fishable size until the hamlet of Saratoga (you'll miss it if you blink). Most anglers consider Troy, where Winona County Road 6 comes in from the east, to be the top of the best mileage.

At Troy, take County Road 43 south. Trout Run flows west of the road but then loops back to the east and crosses under a bridge. The next road to the east drops down to the creek. Below the bridge is a heavily fished pool where you can watch small browns rise almost all day. Across the creek is one of the few surviving round barns in the region, designed so that a hay wagon could enter the upper level and off-load its cargo on the floor above the livestock. Upstream, a thick patch of woods makes casting challenging, to say the least. But the canopy thins quickly as the stream crosses open pasture. Downstream, a trail leads over a small knoll onto mileage that once flowed through a now defunct Boy Scout Camp.

At the boundary between Winona and Fillmore counties, CR 43 becomes CR 11. The first intersection south of the county line takes you to a one-time vacation hamlet—Bide-a-wee (yup!)— where a long green pool stretches north above the bridge and the pocket water run below cuts through a brushy field. Banks in this section are frequently undercut and draped with vegetation. When the sun is on the water, you'll find fewer fish in the open. In summer, cast terrestrials upstream against the bank. CR 11 runs into State Route 30, and just south is another side road that

TROUT RUN CREEK

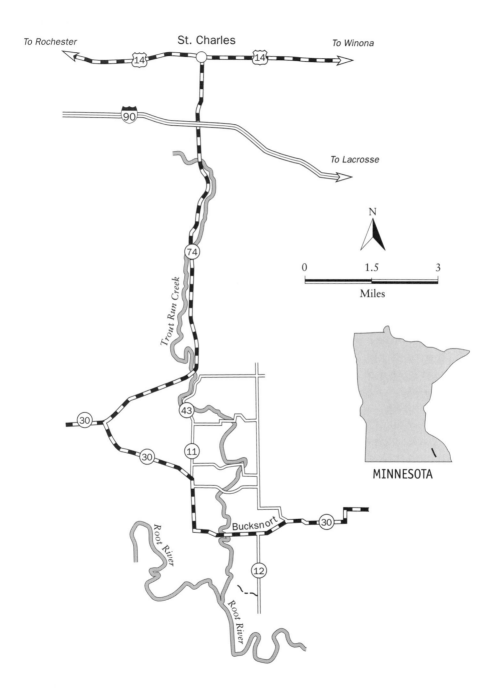

takes you to the river. Making a sharp right-angle turn to the east, State Route 30 drops down a hill and crosses below a low dam and picnic area at Bucksnort. The mileage above the little pond impounded by the dam is some of the best on the creek, as are the two miles or so downstream that eventually flow into the North Branch of the Root.

With natural propagation of browns and brook trout, this creek is said to have populations between 2,000 and 5,000 fish per mile, and it is one of the premier streams in the state. Alas, it too is threatened by agricultural pollution. A farmer whose land lies along the stream at Bucksnort maintains a manure lagoon, which, if it fails, could cause serious damage to the downstream watershed. TU and the Minnesota Department of Natural Resources are working with agricultural interests to find a process which will allow safe use of the fertilizer without jeopardizing the creek.

RESOURCES

Gearing up: Gander Mountain, 1201 S. Broadway, Rochester, MN 55902; 507-285-7427.

Accommodations: Lanesboro Visitor Center, P.O. Box 348, Lanesboro, MN 55949; 800-944-2670.

Books: *Wisconsin and Minnesota Trout Streams*, Jim Humphrey and Bill Shogren, Backcountry Publications, Woodstock, VT, 1995.

46 WHITEWATER RIVER

Location: Southeastern Minnesota.
Short take: Would you believe a winter trout fishery where it's 10 degrees below zero?
Type of stream: Freestone.
Angling methods: Fly, spin.
Species: Brown, rainbow, brook.
Access: Easy.
Season: Mid-April through September; January through March.
Nearest tourist services: Rochester.
Handicapped access: None.
Closest TU chapters: Hiawatha, Win Cres.

THE WHITEWATER IS A MISNOMER. You'll find no torrential cataracts, swirling plunge pools, or deadly falls. Nope. Just a wonderful trio of streams that tumble down from the prairie into a widening cottonwood valley that grows ever broader between high hills topped with cliffs of limestone. Pioneer farmers, trying to wrest a living from the valley floor, had stripped it of its timber, burned its thick sod, and tilled its topsoil until it could stand no more. Massive floods blasted through the valley, leaving devastation and little hope of recovery. In 1919, the state acquired its first parcel in the valley and by 1931, after a petition from the Izaak Walton League in Rochester, began actively purchasing property to form what is now a 27,000-acre wildlife management area.

Managed for wild turkey, grouse, and deer, the area holds a special place in the hearts of many TUers from the nearby Hiawatha chapter in Rochester and Win Cres in Winona. For more than a generation, they have worked at restoring stream habitat and argued for land use policies and practices that would protect and enhance the environment. Thanks to the efforts of Minnesota's Department of Natural Resources and a plethora of local, regional, and state organizations, anglers have at their disposal more than 50 miles of first-class small-river fishing. And the work continues: just recently Hiawatha and Win Cres, working together with DNR, installed cribs and created plunge pools on the Middle Branch above state park waters.

Three main branches—North, Middle, and South—and two tributaries—Trout Run and Beaver Creek—offer similar yet varied angling. Aside from the upper reaches of Middle and South Branches, the streams contain few little rock outcrops. For the most part, the mileage consists of gravel runs and pools running along banks sparsely forested by cottonwoods and aspen. Cold springs feed the headwaters and seep into the branches at numerous points, giving birth to the most unusual aspect of the Whitewater fishery. Its open waters can be fished with barbless hook on a strict catch-and-release basis from New Year's Day until the end of March. Spring,

WHITEWATER RIVER

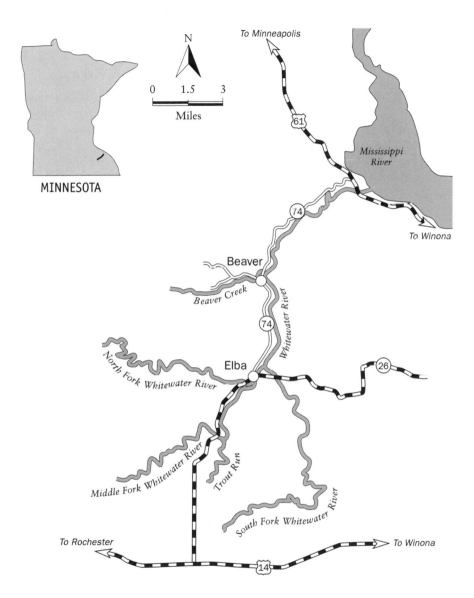

MINNESOTA

JOHN ROSS

Spring-fed, the Whitewater offers a surprisingly good mid-winter fishery.

in the form of midge hatches, comes early to Southeast Minnesota, even if the temperature is hovering at 0 degrees F. Typically from noon to 2 P.M. on even the coldest of sunny days without wind, you'll find a hatch in the riffles. In pools, a nymph fished oh-so-slowly with a strike indicator will attract browns to 16 inches and more. Dressed with fleece and 5 mil neoprenes, anglers seem undeterred by the frigid temperatures. "But it's dry cold," they'll tell you if asked.

Whitewater State Park, at the head of the valley, with 3.3 miles of catch-and-release water offers excellent angling both winter and summer. Diehard fly fishers enjoy the challenge of angling in the little shady runs of Beaver Creek, but it's the complicated currents in the runs and pools of the South Branch that draws much of their attention. Fish shaded woods in deep summer or splash hoppers along grassy banks in the meadows. Numerous roads and trails criss-cross the valley and maps are readily available at the state park headquarters.

RESOURCES

Gearing up: Gander Mountain, 1201 S. Broadway, Rochester, MN 55902; 507-285-7427.

Accommodations: Winona Convention and Visitors Bureau, 67 Main Street, P.O. Box 870, Winona, MN 55987; 800-657-4972. Rochester Convention/Visitors Bureau, 150 South Broadway, Suite A, Rochester, MN 55904-6500; 800-634-8277.

Books: *Wisconsin and Minnesota Trout Streams*, Jim Humphrey and Bill Shogren, Backcountry Publications, Woodstock, VT, 1995.

47 Bois Brule River

Location: Northwestern Wisconsin.
Short take: Presidents fish the "real" Brule. You can too.
Type of stream: Freestone.
Angling methods: Fly, spin.
Species: Brook, brown, rainbow, Chinook, Coho.
Access: Moderate.
Season: April through mid-November.
Nearest tourist services: Brule, Superior, Iron River.
Handicapped access: Yes.
Closest TU chapter: Wild River.

EVER THINK OF ULYSSES S. GRANT as an angler? He was the first of a handful of presidents that include Cleveland, Coolidge, Hoover, and Eisenhower to fish the Bois Brule, that river of many faces first known for its large brook trout and now for its browns, steelhead, and salmon. You may fish it as well, canoeing a dozen or so miles on the upper river casting for native brookies, battling early and late season snows for salmon and steelhead, seducing fat browns from their summer lies beneath sweepers that swing in the current. This river (Burnt Woods in French) differs considerably from the Brule which rises in Michigan and forms the border with Wisconsin for several miles before joining the Menominee which empties into Lake Michigan above Green Bay.

The Bois Brule gathers its waters from a boggy height of land in the middle of Douglas County and flows northeast through a state forest, established in 1907, before emptying into Lake Superior. The upper waters are slow, forming in a swamp and nourished by springs along its route. The bottom is sandy silt, and here the river is a rich soup of aquatic life. Brook trout, descendants of the original char that have inhabited the watershed since the last glaciation, thrive in these waters. To fish these waters effectively, one must make use of a canoe. Launch at Stone's Bridge on County Road S and drift a dozen miles to a take-out at Winneboujou. The first few miles are placid; the middle is studded with sharp rapids but not enough to cause undue concern, and the lower reaches include a pair of sinuous lakes where huge brown trout may come out to play. In the midst is venerable Cedar Island, the 4,500-acre-estate where presidents came to fish.

A number of summer homes are found in the vicinity of the bridge where County Road B crosses the river at Winneboujou. Less than a mile downstream the Nebagamon enters from the west and swells the river. Farther down comes the confluence of the Little Bois Brule and a set of rapids. The intervening waters are reputed to fish well in summer for rainbows and browns. Trout authors Humphery and Shogren also report good angling for browns and rainbows in the waters near Copper Range Campground and Pine Tree Landing.

Bois Brule River

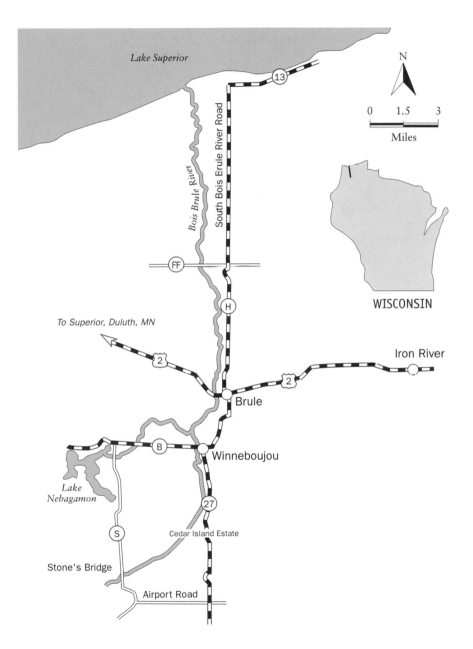

Lake Superior

Bois Brule River

South Bois Brule River Road

13

To Superior, Duluth, MN

2

2

Iron River

Brule

FF

H

B

Winneboujou

Lake
Nebagamon

27

Cedar Island Estate

S

Stone's Bridge

Airport Road

N

0   1.5   3
Miles

WISCONSIN

County Road FF marks the practical limit of wade fishing on the river. Below the bottom is difficult—lots of rock, ledges, and drop-offs into deep runs. And, hard rains tend to sweep clay from its banks into the river. The lower section is water favored by salmon and steelhead anglers who fish the fall run in September and the spring run which begins in March. Access to the lower third of the river is ample from a number of side roads heading west from County Road H which becomes State Route 13 as you drive straight north. Below the junction of Trask Creek, South Brule River Road intersects with SR 13 heading west and north along the river all the way to its mouth.

Hatches on this river vary dramatically with location and they tend to be somewhat inconsistent. March Browns and species of *Hexagenia* are found in the slow water between the CR S and Winneboujou accesses. The lakes see hatches of *Callibaetis*, and caddis are generally prevalent. Large stonefly nymphs are effective as are attractors and terrestrials. You'll also find some action on streamers.

The region is easily reached by car from Duluth and accommodations may be found in the small city of Superior or at a number of motels and bed-and-breakfasts in the areas along the river.

RESOURCES

Gearing up: Brule River Classics, 6008 S. State Rt. 28, Brule, WI 54820; 715-372-8153.

Accommodations: Superior/Douglas County Chamber of Commerce, 305 Harborview Parkway, Superior, WI 54880; 715-394-7716.

Books: *Wisconsin & Minnesota Trout Streams*, Jim Humphrey and Bill Shogren, Backcountry Publications, Woodstock, VT, 1995.

Exploring Wisconsin Trout Streams, Steve Born, et al, Univ. of Wisconsin Press, Madison, WI, 1997.

48 KICKAPOO RIVER, WEST FORK

Location: Southwestern Wisconsin.
Short take: Great browns in the most pastoral of settings.
Type of stream: Freestone, spring creek.
Angling methods: Fly, spin.
Species: Brown, brook.
Access: Easy.
Season: March through September.
Nearest tourist services: Avalanche, Coon Valley, LaCrosse.
Handicapped access: None.
Closest TU chapter: Coulee Region.

BECAUSE THE TERRAIN IN SOUTHWESTERN Wisconsin was somewhat higher than the surrounding countryside, geologists surmise, continental glaciers flowed around rather than over it. Instead of being worn down and filled up with boulders, sands, and clays, valleys here are steep and bounded by cliffs. At the base of rock bluffs, countless springs percolate to the surface and their cold waters drain into a maze of creeks that at one time supported wonderful populations of wild brook trout. No more. A century of intensive and ill-advised farming practices allowed erosion to flush silt into streams clogging gravelly bedding runs. When chemical fertilizers, herbicides, and pesticides first came into vogue, their indiscriminate use added toxins and unnatural nutrients to the streams that slowly poisoned the fish. Yet a generation ago, farmers, anglers, and environmentalists recognized that no one benefits from wanton stream degradation. Agricultural practices began to change. Stringent management was applied to the fishery, and corps of volunteers, TU members among them, began the hands-on work of rehabilitating the watershed. Nowhere is that success more apparent than on Timber Coulee Creek near Coon Valley.

Now the West Fork of the Kickapoo River, in the next watershed to the east, is seeing a tremendous rejuvenation. Browns of 16 to 18 inches are fairly common in the nine miles of catch-and-release water from the State Route 82 bridge upstream to the bridge at Bloomingdale. This section represents fairly small water, ranging from 15 to 30 feet in width. For the most part if flows through grassy pasture, terribly exposed to the sun until a number of lunker structures were installed by the West Fork Sportsman's Club to provide cover. Some sections are naturally shaded by stands of 100-year-old cottonwoods. In other runs, banks are heavily brushed. In many spots the river is easily wadeable, but often stealthy casting from the bank is more effective. Patience can bring anglers some of those phenomenal days of a dozen fish no smaller than 12 inches.

Dry fly fishing is great fun on this river whether you're working March Browns in May, Sulphurs in June; Light Cahills, Yellow Sallies, or Caddis (Elk Hair Caddis

KICKAPOO RIVER, WEST FORK

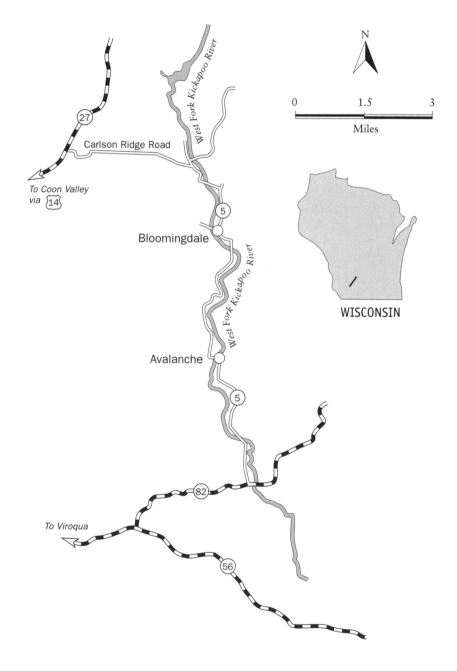

A stealthy approach is essential if you intend to fool 16- to 18-inch browns on the West Fork of the Kickapoo.

are good almost throughout the season). Terrestrials from July on are very important. Hoppers, beetles, crickets, and ants plopped right next to the bank will often draw strikes even on the stillest of days. Anglers seeking big fish throw muskrats, gray Woolly Buggers, and Muddlers as dark settles into the valley. Many of the streams that feed the West Fork are themselves excellent fisheries, and they provide a bit of a safety valve for the number of anglers who have discovered the main river. And, while the premier water is that centered on the small hamlet of Avalanche, the mileage downstream from the Route 82 bridge holds some very big browns. You'll catch fewer fish south of the highway bridge, but they will be bigger.

Kudos for the rehabilitation of the West Fork go to the West Fork Sportsman's Club and its president, Robert Widner, Jr. Club members, occasionally with an assist from TU's Blackhawk and Coulee chapters, have devoted thousands of dollars and volunteer hours to restoration of this trout fishery. Their work is without peer. Because of their high level of community commitment, and of the importance of the watershed to the economic health of the region, TU selected the Kickapoo watershed for its second Home Waters Initiative. More than $200,000 has been raised from a number of national foundations and private individuals to conduct a thorough baseline study of the watershed, accelerate enhancement of instream and riparian habitat, and provide educational and informational outreach to area residents, school children, tourists, and anglers of the importance of improving and preserving the watershed. Like the premier Home Waters Project on the Beamoc drainage, the Kickapoo project is becoming a national model.

RESOURCES

Gearing up: Spring Creek Anglers, P.O. Box 283, 219 Coon Valley, WI 54623; 608-452-3430.

Accommodations: Vernon County Chamber of Commerce, 220 S. Main St., Viroqua, WI 54665; 608-637-2575.

Books: *Exploring Wisconsin Trout Streams,* Steve Born, Jeff Mayers, Andy Morton, and Bill Sonzogni, Author, Univ. of Wisconsin Press, Madison, WI, 1997.

49 WOLF RIVER

Location: Upper Northeastern Wisconsin.
Short take: Gentle and lovely, this is a river of dreams.
Type of stream: Freestone.
Angling methods: Fly, spin.
Species: Brown, rainbow.
Access: Moderate.
Season: March through mid-November.
Nearest tourist services: White Lake, Green Bay.
Handicapped access: Yes.
Closest TU chapter: Wolf River.

SPRING DRAWS THE WATER OUT OF Wisconsin's northcountry, filtering it first into tiny rivulets beneath the conifers, including those of Nicolet National Forest. These tiny brooks coalesce into the headwaters of streams that grow into rivers that carry trout—the Brule (shared later with Michigan's Upper Peninsula), the Peshtigo, and the Wolf, which is the best of them all. Whelped by feeders of Hiles Mill Pond and Pine Lake, the Wolf emerges as a stream in its own right at the outflow of Post Lake. But it is not until the Hunting River runs into the Wolf at Pearson, that the river becomes fishable. For 60 miles, to the southern boundary of the Menominee Indian Reservation, the Wolf is first-class trout water. The upper 34 miles of the river are accessible to all anglers, and the remainder of the mileage is reserved for Indians. Anglers respect the boundary to be sure, but the trout are not so responsible.

In the reach from Pearson to Lily where State Route 52 crosses the river, the Wolf is slow and cold. The silty bottom in the upper section gives birth to the river's hatch of *Hexagenia atrocaudata* (also known as Slate Drakes), a smaller Hex species than the more common *limbata* that comes off in mid-July. Below Lily the rapids, beginning with Saint Claire and ending with Gilmore's Mistake (we can only wonder what it was) at the reservation boundary, change the character of the river. The pace quickens with increasing gradient as the river swirls over submerged boulders, skips along through pocket water, and slides through deep runs. Occasionally boulders, erratics left by glacial ice, break the river's flow, as do infrequent islands. Where flats widen and shallow the river, braided channels form.

In the main, the Wolf wades easily. And the Wisconsin Department of Natural Resources has purchased or otherwise secured access for most of the mileage upstream of the Menominee Reservation. But getting to the river can be a challenge. Only highway bridges cross the river—County Road T at Lily, State Route 52 at Lily, State Route 64 at Langlade, and County M just above the reservation boundary. Military Wayside on State Route 55 about six miles northwest of Lily offers good access, as does Wood River Road off SR 55, about three miles south of Lily, and Hollister Road, about four miles down the highway toward Langlade. The Soo Line

WOLF RIVER

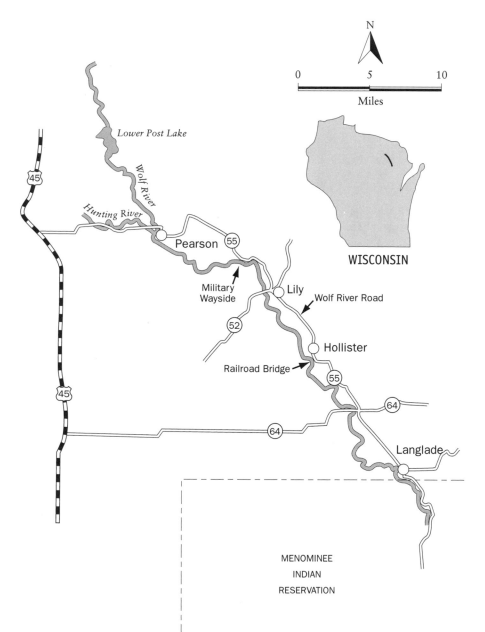

N

0   5   10
Miles

Lower Post Lake

Wolf River

Hunting River

45

Pearson   55

Military
Wayside

Lily

52

Wolf River Road

Hollister

Railroad Bridge

55

45

64

64

Langlade

WISCONSIN

MENOMINEE
INDIAN
RESERVATION

Railroad Bridge, about seven miles north of Langlade, marks the upper reach of five miles or so of catch-and-release water restricted to artificial lures with single barbless hooks. Water is elegant for waders who enjoy a challenge.

Hatches on the river are substantial. After the high flows of spring have washed through the system, you'll see Hendricksons, sulphurs, and gray and brown drakes from mid-May into June. Then come tricos, and mahogany duns. Stoneflies, black and yellow, are also important on the river in June. August brings massive hatches of *Ephoron leukon*—#8 to #10 White Wulffs. Terrestrials are also good, as are streamers and various Muddlers.

TU chapters once float-stocked the upper reaches of the river, but of late the Wolf River Chapter has been working hard on habitat improvement projects designed to deepen stream runs in an effort to mitigate threats to propagation from slush ice and from warm shallow flows in summer. TU was also an eloquent advocate in establishing a moratorium on the future operation of a zinc and copper mine at Crandon which threatens to both pollute and reduce flows in the river. Folks along the river know the river's value, are accommodating to anglers, and fight tooth and nail to protect it.

RESOURCES

Gearing up: Mike's Mobil Service, N4505 Hwy 55, White Lake, WI 54491; 715-882-8901.

Accommodations: Antigo Area Chamber of Commerce, 329 Superior St., P.O. Box 339, Antigo, WI 54409; 715-623-4134; www.newnorth.net/ antigo.chamber. Bear Paw Inn, N3494 Hwy 55, White Lake WI 54491; 715-882-3502. Wild Wolf Inn, 2850 Hwy 55, White Lake, WI 54491; 715-882-8611.

Books: *Wisconsin & Minnesota Trout Streams*, Jim Humphrey and Bill Shogren, Backcountry Publications, Woodstock, VT, 1995.

Exploring Wisconsin Trout Streams, Steve Born et al, Univ. of Wisconsin Press, Madison, WI, 1997.

River Rap (audio tape with map),Wolf River, Wayne Anderson and Gary LaFontaine, Greycliff Publishing, Helena, MT, 1992.

MISSOURI

51   **52**

50

ARKANSAS

50. WHITE RIVER
51. CRANE CREEK
52. NORTH FORK RIVER

MIDWEST

ARKANSAS

MISSOURI

50 WHITE RIVER

Location: North-central Arkansas.
Short take: The most popular trout river in the Midwest.
Type of stream: Tailwater.
Angling methods: Fly, spin.
Species: Brown, cutthroat, rainbow, brook.
Access: Easy to moderate.
Season: Year-round.
Nearest tourist services: Midway, Mountain Home.
Handicapped access: None.
Closest TU chapter: North Central Arkansas.

TIME WAS, WHEN ANGLERS thought of Arkansas they thought of lazy khaki-green rivers gliding past limestone cliffs topped with stands of oak and hickory. Smallmouth was the fish that came to mind. The artificial boys tossed jig 'n pigs or crankbaits. Hellgrammites and minnows were favored by the live bait set. The conveyance of choice was a johnboat, flat-bottomed and most likely of aluminum, but often built of wood. A five-pound bronzeback was king of the hill.

No more, of course. Along with smallmouth, when fishing folk think of Arkansas they think of trout—big brown trout—particularly the 10- to 30-pound spawners that wrestle flank-to-fin in the redds below Bull Shoals Dam from November through January during the height of the run. For flood control and power generation, Corps of Engineers dams on the White and its principle tributaries were constructed in the late 1940s and early 1950s. Resultant bottom draws produced cold tail waters ideal for trout. They were heavily stocked and fished on a put-and-take basis, but no one imagined these waters could become a world-class, self-sustaining fishery.

And it didn't happen overnight. Browns were introduced to the river in the late '40s, but the program terminated a decade later. Convinced that the White and Norfork Rivers could potentially produce wild browns, the Northeast Arkansas Fly Fishers used Vibert boxes to introduce fertile brown trout eggs to the rivers in 1975. A few years later, Arkansas Game and Fish Commission reinstated its brown trout stocking program. In the late '80s, the fly fishers, boat dock operators, and TU mounted a charge resulting in a 2-fish, 16-inch minimum limit on browns. And TU also sponsored efforts to establish a single-hook, artificial lure, catch-and-release policy for the spawning beds below Bull Shoals Dam from November through January.

The 44 miles from Bull Shoals to Norfork, Arkansas is regarded as the best stretch of trout water in the White River system. Its long runs, gravel bars, pools, and eddies are among the richest trout water in the world. And, as in the late and not widely lamented smallmouth days, the best way to fish it is to float and camp overnight.

WHITE RIVER

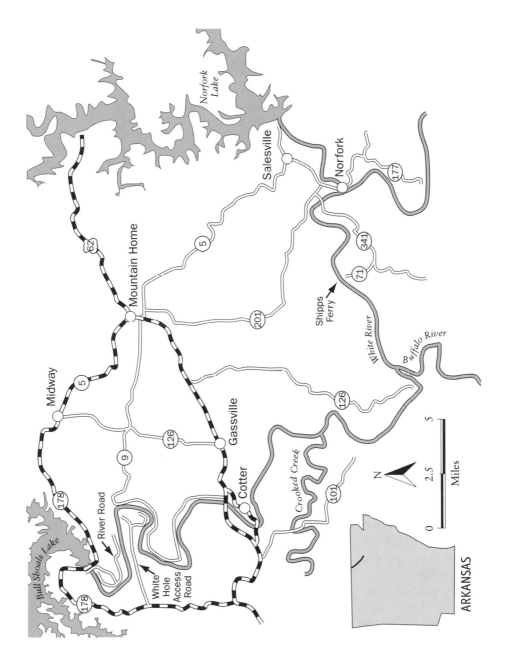

SPENCER E. TURNER

Traditional john boats have given way to modern drift boats on the White River at Bull Shoals.

Why? Floating puts anglers on the best water when browns, nocturnal feeders in the main, are at their most ravenous. Sure, you'll catch them rising to mayfly hatches. But crustaceans and minnows are primary foods and nymphs and streamers are the most effective patterns. If renowned angler Dave Whitlock, who works out of Midway, were to name the most popular streamer for the White, he'd steer you to a #8 or #10 Olive Woolly Bugger. Whitlock's own design, Dave's Red Fox Squirrel Nymph, is one of those all-things-to-all-fish kind of flies. In small sizes it looks a bit like a sowbug or scud or mayfly nymph. Tie it larger and you've got a crawdad or stonefly nymph. Sculpins are staples of trout longer than 16 inches. Not only is the typical russet and olive pattern effective, but so is white. Those diehards or fanatics who insist on fishing dries will have to make do with #20 to #24 midges which hatch every day of the year.

The long tailwater below Bull Shoals Dam is not the only stellar trout water in this corner of the state. Another—if the 38-pound, 9-ounce brown taken in 1988 is any indication—is the 4.8 miles of cold released water from Norfork dam to the town of the same name at its junction with the White River. The newest White River impoundment, Beaver Lake, has produced an eight-mile tailwater where ten-pound browns and big rainbows are not uncommon. TU members from Arkansas and Oklahoma, with a $10,000 Embrace-a-Stream Grant, have been instrumental in establishing habitat in the Beaver Dam tailwater. Below Table Rock Dam in Missouri, is another 22 miles of good brown and rainbow trout fishing, Lake Taneycomo, which flows past Branson, the nation's new country music capital. And while the 44 miles of river from Bull Shoals to Norfork are the premier waters on the lower White, the mileage immediately downstream also offers some possibilities.

RESOURCES

Gearing up: Blue Ribbon Flies, 1343 Hwy. 5, Mountain Home, AR 72653; 870-425-0447; www.stlweb.mtnhome.com/brf/.

White River Angler, 577 E. Millsap Road, Fayetteville, AR 72703; 800-544-1420.

Accommodations: Mountain Home Area Chamber of Commerce, Highway 412/62, P.O. Box 488, Mountain Home, AR 72653-0488; 870-425-5111; 800-822-3536; www.mtnhomechamber.com.

Books: *Ozark Trout Tales: A Fishing Guide for the White River System*, Steve Wright, White River Chronicle, Fayetteville, AR, 1995.

51 CRANE CREEK

Location: South-central Missouri.
Short take: Delicate little stream with big, western 'bows.
Type of stream: Spring creek.
Angling methods: Fly, spin.
Species: McCloud Strain rainbow.
Access: Easy.
Season: Year-round.
Nearest tourist services: Springfield.
Handicapped access: None.
Closest TU chapter: Branson.

LOCATED JUST 25 MILES SOUTHWEST of Springfield, this jewel of a trout stream is as diminutive in size as its fish are hearty. Here you'll find rainbows—pure strain McCloud River rainbows—first stocked in 1880, then allowed to go wild. And that's what they've done; they thrive in the cold flows fed by springs and limestone sinks. Clear as proverbial glass, the water roils over a pebbly bottom, tufted here and there with patches of aquatic grasses that wave in the current. The main section of fishable waters—two miles in the Wire Road Conservation area north and west of the little hamlet of Crane—is largely protected by a brushy canopy of box elder and sycamore. That helps keep the waters cool even on those scorching 100 degrees F days of mid-summer. Vegetation overhangs cut banks, providing additional shelter, and the riffles are just aggressive enough to oxygenate the water.

Because of its origins in carbonate rock, Crane has a relatively high pH level. Rich in crayfish, scuds, and nymphs, the river produces excellent hatches of mayflies, caddis, and sedge. Starting in March, use Blue-Winged Olives, Light Cahills and black caddis. By mid-June, terrestrials—namely ants, beetles and inchworms—make their appearances and you can fish them into the fall. Another good fly is the Little Sister Sedge, according to Meck and Hoover in their book *Great Rivers, Great Hatches*. And many good fish are taken on Elk Hair Caddis and various nymphs in the #12 to #16 range.

While some of the stream is held privately, the Missouri Division of Conservation's mileage above the town and another mile or so downstream give anglers reasonable access. Because the stream averages no more than 25 feet in width and its banks are made of loamy soils, a stealthy approach is a must. Precision in the placement of moderate-sized flies tied on 12- to 15-foot tippets of 4X and finer are required for top water success. Shorter leaders can be used with nymphs. All fishing on the Crane from the bridge at Quail Stop upstream is strictly via artificial lure. Catch-and-release is required as well.

Crane Creek is a delightful but very difficult counterpart to Missouri and Arkansas tailwaters that flow from impoundments in the Ozark Plateau, which rises

CRANE CREEK

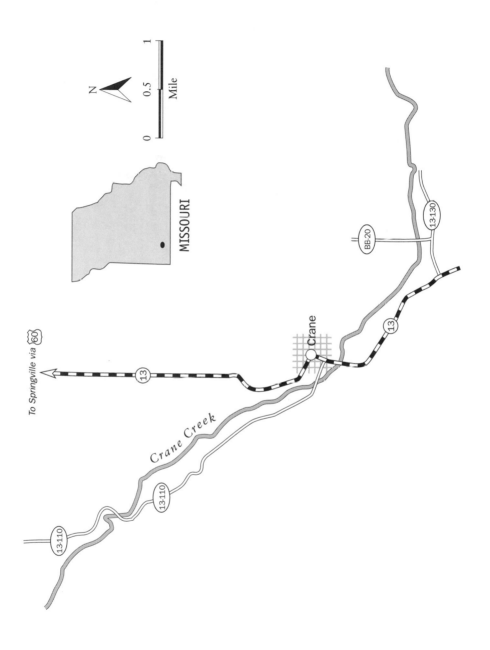

This chunky rainbow shows the health and tone typical of the trout in Crane Creek.

20 miles to the south. To reach this gem of a creek, drive south from Springfield on U.S. Highway 60, then bear left on State Route 13 just beyond Billings. Follow your nose to Crane and the signs there for the Wire Road Conservation Area. If you need tackle, supplies, or information, stop at Bass Pro Shop in Springfield. While these good ol' boys speak largemouth with more than a little southern drawl, you'll find that they can talk trout with the best of them.

RESOURCES

Gearing up: Bass Pro Shop, 2500 E. Kearney, Springfield, MO 65898; 800-227-7776.

Accommodations: Aurora Chamber of Commerce, P.O. Box 257, Avnona, MO 65605; 407-678-4150.

Books: *Fly Fishing for Trout in Missouri*, Chuck and Sharon Tryon, Ozark Mountain Fly Fishers, Rolla, MO, 1992.

52 North Fork River

Location: South-central Missouri.
Short take: Big river. Big browns, good rainbows.
Type of stream: Freestone.
Angling methods: Fly, spin.
Species: Brown, rainbow.
Access: Moderate.
Season: Year-round.
Nearest tourist services: Tecumseh.
Handicapped access: None.
Closest TU chapter: Mid-Missouri.

WHILE ON THE MAPS IT'S NAMED the North Fork of the White River, most folks in the Show Me State just call it the North Fork. Rising east of the little town of Mountain Grove on U.S. Highway 60, the North Fork flows almost due south, draining a forested highland capped by 1,342-foot Bald Knob Mountain. Below the little crossroads of Ann, the river enters the Mark Twain National Forest and gathers more flow from numerous tributaries. You'll find some trout in this mileage, but the best water, that which draws most of the national attention, is lower in the system, beginning below the double springs, North Fork and Rainbow, that add heavy flows of cold water into the river.

For the next dozen miles, down to Blair Bridge, the North Fork is managed for trophy trout. Using artificial lures only, anglers are allowed to keep three fish per day as long as each is 18 inches or longer. From the springs south, classic freestone pocket water characterizes the river. A few limestone ledges, particularly at The Falls, a mile and a half below McKee Bridge, transect the channel. And along the way you'll find pools fed by long smooth gravel runs and mileage where the river surges over and around big boulders. The best way to fish the river is to float it in a canoe, johnboat or small drift boat. The river, ranging from 50 to 100 feet in width, is big enough. Fine diatomaceous algae covers rocks. Even caulked felt-soled wading shoes are scant insurance against a quick plunge. Access to the river in this section for non-floaters is limited. The best bet is Kelly Ford, about a mile downstream from The Falls. You can also reach the river at Blair Bridge at the end of the special regulations section.

Evidently, big browns and rainbows don't care about special regulations. Why else would so many in the five-pounds-and-up range be taken between Blair Bridge and James Bridge, not far upstream from Tecumseh? There's good wading access to the upper third of this stretch at Patrick Bridge on Highway H.

Small insects are not the main staple in the diet of these big trout, though late July and August mornings witness reasonably good trico hatches, and slate and golden drakes are around from May into July. A few Blue-Winged Olives and

NORTH FORK RIVER

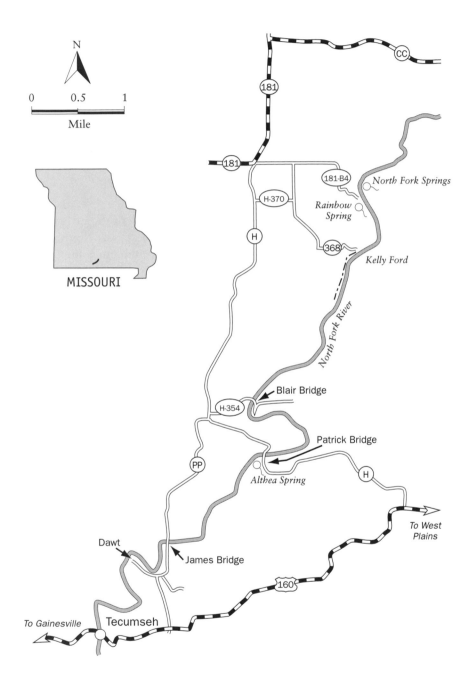

N

0   0.5   1
Mile

MISSOURI

CC

181

181

181-B4   North Fork Springs

H-370   Rainbow Spring

H

368   Kelly Ford

North Fork River

Blair Bridge

H-354

Patrick Bridge

PP   H

Althea Spring   To West Plains

Dawt   To Gainesville   Tecumseh   James Bridge   160

hendricksons come off in spring, and PMDs seem to do the number from mid-May into June. This is primarily a river for nymphs or emergers. Shawn Taylor, impresario of Taylormade River Treks, a guide service-cum-bed-and-breakfast on the river near Tecumseh, swears by Prince and similar nymphs.

As one would expect, the river is popular with canoeists and they float it mightily in summer months. But in spring and fall, when the fishing is arguably best, they are mostly gone. And in the winter, when the fishing can be superb, canoes are a rarity.

RESOURCES

Gearing up: Blue Ribbon Flies, 1343 Hwy. 5, Mountain Home, AR 72653; 870-425-0447; www.stlweb.mtnhome.com/brf/.

Accommodations: Taylormade River Treks, HC 1, Box 1755, Tecumseh, MO 65760; 417-284-3055. Twin Bridges Canoe & Campground, HC 64, Box 230, West Plains, MO 65775; 417-256-2726.

Books: *Fly Fishing for Trout in Missouri*, Chuck and Sharon Tryon, Ozark Mountain Fly Fishers, Rolla, MO, 1992.

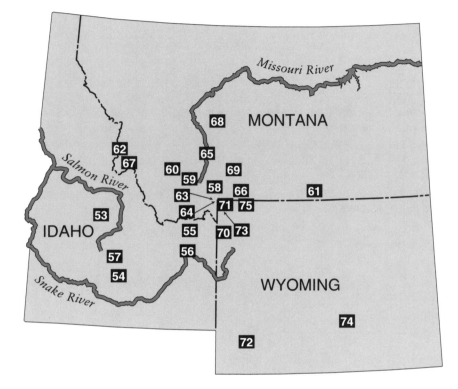

NORTHERN ROCKY MOUNTAINS

IDAHO

MONTANA

WYOMING

53 SALMON RIVER, MIDDLE FORK

Location: West Central Idaho.
Short take: Run 100 miles of whitewater through the country's largest mountain wilderness.
Type of stream: Freestone.
Angling methods: Fly, spin.
Species: Westslope cutthroat, rainbow.
Access: Extremely difficult.
Season: Late May through November.
Nearest tourist services: None.
Handicapped access: None.
Closest TU chapter: Reed Gullespie/Central Idaho.

FORMING BELOW CAPE HORN, the Middle Fork of the Salmon River plunges more or less due north in its 104-mile journey to the main stem. It flows through the southeastern quadrant of the Frank Church River of No Return Wilderness, which with 2.4 million acres is the second largest wilderness area in the United States. (The largest is Death Valley.) No roads penetrate far into the drainage. One rugged trail follows the river for 70 miles then veers away as the Middle Fork dives into a canyon of Class IV rapids. Other trails do reach the river, but only after hikes of 20 to 25 miles from the nearest gravel road.

To the east of the river rise the jagged Bighorn Crags, and between the river and these 10,000-foot peaks are an endless succession of ridges, some forested with Douglas-fir and lodgepole pine, others awash in sun-soaked aspen and mountain grasses. Along the river are stands of ponderosa pine and little parks where you're apt to see elk and black bear. Bighorn sheep are commonly sighted and occasionally you'll see the white dots of mountain goats working their way across cliffs and slopes of talus.

Over its run to the main fork of the Salmon, the Middle Fork drops some 2,700 feet. The gradient is constant, not the brawling life-threatening rapids of the big river which earned it the sobriquet River of No Return. Innumerable chutes rushing past gravel bars empty into runs studded with boulders. West slope cutthroat and rainbows ply these waters, and they readily take dry flies. Aside from a stonefly hatch in early July, it makes little difference what you toss. Attractor patterns including Wulffs and Stimulators are very effective. Elk-hair Caddis in brown and olive are good choices as well. Few fish are taken on nymphs, though at times a small Hare's Ear or Pheasant Tail fished as a dropper below a dry will pick up a cutty. In late summer and early fall, terrestrials, especially hopper patterns, are productive. A 4-weight rod carrying a disk drag reel loaded with 50 yards of backing and a floating weight forward line is an ideal outfit. Leaders need not be overlong or very fine. Four-pound test line and small Mepps, Rooster Tails, Panther Martins, or other

SALMON RIVER, MIDDLE FORK

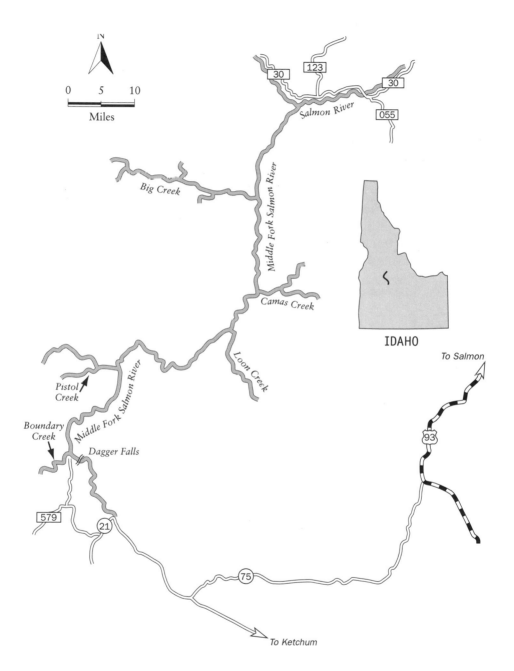

C. LARRY PROSER

Renowned as a classic white water run, the Middle Fork of the Salmon also provides a top-notch wilderness experience fishing for cutthroat and rainbow trout.

spinners will work well on ultra-light systems. Average fish will range between 10 and 14 inches, and you may catch one of 16 inches or so. Sophisticated these trout are not.

There is but one way that most of us could ever fish this river, and that is to hire a guide who is permitted to outfit on the Middle Fork. You can, of course, try to run the river yourself in a rubber raft or drift boat. To do so is foolish, unless you know the river intimately. One such guide is Kurt Selisch of Middle Fork River Tours. Kurt launches at Boundary Creek. A camp boat hurries ahead as anglers fish their way down in drift boats. As the fishers round the last bend of the day, they find tents erected, a fire burning, and wines chilled or breathing as is their wont. Settle down to dinner of grilled pork and duck with apple and fig sauté accompanied by fruit chutney. All you need to bring is your imagination and appetite.

RESOURCES

Gearing up: Lost River Anglers, P.O. Box 3445, Ketchum, ID 83340; 208-726-1706.

Accommodations: Middle Fork River Tours, Hailey, ID 83333; 800-445-9738.

Books: *Fly Fisher's Guide to Idaho,* Ken Retallic and Rocky Barker, Wilderness Adventure Press, Gallatin Gateway, MT, 1996.

54 SILVER CREEK

Location: South-central Idaho.
Short take: Toughest spring creek you'll ever love.
Type of stream: Spring creek.
Angling methods: Fly, spin.
Species: Rainbow, brown, odd brook.
Access: Easy.
Season: Late May through November.
Nearest tourist services: Tackle shops, accommodations in Sun Valley.
Handicapped access: Limited.
Closest TU chapter: Hemingway.

LIKE A RIVER OF MERCURY, Silver Creek slides through the tawny and arid plateau 30 miles south of Sun Valley. This is the Letort of the West. A spring creek where trout, in this case mostly rainbows, lurk in waving aquatic grasses or beneath bankside vegetation, waiting for just the right pattern to drift into their feeding lanes. The river's stately flow seems, at times, to be almost laminar, a sheet of water moving at a consistent speed. But watching micro cross currents catch your tippet and turn your fly this way and that soon disabuses you of that notion.

Not only is this water incredibly challenging to fish, but wading has its moments as well. The bottom is mainly muck with small lenses of pea gravel where encroaching banks constrict the river. With each step, you'll sink a foot or two, maybe more. Wading here is a slow and bad business, which is why many who fish Silver Creek do so from belly boats. With the exception of a five-mile stretch owned by The Nature Conservancy, the best portion of the creek flows through private lands. Floating is the only way to access this water and that's best achieved via canoe. But you have to get out to fish; Idaho law prohibits fishing Silver Creek directly from a boat. Canoes are favored over larger, heavier craft because any float on Silver Creek involves a portage around or over fences.

OK, so what's the allure? Large rainbows and a few browns with small heads and fat bodies that take very small dry flies and then run and jump like hell. Typical fish run in the 12- to 18-inch class, but behemoths of 20-inches-plus are not uncommon. Netting them is. The Nature Conservancy owns the best mileage of the creek, and it's restricted to fly fishing only. Other lures with barbless hooks may be used downstream, but all the way east to the U.S. Highway 20 bridge, the stream is catch-and-release. Downstream from the US 20 bridge to Picabo (peek-a-boo), anglers may retain two trout but none between 12 and 16 inches.

Best known for showers of tricos that hatch from mid-July through mid-August, this is mayfly water. Other major hatches include PMDs, brown drakes, *baetis*, and *calibaetis*. Hatches in mid-summer are best on cloudy days. In fall, arguably the best time to fish the river, sun triggers the *calibaetis* hatch, often at mid-day. Caddis

SILVER CREEK

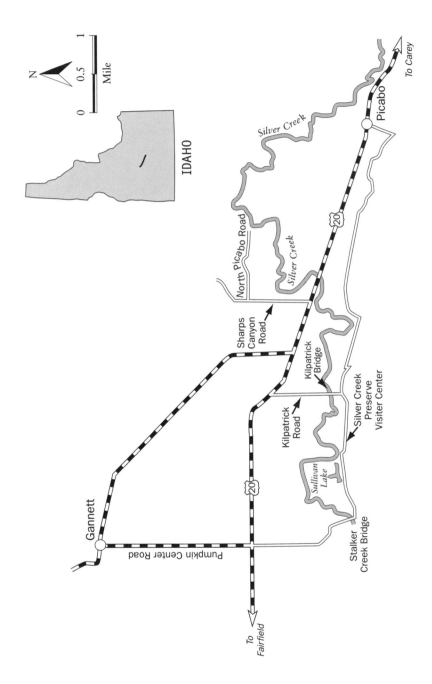

are not an important fly on Silver Creek; those that do come off hatch right at dark. Heavy moss makes fishing nymphs so difficult that most anglers don't bother.

Most anglers come to Silver Creek for the fishing. But little yellow lady slippers bloom along the creek in June, and sandhill cranes, long-billed curlews, and white ibis nest nearby. The Hemingways—Ernest and son Jack—were among the first to appreciate the importance of this high-desert, cold water ecosystem. Jack brought the creek to the attention of The Nature Conservancy which now holds conservation easements along more than 30 miles of the stream and its tributaries.

RESOURCES

Gearing up: Silver Creek Outfitters, P.O. Box 418, Ketchum, ID 83340; 208-726-5282. Idaho Angler, 1023 W. Bannock, Boise, ID 83702; 800-787-9957.

Accommodations: Ketchum/Sun Valley Chamber of Commerce, P.O. Box 2420, Ketchum, ID 83353; 800-634-3347.

Books: *Silver Creek: Ideal Fly Fishing Paradise*, David Glasscock and David Clark, Claxton Printers, Caldwell, ID, 1997.

55 SNAKE RIVER, HENRY'S FORK

Location: Eastern Idaho.
Short take: Number one in TU poll. Drought and erratic water flows once plagued the fishery, which is famed for big, tough rainbows, but it's coming back.
Type of stream: Spring creek, freestone.
Angling methods: Fly, spin.
Species: Rainbow in upper reaches, brown and rainbow below Mesa Falls.
Access: Easy to moderate.
Season: Down to Vernon Brige: late May through November; below: year-round.
Nearest tourist services: Last Chance, Island Park.
Handicapped access: Below Island Park Dam.
Closest TU chapter: Upper Snake.

WHEN A TROUT STREAM IS VOTED number one in the nation, it's got to be pretty good or awfully famous. Henry's Fork is both. Rising in huge springs and crisp mountain cascades, Henry's Fork cuts across the crater of a dormant volcano (caldera) before plunging through its rim some 180 feet to the flat prairie below. The most popular section of the river is the stretch of about 15 miles from Island Park Dam, through the famed Box Canyon and Harriman State Park, to Riverside take-out. All of this is roughly paralleled by U.S. Highway 20 which runs from Idaho Falls, Idaho, to West Yellowstone, Montana. In this section, for the most part, Henry's Fork flows through public land and access by wading or floating anglers is reasonably easy.

But there's more to Henry's Fork than these easily reached runs. From its primary headwaters at Henry's Lake, the stream follows a narrow course for seven miles through Flat Ranch where TU volunteers from the Idaho Council worked to repair riparian vegetation with the help of an Embrace-A-Stream grant. Below the ranch, the Fork meets the icy waters from Big Springs. There's no fishing in the springs. Its gravel channel is a prime nursery for the stream's rainbows, and you can see really huge 'bows cruising back and forth at the observation walkway over the spring at any time of year. Downstream, in the nine miles above Island Park Reservoir, there is some fishing, particularly in the vicinity of the hamlet of Mack's Inn, and it can be good. The Buffalo River, a reasonable piece of water that is often underfished, joins Henry's Fork just below Island Park Dam. Nymph fishing in the runs south of the dam when the water is off can be very productive, but watch out for quickly rising flows.

The Box Canyon, so called because it traverses a shallow cut in the floor of the caldera, is classic big freestone pocket water. Rainbows of 20 inches or more are often hung in these stretches on big nymphs—rubberlegs, stones, Bitch Creek are all good—and, once in a while, dries. This section is catch-and-release, but it's open to

196

SNAKE RIVER, HENRY'S FORK

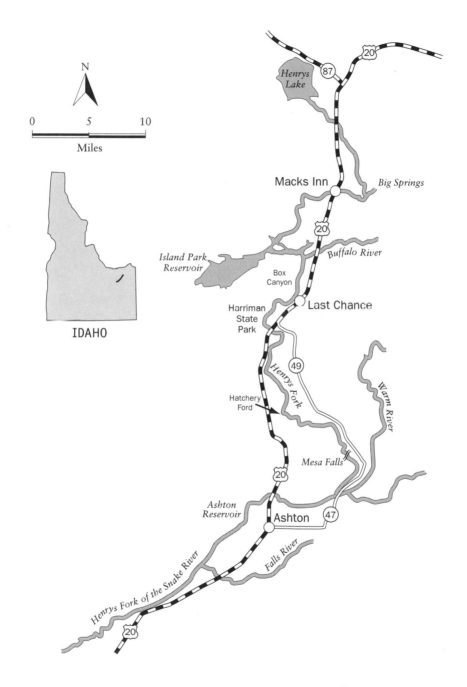

N

0   5   10
Miles

IDAHO

Henrys
Lake

87
20

Macks Inn   Big Springs

20

Island Park
Reservoir

Buffalo River

Box
Canyon

Harriman
State
Park   Last Chance

49

Henrys Fork

Hatchery
Ford

Warm River

Mesa Falls

Ashton
Reservoir   Ashton   47

20

Henrys Fork of the Snake River

Falls River

20

BARRY AND CATHY BECK

Fishing a rise on the Railroad Ranch section of the Henry's Fork is something every trout angler needs to experience at least once in an angling career.

spin anglers, though very few fish it. The angler who hurls a zero-sized Mepps or tiny Panther Martin won't be disappointed. Most serious anglers float through the Box, launching just below the dam and taking out at Last Chance.

You'll find more big fish in the Box than elsewhere on the river, but if stalking trout is your game, you'll have more fun on the 13-mile section that runs through Harriman State Park to Riverside Campground. Here is Henry's Fork at its most challenging. Above Last Chance, a wide spot in the road known for its great flyshops and a streamside restaurant that serves a chili and onion ring combination that's guaranteed to warm your waders, the river gradient flattens and the stream takes on the characteristics of a spring creek. Aquatic grasses undulate with the current. Trout, some of them huge, lie and wait for just the right pattern and presentation. If you have the innate coordination that allows long, graceful, and accurate casts, fire away. You're in Fat City. But the angler who wades carefully will generally get close enough to deliver the pattern *du jour* with ample subtlety for a the requisite drag-free float. You won't catch many fish by being sloppy here. Float tubes are also used on this stretch and many outfitters run drift boats through. Still, there's nothing like spotting a fish, working it, and then getting the take.

Downstream from Osborne Bridge, the river begins to pick up steam. The bed is increasingly rocky. Most float trips on the upper section take out at Riverside, but the next four miles or so to Hatchery Ford can be very good during the golden stone hatch in June. And later, nymphs and streamers produce. Nobody floats the next section; there are no other takeouts above Mesa Falls. Floating begins again at the mouth of the Warm River, and the next 11 miles to the upper reaches of Ashton Reservoir is very good water for both rainbows and browns.

The native trout in this system were Yellowstone cutthroat. Sadly they are all but gone. You'll find some lovely natives high in the thin tributaries on the flanks of the mountains, but everyone leaves them alone. They're hard to get to, quite small, and it's kind of nice just to know that natives still exist in the watershed. Rainbows are the fish of fame in Henry's Fork, and their much-vaunted size, which caught everyone's attention in the '70s and early '80s, was largely a fluke.

As in most western rivers, agricultural interests control water levels. In the 1970s it was not uncommon to count 18,000 trout in the three-mile Box section, and more than a few ran in the four- to six-pound class. In a few cases, these behemoths were naturally spawned and raised in the river. But most were spawned in the Big Spring Creek and reached maturity in Island Park Lake. When the gates were opened and the reservoir was drawn down, hundreds of huge rainbows sluiced through the openings and found themselves on a wild ride down the Box.

In the 1980s, thanks to erratic water flows and drought, fish populations plummeted. By 1991, the number of trout in the Box was less than a quarter of that of a decade earlier. A nearly disastrous release from the Island Park dam in 1992 dumped more than 50,000 tons of sediment into the Fork, clogging areas needed by first-year fish to overwinter and survive. The same discharge flushed some 10,000 fat, lake-fed rainbows into the section, creating a ruddy glow of apparent health.

Work by the Henry's Fork Foundation, begun in 1984 and expanded with the hiring of an executive director in 1991 and the recent creation of a 22-agency watershed council, supported by Trout Unlimited and a number of other organizations, is beginning to stabilize the fishery. Much initial effort has gone and will go into establishing baselines, which will lead to a clear understanding of populations of trout that can be naturally sustained throughout the entire 163 mile watershed, not just the famous upper 20 miles of the river. The watershed council is working to bring forth a more natural flow of water in the river, and is also beginning to address questions of real estate development along the river.

There's no doubt that Henry's Fork is coming back. Today, with no stocking, trout density in the Box has reached the 7,000-fish level. The bad reputation the river earned in the late '80s has dispersed the angling crowd. Anglers are learning that beats on the river other than those in the Box or ranch can consistently produce trophy rainbows and a sense of solitude valued by so many. In addition, some anglers are discovering the section centered on Saint Anthony. Fed by unfettered run-off of the Warm, Teton, and Fall rivers, the lower section of Henry's Fork experiences a more natural cycle. While flowing through heavily farmed lands, the river still benefits from the lush reparian vegetation so essential for a healthy fishery. Much of the river is bounded by private lands, but access can generally be had for the asking.

And the fishing makes it worthwhile. Native cutthroat are present in significant numbers as are a mixed population of rainbows and browns. Spring opens with early hatches of pale morning duns and by late May salmon flies come off regularly along with some caddis. The gray drakes of June signal the *finis* of the prolific hatches. Thereafter anglers rely on terrestrials until fall brings cooler weather and a resurgence of mayflies. How good is the fishing, really? Just ask Mile Lawson, founder of Henry's Fork Anglers, where he prefers to fish. Anglers who visit this area and neglect a trip to the lower section are missing at least half the fun.

For more stream information, contact Henry's Fork Foundation, P.O. Box 61, Island Park, ID 83429; 208-558-9041; e-mail: hff@desktop.org. The group has a Web site at www.srv.net/~henrys.

RESOURCES

Gearing up: Henry's Fork Anglers, HC66, Box 491, Island Park, ID 83429-0491; 208-558-7525; e-mail: henfork@srv.net; www.henrys-fork.com/. Jimmy's All Seasons Angler, 275 A Street, Idaho Falls, ID 83402; 208-524-7160.

Accommodations: Island Park Area Chamber of Commerce, Box 83, Island Park, ID 83429; 208-558-7751, 800-543-1895.

Books: *The Montana Angling Guide*, Fothergill and Sterling, Stream Stalker Publishing Co., 1988.

River Journal: Henry's Fork, Larry Tullis, Frank Amato Publications, Portland, OR, 1995.

Fly Fisher's Guide to Idaho, Ken Retallic and Rocky Barker, Wilderness Adventure Press, Gallatin Gateway, MT, 1996.

56 SNAKE RIVER, SOUTH FORK

Location: Southwestern Idaho.
Short take: Erratic water releases make this river difficult to wade, but great to float.
Type of stream: Tailwater.
Angling methods: Fly, spin.
Species: Cutthroat, brown, rainbow.
Access: Moderate.
Season: Year-round.
Nearest tourist services: Tackle shops and accommodations can be found along the river.
Handicapped access: Yes.
Closest TU chapter: Upper Snake.

ISSUING FORTH FROM PALISADES DAM near the Wyoming Border, the South Fork flows westward nearly 60 miles to its junction with Henry's (North) Fork of the Snake. All of it is good, albeit different, trout water. For the first 14 miles from the dam to Conant, the river runs through the Swan Valley, a narrow flood plain. Eagles nest in the tops of cottonwoods. Some of these trees have survived more than three centuries, making them among the oldest species in the country. Beyond the plain rise palisades capped with basalt, a precursor to the forest which strives to climb Teton-like peaks. Below Conant, the Snake enters the section called the "Canyon," but in reality this mileage passes a number of small 300- to 400-foot canyons—Dry, Ladder, Black, Bums—before emerging at Byington launch ramp near the town of Poplar. In the upper and middle sections, the river bed is similar, characterized by gravel bars, slick runs, and backwater eddies.

Below Byington, the river braids in a manner similar to the runs above Jackson in Wyoming. Channels fork to the left and right, and many lead to log jams impassable by drift boat, the preferred way to fish the river. It can be waded in some spots, but sudden increases in water flow from the dam have swept more than one angler to death. Rowers must be ever-vigilant, for big sweepers lie just under the surface ready to startle and perhaps upset the unwary. The river is deeper here, the fish generally larger, and browns tend to dominate over rainbows and cutthroat.

The upper and canyon sections of the river are preferred over the lower because they tend to fish more consistently day in and day out. Twenty-fish days are not at all unusual on the upper and middle reaches, and even on a lousy day, anglers still catch some fish. When the lower river is "on" it's really on, but when it's "off" it's as if the fish have lockjaw. And nobody seems to be able to predict how lower-section trout will feed from day to day.

Dry flies are the favorite game here—Sulfur Duns all year, Blue-Winged Olives early and late, and when it's cloudy and rainy, stoneflies, Golden Stones, and Yellow

SNAKE RIVER, SOUTH FORK

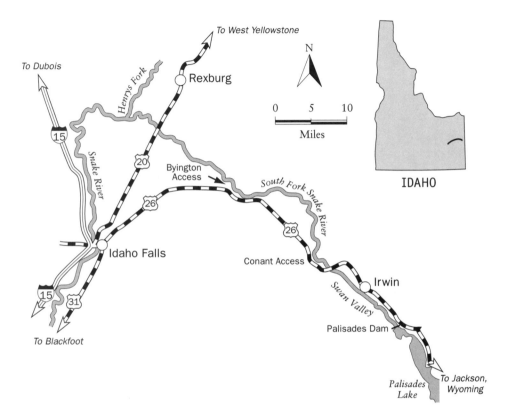

Sallies in late June and July, when run-off begins to recede. Caddis show up from August through September and terrestrials fish well into the fall. When all else fails, you can pound the water with nymphs, weighted or not, depending on flow.

The South Fork is one of those rivers that, if water flows were ever stabilized, would be one of the finest trout rivers in the world. Still, despite incessant variation in releases from Palisades Dam, the river has a reputation for producing lots of browns, cutthroat, and rainbows, most in the 12- to 16-inch range. At one time, it wasn't unusual to see a pod of 18-inch cutthroats sipping Sulfur Duns in still water behind one of the river's countless cobble bars. Those days are gone, though. In 1997, a 43,000 cfs flood release from Palisades Dam (normal flow for the river is 12,000 to 15,000 cfs) blew out gravel bars, eroded banks, toppled cottonwoods, and may have washed out most of a year-class of trout. And, as this is being written, the Idaho Water Resources Board wants to set a minimum flow of 550 cfs for the South Fork during spring run-off when normal volumes range between 15,000 to 25,000 cfs. Coming at the behest of agricultural interests worried about depletions to the Eastern Snake River Plain Aquifer, this feast-or-famine approach to water management could cripple the South Fork and Henry's Fork, which also faces similar strictures.

Anglers headed for the South Fork have their choice of motels in Idaho Falls or a pair of lovely lodges in Swan Valley up near the dam. Most anglers fish with guides who hold permits for the South Fork. To fish with a guide who is not licensed for the South Fork (and some anglers unwittingly or otherwise do it) is to risk a hefty fine. The South Fork, like Henry's Fork, is a great destination river. Plan on spending a week.

RESOURCES

Gearing up: Flyshop at The Lodge at Palisades Creek, P.O. Box 70, Irwin, ID 83428; 208-483-2222. Jimmy's All Seasons Angler, 275 A St., Idaho Falls, ID 83402; 208-524-7160.

Accommodations: Greater Idaho Falls Chamber of Commerce, P.O. Box 50498, 505 Lindsay Blvd., Idaho Falls, ID 83405; 800-634-3246.

Books: *Snake River Country and Flies*, Bruce Staples, Frank Amato Publications, Portland, OR, 1991.

Snake River Secrets, Bruce Staples, Frank Amato Publications, Portland, OR, 1996.

57 BIG WOOD RIVER

Location: Central Idaho.
Short take: Takes its name from downed and drowned cottonwoods, cover for multitudes of trout.
Type of stream: Freestone.
Angling methods: Fly, spin.
Species: Rainbow, brown.
Access: Easy.
Season: End of May through November.
Nearest tourist services: Ketchum.
Handicapped access: None.
Closest TU chapter: Hemingway.

ANY TROUTER WHO'S SKIED SUN VALLEY knows the Big Wood River. For about 50 miles, it flows more or less alongside Idaho Route 75 from U.S. Highway 20, winding (but not meandering) through high desert from its headwaters in the gulches below 8,990-foot Galena Summit to Magic Reservoir. You can't miss its cottonwoods, many on shore but some of them fallen into the river, from which it takes its name. The rainbows in the upper reaches and the browns down below are not huge by any measure, an average fish is 13 inches, but they are plentiful and, under the right conditions, willing. And that's about all one can ask.

The upper reaches of the river are quite steep and boulders there may be six feet in diameter. As the gradient lessens, so does the size of the river rock. From the headwaters to the confluence of the North Fork, the Wood is heavily stocked. But from where the fork joins the main stem down to Magic Reservoir, a distance of about 40 miles, the river is populated by wild fish. In spring, rainbows come up from Magic Reservoir to spawn and in the fall, so do browns. Below Magic Dam is a short tailwater that holds some of the biggest fish in the river. Despite heavy brush, the tailwater is well worth the effort. Idaho mandates a policy of catch-and-release from the junction of the North Fork downstream to the bridge at Greenhorn Gulch. A 12- to 16-inch slot limit applies from Greenhorn to Glendale Bridge, and below Glendale Bridge, standard regulations apply.

Perhaps the best time to fish the river is in October during red quill and *baetis* hatches. But also significant are the stonefly hatches of late June and early July, the green drakes beginning in early July, caddis on summer afternoons in July and August, and terrestrials in late summer and early fall. Not to be ignored are excellent midge hatches through out the winter. Skiing anglers ought to pack a travel rod and cold weather gear. Angling for large far-weight rainbows can be superb. Streamers can also be fished with success then.

With the exception of the spring run-off, which begins in May and normally clears the system by late June, the Big Wood cannot be successfully float fished.

Big Wood River

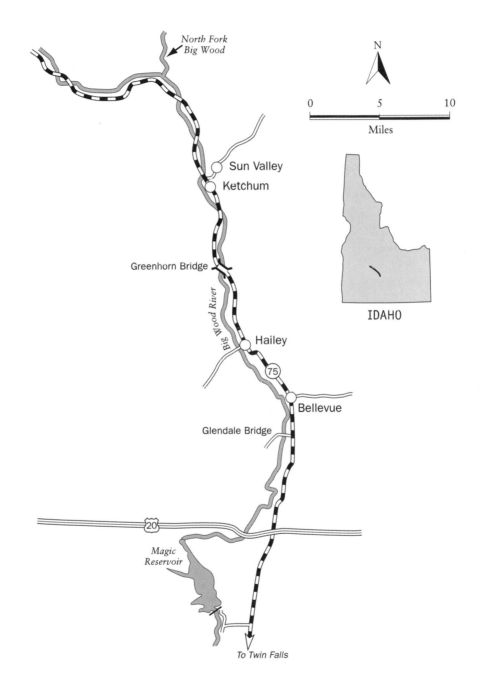

North Fork
Big Wood

N

0   5   10
Miles

Sun Valley
Ketchum

Greenhorn Bridge

Big Wood River

IDAHO

Hailey

75

Bellevue

Glendale Bridge

20

Magic
Reservoir

To Twin Falls

Wading is the name of the game here, and an abundance of riffles provides ample opportunity for anglers to become dispersed. The regular season on the river begins at the end of May and continues through November. Then, the entire river becomes catch-and-release and stays that way until closing at the end of March. Best time to fish the river, as it always seems to be on western rivers, is fall when trout are gorging on *baetis*, and most other anglers, besides you and me, have gone home.

The Big Wood and Silver Creek, a couple dozen miles east, present an interesting contrast. Silver, secluded and tough, challenges the most accomplished angler. The Big Wood is easier. It's hypothesized that water from the Big Wood sinks into the high desert only to emerge in the springs of Silver Creek. If you're spending time on one, it would be a shame not to give the other a tumble.

RESOURCES

Gearing up: Lost River Anglers, P.O. Box 3445, Ketchum, ID 83340; 208-726-1706.

Bill Mason Outfitters, Sun Valley, ID 83353; 208-622-9305.

Accommodations: Ketchum/Sun Valley Chamber of Commerce, P.O. Box 2420, Ketchum, ID 83353; 800-634-3347.

Books: *Fly Fisher's Guide to Idaho,* Ken Retallic and Rocky Barker, Wilderness Adventure Press, Gallatin Gateway, MT, 1996.

58 ARMSTRONG'S SPRING CREEK

Location: South-central Montana.
Short take: A controversial berm preserved this bit of dry-fly heaven, albeit for a price. Reservations required; 406-222-2979.
Type of stream: Spring creek.
Angling method: Fly.
Species: Rainbow, brown.
Access: Easy.
Season: Year-round.
Nearest tourist services: Livingston.
Handicapped access: Possible.
Closest TU chapter: Joe Brooks.

AS YOU STAND ON THE WEST BANK, the Yellowstone is running high, wide, handsome, and brown—brown with meltwater, streaming from the Yellowstone caldera and the peaks of the Absaroka and Gallatin Mountains which form the river's valley. But in front of you on this late June day is a small stream, little more than 30 feet wide, that's flowing clear as a soprano's highest note. Aquatic grasses sway with the steady currents that trip happily through runs of cobbly rock. Here and there anglers work PMDs for rising fish. That's where the action is. Fed by a massive spring of cold and constant flows, Armstrong's Spring Creek fishes well all the time, except when the flooding Yellowstone ploughs across its narrow flood plain and invades the spring creek's channel.

That's just what happened in June of 1996. The Yellowstone, gorged with rain and heavy with snowmelt, overflowed about 300 yards of gravel bar and poured into Armstrong's Spring Creek. As the flood abated, it was clear that the river had eaten down through the bar, creating a new channel that allowed water from the river to flow into the spring creek. Owners of the O'Hair Ranch, where the breach occurred, sought and received permission from the Corps of Engineers to construct a rock dike that would divert the river back into its original channel. Construction sparked a huge debate; should the river be allowed to meander as it chooses, or do landowners have the right to protect their properties from the ravages of flood? The debate has not been resolved; such discussions seldom are. However, the dike and a second designed to protect Armstrong's from ice-jam induced flooding do stand, and Armstrong's is fishing as well as ever with promises of better things to come. Why? The flood flushed accumulated silt from the channel and deepened pools along the way.

Both sections of Armstrong's Spring Creek, O'Hair's one-and-a-half miles at the top and DePuy's three miles below, are open to the public, but for a rod-fee which varies with the season. The O'Hair section is essentially riffles and runs; DePuy's offers more pools, some of them broad enough to make float tubing viable. Aquatic

ARMSTRONG'S SPRING CREEK

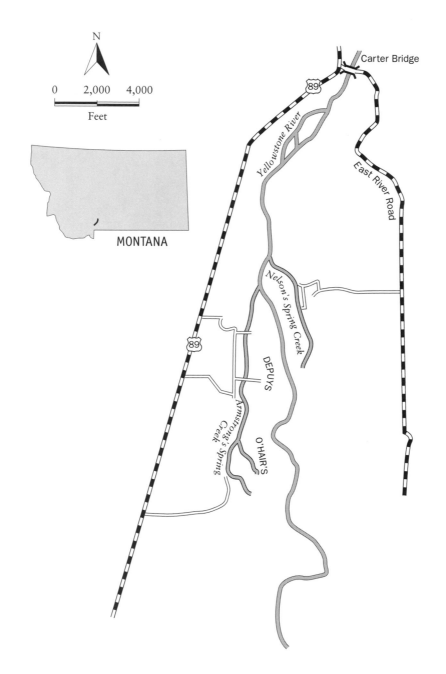

N

0   2,000   4,000
Feet

MONTANA

Carter Bridge

89

Yellowstone River

East River Road

Nelson's Spring Creek

89

DEPUYS

O'HAIR'S

Armstrong's Spring Creek

vegetation thrives in the creek. As summer progresses, angling becomes more technical as drag-free floats are more difficult to achieve among micro-currents weaving through barely submerged weeds. Though the creek is shallow, chest waders are required for ease in getting around. Later in the season, you'll find that the fish are increasingly spooky. Careful stalking, and short, precise casts, become the keys to taking the rainbows and browns over 16 inches.

An all-season fishery, you'll find midges and small Blue-Winged Olives to be productive from January into June. An early hatch of caddis comes off in early June, followed by pale morning duns and a few brown drakes. Sulphurs open in mid-July and hatch throughout the afternoon until dusk. August brings terrestrials—ants, beetles, crickets, and hoppers—as well as a hatch of micro-caddis and, on slow-moving flat water late in the month, tricos. September sees the end of the sulphurs and the start of the famed fall blue-winged olive hatch. Rates are highest during the peak of the dry-fly season from mid-June to mid-September. Anglers who time their fishing on Armstrong's for late September and early October have the best of everything: great hatches, stunning scenery, and few crowds.

RESOURCES

Gearing up: Yellowstone Angler, P.O. Box 660, Livingston, MT 59047; 406-222-7130. Dan Bailey's Fly Shop, 209 West Park Street, Livingston, MT 59047; 800-356-4052; www.dan-bailey.com.

Accommodations: Livingston Area Chamber of Commerce, 208 West Park, Livingston, MT 59047; 406-222-0850. Travel Montana, P.O. Box 7549, Missoula, MT 59807-7549; 800-VISIT MT; www.visitmt.com.

Books: *The Montana Angling Guide*, Chuck Fothergill and Bob Sterling, Stream Stalker Publishing Co., Woody Creek, CO, 1988.

59 Beaverhead River

Location: Southwestern Montana.
Short take: This river of contrasts yields rainbows in the upper runs and browns below to those who figure it out.
Type of stream: Tailwater.
Angling methods: Fly, spin.
Species: Brown, cutthroat, rainbow.
Access: Moderate.
Season: Year-round.
Nearest tourist services: Dillon, Twin Bridges.
Handicapped access: None.
Closest TU chapter: Lewis & Clark.

ISSUING FROM THE BASE of Clark Canyon Reservoir 20 miles or so south of Dillon, the Beaverhead flows north-by-northeast for more than 50 miles before joining the Big Hole below Twin Bridges to form the Jefferson. The upper stretch from the reservoir down to Barrett's diversion dam is considered to be prime rainbow water. Below the dam, the river warms and brown trout predominate. The Beaverhead is literally two different rivers.

Releases from Clark Canyon Reservoir are reasonably consistent even during the peak of the run-off in June. Then the lake fills, building a pool that will be drawn down as July moves into August, and farmers' needs for water increases. Steady flows and stable temperatures create a year-round fishery on the upper reaches. In spring, some of the sediment from the reservoir escapes into the river providing just enough color to camouflage heavy leaders. You'll need them. The river follows a fairly tight channel between banks heavily brushed with cottonwoods and willow. Wading is extremely difficult; most anglers fish from drift boats. The biggest rainbows lie under cover along the bank, and one accepted strategy for seducing them is to blast a weighted Woolly Bugger or nymph into pockets beneath the branches where the 'bows may be holding. Unless you are a phenomenally proficient caster, you'll hang up as often as you hit the sweet spot. The heavy leader seems not to spook the fish, and it sure helps in retrieving flies as your drift boat races on with the current.

But that's only one side of the coin. On the other are the Blue-Winged Olives that hatch in March and April and again in September. You'll find caddis in July and August, as well as pale morning duns, yellow sallies, and golden stones. A massive crane fly hatch opens in mid-August and continues into September. If dry flies are your game, try to time your visit for a glowering overcast day in summer or early fall.

Barrett's diversion sucks most of the water from the river from July into fall. While flows above may be running 500 cfs and above, those below may be half or less of that. Yet, this makes the river more wadeable, and anglers willing to fish

BEAVERHEAD RIVER

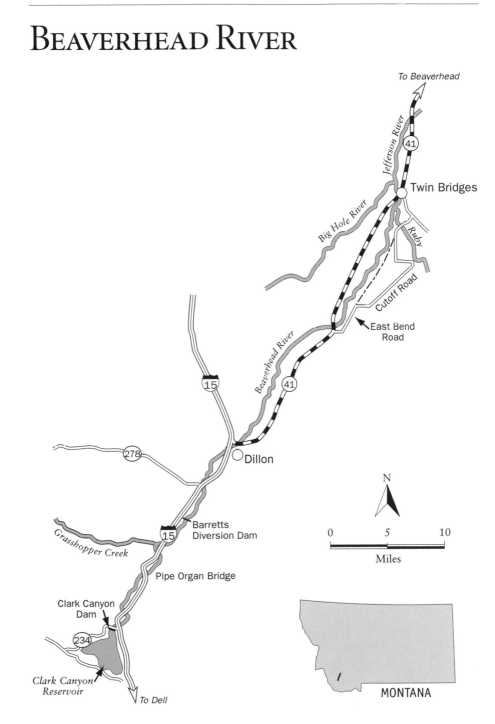

To Beaverhead

Jefferson River

41

Twin Bridges

Big Hole River

Ruby

Cutoff Road

East Bend Road

Beaverhead River

15

41

278

Dillon

N

0   5   10

Miles

Barretts Diversion Dam

15

Grasshopper Creek

Pipe Organ Bridge

Clark Canyon Dam

234

Clark Canyon Reservoir

To Dell

MONTANA

morning and evening can often do quite well on browns up to 15 inches. The lower river receives less pressure than the upper runs because big fish are fewer. Yet an abundance of wildlife, relative solitude, and a slower and gentler place do attract anglers to the water from the diversion into Dillon. Below Dillon, turbidity is occasionally a problem in summer, and that limits angling for spin and fly fishers alike.

As of this writing, no tackle restrictions exist on the Beaverhead. But possession downstream from Pipe Organ Bridge, about half-way from the reservoir to Barrett's, is restricted to three fish per day, one rainbow, and only one fish over 18 inches. Regulations are, of course, subject to change, but any one of a number of tackle shops in Dillon or Twin Bridges (home of Winston Rods) can set you straight, provide guides and gear, and steer you toward your choice of motel, bed-and-breakfast, or full-service fishing lodge as your preference and pocketbook dictate.

RESOURCES

Gearing up: Last Chance Lodge and Outfitters, P.O. Box 529, 409 N. Main St., Twin Bridges, MT 59754; 888-434-5188. Fishing Headquarters, 610 N Montana, Dillon, MT 59725; 800-753-6660.

Accommodations: Beaverhead Chamber of Commerce, 125 S. Montana St., Dillon, MT 59725; 406-683-5511. Travel Montana, P.O. Box 7549, Missoula, MT 59807-7549; 800-VISIT MT; www.visitmt.com.

Books: *Fishing Montana*, Michael S. Sample, Falcon Publishing, Helena, MT, 1999.

The Montana Angling Guide, Chuck Fothergill and Bob Sterling, Stream Stalker Publishing Co., Woody Creek, CO, 1988.

60 Big Hole River

Location: Southwestern Montana.
Short take: Upper reaches hold brookies and among the last fluvial grayling in the continental United States. Lower waters, great browns.
Type of stream: Freestone.
Angling methods: Fly, spin.
Species: Brown, rainbow, cutthroat, brook, grayling.
Access: Moderate.
Nearest tourist services: Wisdom, Wise River, Twin Bridges.
Handicapped access: None.
Closest TU chapters: Lewis & Clark, George Grant.

WITH 150 MILES OF OUTSTANDING free-flowing trout water, and much more in its tributaries, the Big Hole River provides angling diversity not found on any other river in the West. Broad statement? Well, here are the facts. Not only do you encounter rainbows and browns, some of them trophy sized, but also brook trout, a smattering of cutthroat, and one of the few populations of fluvial grayling in the United States. Whitefish are also abundant. Flowing in a broad arc north around the Pioneer Mountains, the river winds its way through a wide, flat valley of gravel runs and gentle pools, before picking up volume and velocity with the added waters of the Wise River. The upper reaches see relatively little fishing pressure, while the center stretch gets hammered pretty hard. Still, there's nowhere near the pressure on this river that's found, for instance, on the Yellowstone or Madison or the Snake across the mountains. As it goes when rivers serve multiple masters, the Big Hole has seen its share of water-flow problems. In the summer of 1994, the Big Hole dropped to a mere 2 cfs in its upper mileage with devastating affects on trout. At the initiative of the George Grant Chapter in nearby Butte, anglers and ranchers began meeting in 1995 and formed the Big Hole Watershed Committee. In 1998, the committee signed an agreement which ensures water flows for agricultural needs while, at the same time, protecting the fishery.

Were I planning a trip to the Big Hole, I'd start in Wisdom, a little town with a fabulous general store and tackle shop, a couple of good restaurants, and accommodations that won't break your bank. The river in this vicinity is small, winding through pasture from riffle to pool to riffle again. Brook trout offer the most fun here. Fish undercut banks shaded by cottonwoods, and don't pass up tributaries. A polite request for permission to fish is the best access to private land. In the upper river, you'll find grayling, once the dominant fish of the system, but now greatly diminished in range. Grayling are gullible; they'll hit almost any reasonable artificial lure. Their gullibility; the dewatering of the river for agricultural needs; the introduction of browns, brookies, and rainbows; and siltation from banks trodden to mud by grazing cattle have all conspired against the grayling. If you catch a grayling,

BIG HOLE RIVER

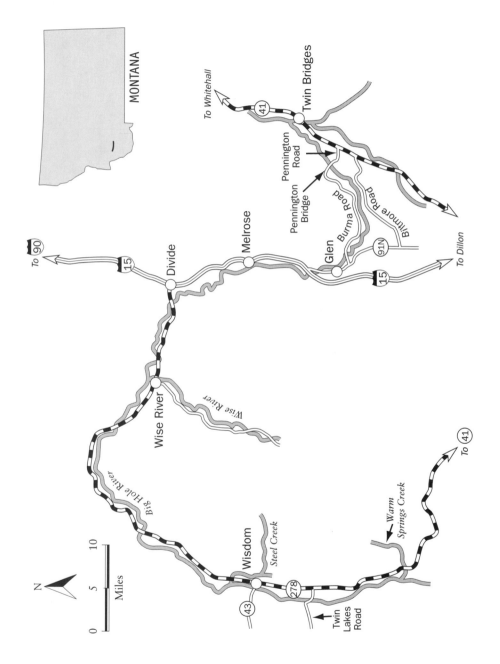

admire its sleek gray body and its flowing dorsal, think of it as a relic of the ice ages, and return it quickly and gently to the river. Current regs require that all grayling or cutthroat caught in the river must be released. Fish with artificial lures and pinch down each hook's barb.

Below its junction with the Wise River, the Big Hole changes character. The gradient steepens and water races over a streambed studded with boulders and shaded by canyon walls. From Wise River to Divide is rainbow water. Montana Highway 43 follows this mileage. Numerous turnouts provide parking for anglers willing to scramble down the bank to the river. The highway leaves the river a mile or so west of Divide. From this point on, the river is best fished by boat, though waders can find access at half a dozen points. At Glen, the river breaks into ranchland and the channel braids into a number of cobbly runs and banks where undercut cottonwoods have tumbled into the river. Access is limited, though a request for permission may get you on the run you like. Drive the Burma Road which follows the river from Glen to Pennington Bridge.

Two surges of meltwater raise the Big Hole. The first, in May, contains run-off from the upper basin and the latter, from mid-June to mid-July, carries run-off from the high Bitterroots to the west. If luck is with you, the Big Hole's signature salmonfly—*Pteronarcys californica*—will hatch between these two high flows. The river below Melrose will be crowded with boats. Still, it's your best shot at big browns. Bring a pair of rods for your week on the Big Hole. A 3-weight will be dandy for the upper mileage, and a 5- or 6-weight will handle chores lower down. Caddis patterns and Adams are the mainstay for fishing the upper river during the evening when fishing's best. Lower down there's some dry-fly action, but in the main, it's nymph and streamer water. Unfortunately, a heavy algae bloom makes angling with spinners and small plugs quite frustrating. Try a fly and a bubble instead.

RESOURCES

Gearing up: Conover's General Store, Box 84, Highway 43, Wisdom, MT 59761; 406-689-3272. Troutfitters, 62311 Hwy 43, Wise River, MT 59762; 406-832-3212.

Accommodations: Beaverhead Chamber of Commerce, 125 S. Montana St., Dillon, MT 59725; 406-683-5511. Travel Montana, P.O. Box 7549, Missoula, MT 59807-7549; 800-VISIT MT; www.visitmt.com.

Books: *Fishing Montana*, Michael S. Sample, Falcon Publishing, Helena, MT, 1999.

The Montana Angling Guide, Chuck Fothergill and Bob Sterling, Stream Stalker Publishing Co., Woody Creek, CO, 1988.

The upper Big Hole supports a healthy population of rare and beautiful Montana grayling. Here a fisheries researcher collects grayling data, weighing a chunky specimen.

61 BIGHORN RIVER

Location: South-central Montana.
Short take: Classic western tailwater *sans* solitude.
Type of stream: Tailwater.
Angling methods: Fly, spin.
Species: Rainbow, brown.
Access: Moderate.
Season: Year-round.
Nearest tourist services: Fort Smith, Hardin.
Handicapped access: None.
Closest TU chapter: Magic City.

ASK ANYONE TO NAME THE TOP western tailwater, and odds are that the Bighorn will make a very short list, right up there with the Green below Flaming Gorge and the Colorado at Lees Ferry. Like the Colorado, the Bighorn's classic water is a short stretch of fewer than 15 miles and most anglers float it in a drift boat, raft, or canoe. Unlike the water below Glen Canyon Dam, no motors are allowed on boats, and foot-bound anglers can walk into the river at numerous points and wade.

Until the late 1960s, the Bighorn River flooded with silt-laden spring run-off and then lowered and warmed and took on the turgid character of a lazy high plains river, worn out from its journey through the mountains. But the construction of Yellowtail Dam, and the creation of a 71-mile impoundment behind it, turned the Bighorn into a clear and cold (and that means long-handles under your neoprenes in every month but August and September) trophy trout fishery. First stocked with rainbows, browns later found their way from tributaries into the river. They compete for food nurtured by highly alkaline waters. Browns probably outnumber the rainbows, but rainbows may be gaining ground. Below the afterbay dam at the head of the tailwater, all rainbows must be immediately released. Typically, browns and rainbows average 16 inches.

Breaking out of Bighorn Canyon below the dam, the river enters a broad river channel that was shaped before its waters were impounded. Though flows can sometimes reach 17,000 cfs, normally they run between 3,500 and 4,500 cfs and do little to modify braids of the stream bed. Gravel islands and bars abound. Here and there, sandstone cliffs rise from the river. On the upper 13 miles of the river, there's little of the brushy jungle you see along the Beaverhead.

Though open all year, the season generally begins in March with Midges and dark Blue-Winged Olives. Standard nymph patterns—Gold-Ribbed Hare's Ears, Prince, Pheasant Tail—produce, if anything, better than dries. This fishing holds up into June when the river typically rises a bit with meltwater. Still quite fishable in June, nymphs, streamers, and scuds carry the day. In July, caddis activity begins and in late August tricos begin to come off. Later in the season nymphs and streamers, like the ever popular Woolly Bugger, become an angler's mainstays. Bait fishing is

BIGHORN RIVER

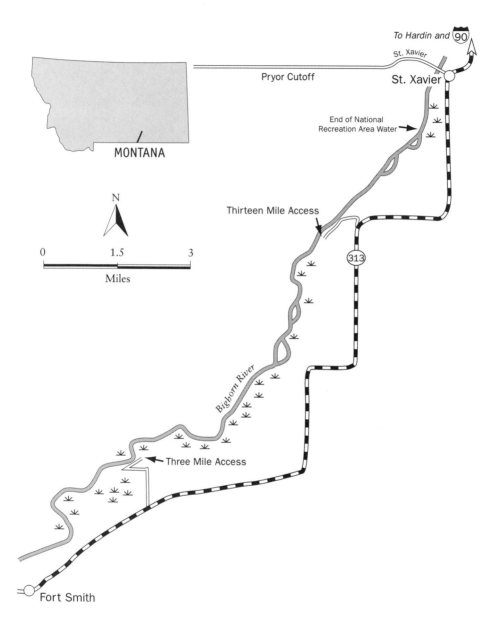

To Hardin and 90

St. Xavier

Pryor Cutoff

St. Xavier

MONTANA

End of National
Recreation Area Water

N

Thirteen Mile Access

0   1.5   3

313

Miles

Bighorn River

Three Mile Access

Fort Smith

MIKE SAMPLE

The Bighorn River below Fort Smith provides trophy for browns and rainbows throughout the year.

curtailed to a short section just below the dam, but spin fishers can ply hardware and plugs the length of the best trout water. Spinners and spoons and shallow-running minnow-like plugs work wonders. Crimping barbs on hooks (and replacing treble hooks with singles) will facilitate required release of rainbows.

Headquarters for fishing the Bighorn are found at Fort Smith, an old and tiny town at the base of the dam, and downstream at Hardin where Interstate 90 crosses the river and SR 313 turns south toward Fort Smith. A private airport is maintained at Fort Smith, but the closest airport with commercial flights is Billings, about 55 miles west of Hardin. If you're in this region, and you haven't yet done so, you owe yourself a drive to the Little Bighorn Battlefield National Monument, 12 miles east of Hardin, and an early morning walk among the white marble stones that mark where each of Custer's men died.

RESOURCES

Gearing up: Bighorn Angler, P.O. Box 7578, Ft. Smith, MT 59035; 406-666-2233. Big Horn Fly and Tackle Shop, 1426 N. Crawford St., Hardin, MT 59034; 888-665-1321.

Accommodations: Hardin Area Chamber of Commerce, Box 1206A, Hardin, MT 59034; 406-665-1672. Travel Montana, P.O. Box 7549, Missoula, MT 59807-7549; 800-VISIT MT; www.visitmt.com.

Books: *Fishing Montana*, Michael S. Sample, Falcon Publishing, Helena, MT, 1999.

The Montana Angling Guide, Chuck Fothergill and Bob Sterling, Stream Stalker Publishing Co., Woody Creek, CO, 1988.

Seasons of the Bighorn, George Kelly, Willow Creek Press, Minocqua, WI 1997.

62 BITTERROOT RIVER

Location: Southwestern Montana.
Short take: A model water agreement brokered by TU ensures the preservation of this magnificent fishery.
Type of stream: Freestone.
Angling methods: Fly, spin.
Species: Brown, rainbow, cutthroat, brook.
Access: Moderate.
Season: Year-round.
Nearest tourist services: Hamilton.
Handicapped access: None.
Closest TU chapter: Bitterroot.

GENERATED FROM SNOWS THAT CLING to the Bitterroot Mountains to the west and the Pintler Peaks of the Sapphire Mountains to the east, the forks of the Bitterroot drain more than 2.5 million acres of wilderness—superb country for elk, mule deer, bear, and cougar. High lakes, as clear and cold as a midnight sky, hold populations of cutthroat and brook trout. And the East and West Forks contain them as well. Lower reaches of these streams are worth fishing, not only for their gaily colored salmonoids, but for the spectacular setting that will steal your heart. If you yearn to explore the headwaters of the East Fork, take SR 43 west from Wisdom through Chief Joseph Pass to Lost Trail Pass where you'll hit U.S. Highway 93. Turn north, and proceed down the hill to Sula, and turn right (east) onto East Fork Road which follows the creek up to Echo Gulch, a trailhead used by many horse packing outfits. US 93 north of Sula follows the East Fork down into Conner where the West Fork comes in. The West Fork also holds small brook trout and some cutthroat and rainbows.

The main stem of the Bitterroot really begins below Conner and runs some 70 miles north through a widening valley to Missoula. When the river comes out of its final canyon above Conner, it dons a gentle personality that supports float fishing as well as wading. Below Darby, the river takes on the personality it will carry to its junction with the Clark Fork at Missoula. The river runs from riffle to pool to riffle, again in a course that generally lacks much in the way of meanders, yet curves enough to create cutbanks held in place by roots of old cottonwoods, aspen, and fir. You'll find pools, log jams, and sweepers along the banks. As is the case with most western rivers, the best flow (and thus the fishing) varies with the water needs of agricultural interests. But over the past 20 years, the Bitterroot Chapter of TU has forged a voluntary coalition with ranchers, anglers, water and power authorities, and state agencies that results in flows that protect the fishery. As a result, cutthroat up to 20 inches are making a huge recovery in the river above Victor, and a similar resurgence of bull trout (*Salvelinus confluentus*) is also being seen. The taking or targeting of bull trout, however, is strictly prohibited by state regs.

BITTERROOT RIVER

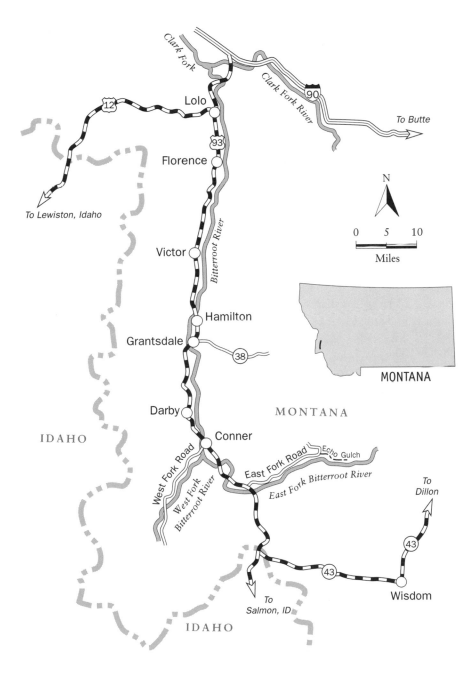

The Bitterroot tends to discharge its load of snow run-off more rapidly than many other rivers in the same part of the state, thus it tends to fish better in late June than most.

The Bitterroot is divided into three segments: the upper river from Conner to Hamilton, the middle reach from Hamilton down to Victor, and the lower section from Victor into Missoula. After spring run-off, which coincides with the salmon fly hatch from Stevensville south toward Conner, water is pulled from the lower reaches for agricultural purposes. Most fishing then focuses on the upper reaches. Though the river is known for its stellar caddis, many anglers work Royal Wulffs throughout the summer, as well as Adams. Nymphs can be productive and so can streamers. Tricos come off in September, and the cooling weather also brings out October caddis and brown drakes. This is one of those feast or famine rivers. Trout concentrate in deeper holds and eschew areas that would otherwise be productive. Finding the fish is the first order of business. Generally speaking, though, they're like trout most anywhere. You'll find most of them tight against the bank, waiting for dinner, like a hopper or ant in August, to drop in.

Even though it's relatively close to population centers, virtually all of the river is less than two hours from the airport at Missoula and a number of fishing lodges and dude ranches occupy its banks, there's a greater feeling of being in the wilderness when you fish this river than you'll find on other Montana rivers. And that's befitting of a river that shares the name of the Montana state flower which casts its blooms from white to deep purple along the river's course.

RESOURCES

Gearing up: Angler's Roost, 815 Hwy 93 S., Hamilton, MT 59840; 406-363-1284. Blackbird's Fly Shop and Lodge, P.O. Box 998, Victor MT 59875; 406-642-6375.

Accommodations: Bitterroot Valley Chamber of Commerce, 105 E. Main St., Hamilton, MT 59840; 406-363-2400. Travel Montana, P.O. Box 7549, Missoula, MT 59807-7549; 800-VISIT MT; www.visitmt.com.

Books: *Fishing Montana*, Michael S. Sample, Falcon Publishing, Helena, MT, 1999.

The Montana Angling Guide, Chuck Fothergill and Bob Sterling, Stream Stalker Publishing Co., Woody Creek, CO, 1988.

63 GALLATIN RIVER

Location: Southwestern Montana.
Short take: Lots of trout, and great for beginners on upper section. Fish become larger and angling more challenging downriver.
Type of stream: Freestone.
Angling methods: Fly, spin.
Species: Rainbow, cutthroat, cuttbow, brown.
Access: Easy.
Season: Year-round.
Nearest tourist services: Big Sky.
Handicapped access: None.
Closest TU chapter: Gallatin-Madison.

RUNNING MORE THAN 100 MILES from its headwaters—a little creek running out of the northwest quadrant of Yellowstone National Park—the Gallatin joins the Missouri just north of its origin, the union of the Madison and the Jefferson at Trident. In between are open riffles, roaring canyon cataracts, and miles and miles of cobble-bedded runs, turns, and pools, shadowed for most of the river's length by U.S. Highway 191. The river holds something for anglers of all skill levels, from the greenest novice who's yet to wet a wader, to the grizzled pro who's been there and done that and plans to keep doing it forever. Roughly a third the size of the Yellowstone River, and without a major entrance to the national park at its headwaters, the valley of the Gallatin lacks the grandeur of its cousin to the east. Even during the height of summer's tourist season, you may have sections of the river all to yourself, save an occasional drift boat or raft and kayak on the middle and lower mileage.

From a point where the river first hits US 191, in a broad basin within the park, north to Cinnamon Station, the Gallatin flows through open meadows. Pools are separated by shallow runs and little streamside brush reaches out to snag errant back casts. Fish in this mileage are not large—a 12-inch rainbow is a good one. Yet, they and their cutthroat neighbors seem willing to forgive a bit of drag or sloppy presentation. Run-off doesn't leave this water until the end of July, and even then it's so cold that the sun must warm the river for a while before it fishes well. Start fishing at noon and stay 'til dusk. National park seasons and regulations govern the water from the park boundary upstream. Check those, and obtain appropriate permits before you fish.

At Cinnamon Station, a one-time rail stop, the Gallatin enters a short canyon about three miles long. You'll find chutes and plunge pools here and some water that holds bigger fish. The canyon opens up into a valley called the Lower Basin and the tourist town of Big Sky, a gateway to the ski resort of the same name, which was established by a consortium spearheaded by the late NBC-TV news anchor, Chet

GALLATIN RIVER

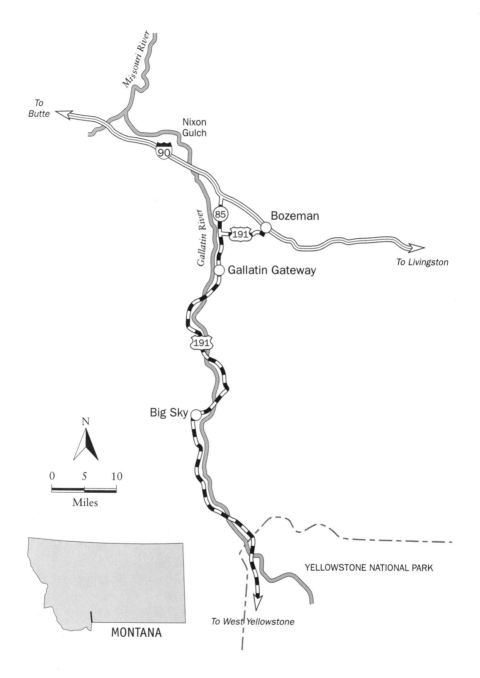

Huntley. The West Fork enters the basin at its northern end, and immediately the river gains volume and drops into a 22-mile canyon of turbulent runs and pools. As lovely as it looks, this water does not hold many large rainbows. The average is a foot or so. But every year a number of 18-inch fish are taken.

The canyon ends at Jack Creek where the Gallatin flows under US 191. From that point, the five miles or so to the bridge over the river at Gallatin Gateway is considered the best fishing on the river. The current has slowed, gravel runs lead to pools that undercut banks creating holds for larger rainbows and cuttbows, a hybrid of 'bows and cutthroats. An occasional brown will show up in this stretch, but they are rare. Rainbows here, however, are larger than those upstream. Downstream, dewatering the river to meet agricultural demands takes a toll on the fishery, though TU is working to establish minimum flows. This section is still worthy of your attention. Browns of five pounds plus are not infrequent.

With the waters of the East Gallatin, the river gains the feel of some of the larger western rivers. For ten miles, the river flows through an intricate riparian zone, heavily brushed, and loaded with wildlife as well as with big browns under cutbanks and 'bows in the riffles. The best way to fish this water is from a drift boat—legal on this stretch—though the angler who's willing to walk a mile or two from access points such as the bridge at Nixon Gulch will find outstanding sport.

Matching the hatch is not of utmost importance on the Gallatin. Caddis and Blue-Winged Olives in spring and fall, with Pale Morning Duns and terrestrials in the height of summer and the usual nymphs and streamers will handle most chores. If run-off has abated (and sometimes it has) the salmon fly hatch in late June and early July can be marvelous. At this writing, no special tackle restrictions are posted on the state-controlled waters, but read the regs before you fish.

RESOURCES

Gearing up: East Slope Anglers, P.O. Box 160249, Big Sky, MT 59716; 406-995-4369. Lone Mountain Ranch, P.O. Box 160069, Big Sky, MT 59716; 406-995-4734.

Accommodations: Big Sky Chamber of Commerce, P.O. Box 160100, Big Sky, MT 59716; 800-943-4111; www.bigskychamber.com. Travel Montana, P.O. Box 7549, Missoula, MT 59807-7549; 800-VISIT MT; www.visitmt.com.

Books: *The Fly Fisher's Guide to Montana*, Greg Thomas, Wilderness Adventure Press, Gallatin Gateway, MT, 1997.

Fishing Montana, Michael S. Sample, Falcon Publishing, Helena, MT, 1999.

The Montana Angling Guide, Chuck Fothergill and Bob Sterling, Stream Stalker Publishing Co., Woody Creek, CO, 1988.

64 THE MADISON RIVER IN MONTANA

Location: Southwestern Montana.
Short take: Close your eyes. Think of a broad trout river chattering down a wide valley between fields of sage. That's the Madison.
Type of stream: Freestone (er…tailwater).
Angling methods: Fly, spin.
Species: Brown, rainbow.
Access: Moderate.
Season: Year-round.
Nearest tourist services: Ennis, West Yellowstone.
Handicapped access: None.
Closest TU chapter: Madison-Gallatin.

YOU KNOW SEVERAL MADISON RIVERS. There's the section in Yellowstone National Park, sired by a pair of wonderful trout streams—the Gibbon and the Firehole and the mileage between the park and Hebgen Lake. There are the waters of Hebgen and Quake Lakes, and the 50-mile run down to Ennis. And there's a warmer stretch of about 30 miles from Ennis to the junction with the Jefferson which forms the Missouri just above Trident.

If you count the fact that Hebgen Lake controls flows into the upper reaches of the Madison outside the park, then it is a tailwater fishery. On the other hand, the river behaves not at all like the Beaverhead or Bighorn, resembling more closely a classic freestone stream. Fothergill and Sterling, noted angling authors, describe the Madison below Quake Lake as one long riffle. In the main, they're correct. You'll find no chutes and plunge pools, no runs slamming hard into rock cliffs, not even many large boulders that create those deep dark holes in which browns love to hold. This section of the river is very homogenous. Flowing over a stable, cobbly bottom at about five miles per hour, the river bends slightly in its ancient channel but it never meanders. Where gradient is steeper, it just runs a little faster. When the river slows, occasional gravel islands appear, but you wouldn't call the channel at all braided. Patches of cottonwood and brush occasionally line the river, but you'll find little structure from submerged logs. The utter consistency of this stretch, easy wading, agreeable browns and rainbows, and more than a dozen points for public access make this wonderful water for a beginning angler.

Spin fishers will throw Mepps, Panther Martins, Roostertails, and minnow or crayfish-pattern crankbaits. Anglers of the fly will open the season on those rare windless days in February when the sun feels good on your shoulders as it warms the riverbed just enough to trigger a midge hatch. Nymphing with the Hare's Ear, Prince, Pheasant Tail, and other similar ties begins in earnest in April. Stonefly nymphs and black, brown, or olive Woolly Buggers pay off as well. After the surge of spring melt passes, usually but not always by the first of July, salmon flies hatch

THE MADISON RIVER IN MONTANA

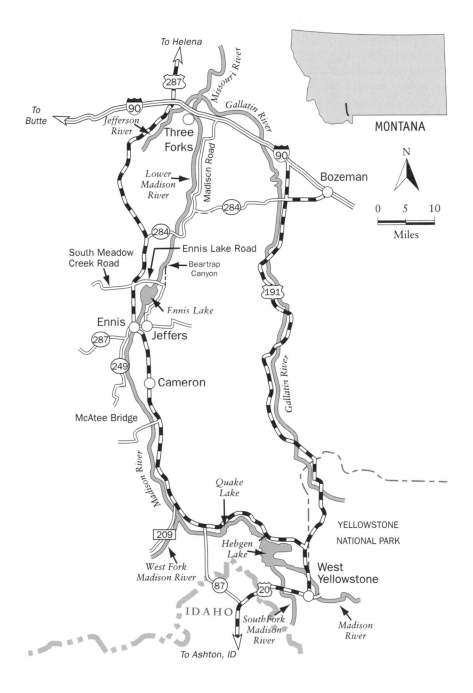

To Helena

287

To Butte

90

Jefferson River

Missouri River

Gallatin River

Three Forks

Lower Madison River

Madison Road

284

MONTANA

N

0   5   10
Miles

Bozeman

90

South Meadow Creek Road

Ennis Lake Road

Beartrap Canyon

284

Ennis Lake

191

Ennis

287

Jeffers

249

Cameron

McAtee Bridge

Gallatin River

Madison River

Quake Lake

209

Hebgen Lake

West Fork Madison River

87

20

IDAHO

South Fork Madison River

Quake Lake

YELLOWSTONE

NATIONAL PARK

West Yellowstone

Madison River

To Ashton, ID

triggering rapacious feeding by rainbows and browns and drawing hundreds of anglers from all over the world. That opens the summer season, and as water levels begin to drop, the first terrestrials— hoppers—appear. Standard attractors also work well. In fall, bring out the streamers and large nymphs.

The river changes character completely below Ennis Lake. Madison Dam, built in 1905, has created a pool that's so shallowed by sediment, that it soaks up radiant heat from the sun and releases the warm water into the river downstream. At times, water temperatures below the dam have reached 80 degrees F, triggering massive fish kills. Up for relicensing by the Federal Energy Regulatory Commission, the dam's current owner, Montana Power Company, in its environmental impact statement denied that the structure contributes to a rise in water temperature, despite several studies to the contrary. TU and a coalition of anglers and fly shop owners are, at the time of this writing, challenging Montana Power's assertions and calling for FERC to require the company to correct the thermal pollution problem.

Below the dam, the Madison gains its only whitewater in Bear Trap Canyon (wading is difficult here) but once beyond the hills, it becomes almost tranquil. Warm and weedy in summer, the lower Madison fishes well both spring and fall. You'll encounter more large browns here. And while this is primarily a fishery for nymphs and streamers, Blue-Winged Olives and caddis do well just before run-off, and a white fly hatch brightens October.

About three miles from the Yellowstone National Park boundary, Hebgen Lake impounds the Madison. Anglers fish it from all manner of watercraft from powerboats equipped with downriggers (the lake is 90 feet deep in spots) to float tubes. The Madison Arm is particularly productive when tricos and *callibaetis* hatch in August. Fishing pressure is heavy here, but downstream in Quake Lake, created during the frightful earthquake of 1959, you'll find some of the same hatches and fewer anglers.

The Madison in Yellowstone National Park is described on page 253.

RESOURCES

Gearing up: The Tackle Shop Outfitters, 127 Main St., Box 625, Ennis, MT 59729; 800-808-2832. Madison River Fishing Co., P.O. Box 627, 109 Main St., Ennis, MT 59729; 800-227-7127.

Accommodations: Ennis Chamber of Commerce, Box 291, Ennis, MT 59729; 406-682-4388. Travel Montana, P.O. Box 7549, Missoula, MT 59807-7549; 800-VISIT MT; www.visitmt.com.

Books: *The Fly Fisher's Guide to Montana*, Greg Thomas, Wilderness Adventure Press, Gallatin Gateway, MT, 1997.

Fishing Montana, Michael S. Sample, Falcon Publishing, Helena, MT, 1999.

The Montana Angling Guide, Chuck Fothergill and Bob Sterling, Stream Stalker Publishing Co., Woody Creek, CO, 1988.

65 MISSOURI RIVER

Location: Central Montana.
Short take: Big river, big tailwater, big trout.
Type of stream: Large river.
Angling methods: Fly, spin.
Species: Rainbow, brown.
Access: Easy.
Season: Year-round.
Nearest tourist services: Craig, Helena.
Handicapped access: None.
Closest TU chapter: Pat Barnes Missouri River.

THE SCALE OF THE MISSOURI RIVER is simply huge. The Missouri is the largest river in the United States. Its upper reaches, so favored by anglers for trout, span more than 100 miles, from the junction of the Jefferson, Madison, and Gallatin at Three Forks to Cascade, high in the Montana's arid steppe. As the river forms above Trident, it's subject to heavy sedimentation, fluctuations of spring run-off, and heat from the persistent rays of the western sun. Yet four dams, all but one relatively minor in size, transform the river from a slow, tepid, prairie stream better suited to warm water species into one of the finest trout fisheries in the west. To varying degrees, each of the reservoirs provides cool holding water for rainbows and browns during the hottest days of summer. And in fall and spring, depending on their species and proclivities, large trout run up out of the impoundments to spawn. And each of the lakes slows the flow, allowing sediment to sift to the bottom, before the water is released into the next section of the river. Without these dams, and increasingly cooperative management by Montana Power Company, which now operates them, there would be few, if any, fishable trout in the Missouri below Three Forks.

The mileage from Trident or Three Forks offers some angling opportunities, but fish are scattered. And it's not until the water below Toston Dam that the fishing is really worthwhile. From U.S. Highway 287, turn east on the Toston Dam Road. If you want to fish the west bank, cross the river at Toston and follow Lombard Road south. Some trout hold in this water year-round but come fall, browns (along with a few rainbows) run up out of Canyon Ferry Lake and in the spring, rainbows do the same. Water levels are lower in the fall, and the fishing is generally best then throughout the reach down to the big lake.

As a lake, Canyon Ferry is wide, shallow, and of scant interest to most trout anglers. But the short mile below it is known for big browns and rainbows, and, as a consequence, sees its share of pressure. County Road 284 (Spokane Creek Road) heads north from US 287 at a blinking yellow light, east of East Helena, crosses Canyon Ferry Dam, and provides some access to its tailwater. Downstream, the water below Hauser Dam flows through a canyon and can be reached on the construction

MISSOURI RIVER

road that heads north from Montana Highway 453 (Hauser Dam Road) on the northeast corner of Lake Helena. Follow Lincoln Road east from Interstate 15, exit 200 to get to Lake Helena.

Below Holter Dam, the last of the impoundments, the river takes on the

BARRY AND CATHY BECK

Below Holter Dam the Missouri takes on the appearance of a huge spring creek—with hatches to match.

appearance of a massive spring creek, punctuated at spots by islands and at Half Breed Rapids, by a number of boulders that wouldn't do your drift boat any good. Cobble generally covers the bottom, and stands of aquatic grasses flourish in summer. This reach boasts a heavy population of sculpins, so Muddlers and similar patterns are very effective, particularly in spring and fall. Standard nymphs fish well in April and May before the first midges and mayflies appear. Golden stones come-off in May. Caddis are the staple in summer along with terrestrials, and then it's time for big streamers.

The lower end of the Missouri's trout water is a fairly desolate place, nearly devoid of towns. Helena is a great jumping-off point for fishing this section, but you'll also find accommodations scattered along the river. Craig, for example, includes an excellent flyshop.

RESOURCES

Gearing up: Missouri River Trout Shop and Lodge, 110 Bridge St., Craig, MT 59648; 800-337-8528. Cross Currents, 326 N. Jackson, Helena, MT 406-449-2292, www.crosscurrents.com.

Accommodations: Helena Area Chamber of Commerce, 225 Cruse Ave., Helena, MT 59601; 406-442-4120. Travel Montana, P.O. Box 7549, Missoula, MT 59807-7549; 800-VISIT MT; www.visitmt.com.

Books: *The Fly Fisher's Guide to Montana*, Greg Thomas, Wilderness Adventure Press, Gallatin Gateway, MT, 1997.

Fishing Montana, Michael S. Sample, Falcon Publishing, Helena, MT, 1999.

The Montana Angling Guide, Chuck Fothergill and Bob Sterling, Stream Stalker Publishing Co., Woody Creek, CO, 1988.

66 NELSON'S SPRING CREEK

(See map on page 208)

Location: South-central Montana.
Short take: Smaller, shorter, tougher sibling of Armstrong's, across the Yellowstone River. Reservations required; 406-222-2159.
Type of stream: Spring creek.
Angling method: Fly.
Species: Rainbow, brown, cutthroat.
Access: Easy.
Season: Year-round.
Nearest tourist services: Livingston.
Handicapped access: None.
Closest TU chapter: Joe Brooks.

IF YOU HAVE ONLY ONE DAY to fish a spring creek in Paradise Valley, it probably ought not be Nelson's, unless you want the supreme technical challenge. Only half-a-mile long, this spring creek rises on the east side of the Yellowstone directly across from Armstrong's. Its course lacks the gradient of the O'Hair mileage of Armstong's Spring Creek, rather resembling some of the slower flows on the DePuy section. As summer's sun warms the gravelly, cobbly bottom, aquatic grasses flourish. By August, were it not for cottonwoods along the bank, Nelson's would resemble an English chalk stream. Undulating in the current, watery cress provides cover for big rainbows—up to 24 inches and more—and a few large browns.

These leviathans dine mainly on nymphs, scuds, and emergers. They will take dries, but only of the smallest patterns presented with 6X or 7X tippet. If you can present a Blue-Winged Olive, a Pale Morning Dun, a Sulphur, or a Trico—or an emerger of this quartet—in such a manner that it rides the currents with no hint of drag for three feet or more, you may succeed in hooking a fish. Anglers who fish this water religiously, and there are several, will spend their time targeting one old boy, identifying his feeding lane and the morsel which brings him to the surface, deciphering the micro-currents that will twist the fly to the right as the leader is tugged left, and creeping into position to make a perfect cast despite winds that swirl through the trees. And with the take, should there be a take, comes the business of playing a 2- to 4-pound trout in what amounts to a riot of submerged weed. Nose first, he'll bury himself, sulking until you work him out, deftly as you can. He has been there before and knows that you probably haven't. If you have supreme patience, and know the snapping point of your tippet, you may bring him to net.

All the water on Nelson's is not like this. Early in the season, in April and May, and late, in October and November, the weeds are diminished. The fishing is easier then and the daily rate is lower. Only six rods are permitted on the stream on any given day.

No, one day is not enough for Nelson's. A week is better. And you can check into one of Ed Nelson's three efficiencies. They're pretty utilitarian, when compared to some of the grand lodges along the Yellowstone. But you can cook your own food, timing your meals to the pattern of that 4-pound rainbow feeding where the current eddies at the base of the cottonwood log beneath the alders along the bank. Fishing may get fancier and the trout more numerous, but it doesn't get any better.

RESOURCES

Gearing up: Yellowstone Angler, P.O. Box 660, Livingston, MT 59047; 406-222-7130. Dan Bailey's Fly Shop, 209 West Park Street, Livingston, MT 59047; 800-356-4052; www.dan-bailey.com.

Accommodations: Nelson's Spring Creek Ranch, 90 Nelson's Spring Creek Rd., Livingston, MT 59047; 406-222-2159. Livingston Area Chamber of Commerce, 208 West Park, Livingston, MT 59047; 406-222-0850. Travel Montana, P.O. Box 7549, Missoula, MT 59807-7549; 800-VISIT MT; www.visitmt.com.

Books: *The Montana Angling Guide*, Chuck Fothergill and Bob Sterling, Stream Stalker Publishing Co., Woody Creek, CO, 1988.

Growing Up in Paradise: The History of Nelson's Spring Creek Ranch, Helen and Edwin Nelson, Clairmont Publishing, Glen Allen, VA, 1998.

67 ROCK CREEK

Location: Southwestern Montana.
Short take: Lovely stream, off the beaten path.
Type of stream: Freestone.
Angling methods: Fly, spin.
Species: Cutthroat, brook, brown, rainbow.
Access: Easy.
Season: Year-round.
Nearest tourist services: Missoula.
Handicapped access: At Valley of the Moon.
Closest TU chapter: West Slope.

TWENTY MILES EAST OF MISSOULA, Rock Creek Road heads due south from Interstate 90, into one of the loveliest mountain valleys in Montana. The road follows the river for most of its 50 miles as it twists and turns through stands of fir, larch, and pine in the Lolo National Forest. This is one of those delightful rivers where anglers of almost any skill will find success. And thanks to special regulations, the population of trout is thriving.

First, the regulations: Only children 14 years and younger can use bait, otherwise artificials are required. Rainbows and cutthroat must be released as must all brown trout over 12 inches in length. Bull trout cannot be targeted or taken. Boats are not allowed on the river from July 1 (end of the spring melt, more or less-through November 30. From December 1 through the third Saturday in May, all trout must be released.

The river divides itself into three areas. From Hogback Creek, just downstream from the old Puyear Ranch, up to the headwaters where Montana Highway 38 cuts across the watershed, and on the river's forks above, the river is made up mainly of tranquil riffles, some pocket water, and smooth runs. Cutts, rainbows, and their hybrids roam these little waters. Fish are aggressive, yet seldom larger than 10 inches. Below the ranch, the gradient increases and with it the river's velocity. Pools are fewer, but pocket water increases. Probing them with a nymph, or better, a double nymph rig, fished upstream, will often produce. Downstream from Butte Cabin Creek which enters the stream above Harry's Flat, the water takes on its mature shape. Riffles run hard against banks, cutting out pools that hold larger fish. So, too, do those heavy swirls that eddy behind boulders. Occasional downed trees provide good cover as well.

Rock Creek is not a dry-fly fisher's dream. For four out of five years, snowmelt will wash out the salmon fly hatch in late May and June. But on the year that it doesn't, Rock Creek is one fine place to be. Check with fly shops in Missoula. Just after salmon flies comes a hatch of green and gray drakes, and then some golden stones. Caddis are good on summer evenings, and Pale Morning Duns in the afternoons. Blue-

Rock Creek

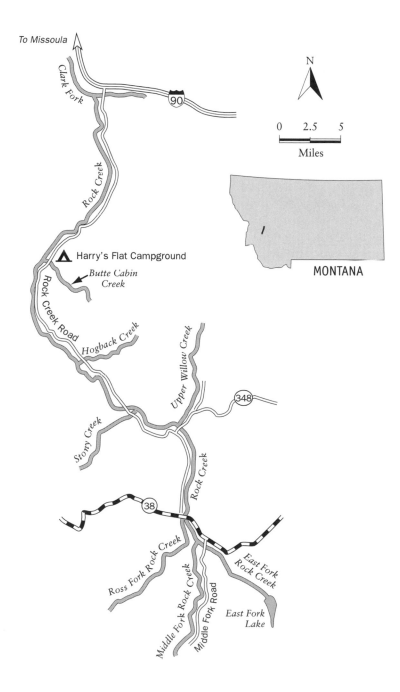

To Missoula

Clark Fork

90

N

0   2.5   5

Miles

MONTANA

Rock Creek

Harry's Flat Campground

Butte Cabin
Creek

Rock Creek Road

Hogback Creek

Upper Willow Creek

348

Stony Creek

Rock Creek

38

Ross Fork Rock Creek

Middle Fork Rock Creek

Middle Fork Road

East Fork
Rock Creek

East Fork
Lake

Winged Olives do well early, before run-off and later in the fall, and hoppers work from August into September.

The angler who really wants to sample Rock Creek's promise will forgo dry flies and concentrate on nymphing. Black stones during the salmon fly hatch and then brown and golden patterns work very well. San Juan Worms are also effective. And a number of anglers will drop a Prince or Pheasant-Tail Nymph beneath a larger Stonefly Nymph and cast upstream into the seams defining pocket water. Arming your five- or six-weight in such a fashion is almost like money in the bank. Browns of 12 inches or more are the standard fare, but watch out for big bull trout. It's not at all unusual to hook a little brown or cutthroat only to have a two-foot bull lumber out from its lair deep in a run looking for an easy meal. But don't worry, these old bulls know how to practice catch-and-release themselves.

While public access continues to be an issue on most stellar western streams, the Rock Creek Trust has been pivotal in securing a 1.5-mile conservation easement on Castle Rock Ranch's section of the creek. TU's Westslope chapter is a key player in the Rock Creek Trust, working in partnership with the ranch owners and Montana's Department of Fish, Wildlife and Parks to obtain other conservation easements that will ensure access for future generations of anglers. Rock Creek is also unusual in that access for physically challenged anglers is available at Valley of the Moon, a few miles upstream from I-90.

RESOURCES

Gearing up: Grizzly Hackle International Fishing Co., 215 W. Front St., Missoula, MT 59802; 800-297-8996. Kingfisher Fly Shop 926 E. Broadway, Missoula, MT 59802; 406-721-6141.

Accommodations: Missoula Area Chamber of Commerce, 825 E. Front St., P.O. Box 7577, Missoula, MT 59807; 406-543-6623. Travel Montana, P.O. Box 7549, Missoula, MT 59807-7549; 800-VISIT MT; www.visitmt.com.

Books: *The Fly Fisher's Guide to Montana*, Greg Thomas, Wilderness Adventure Press, Gallatin Gateway, MT, 1997.

Fishing Montana, Michael S. Sample, Falcon Publishing, Helena, MT, 1999.

The Montana Angling Guide, Chuck Fothergill and Bob Sterling, Stream Stalker Publishing Co., Woody Creek, CO, 1988.

68 SMITH RIVER

Location: Central Montana, south of Great Falls.
Short take: Only one way to fish this water—take a raft.
Type of stream: Freestone.
Angling methods: Fly, spin.
Species: Brown, rainbow.
Access: Difficult.
Season: Year-round.
Nearest tourist services: Great Falls, Helena, White Sulphur Springs.
Handicapped access: None.
Closest TU chapter: Pat Barnes Missouri River.

IF YOU WANT TO GET AWAY FROM IT ALL, try the Smith River, 63 miles of twisting, turning, cold water that flows through the low valley between the Little Belt Mountains to the northeast and the Big Belt Mountains to the southwest. The upper forks of the river run along U.S. Highway 12 in the vicinity of White Sulphur Springs, joining just west of this hamlet to form the main stem of the Smith. No dams constrain the flow of this river, nor do they swell and cool the waters during the heat of high summer. No roads shadow the river's course, and few, if any, trails lead to its banks. Aside from floating the river and camping at designated sites along the route, access is extremely limited.

Fothergill and Sterling report, in *The Montana Angling Guide*, published in 1988, that on weekends in June and July, the Smith might see 100 launches an hour! Not so anymore: Everyone, outfitter and private person alike, must draw a permit. During five days each week, eight private and one outfitter-led party are allowed to launch. On Sundays and Wednesdays, two outfitters and seven private groups may launch. No group can contain more than 15 people. Gone are the crowds of yore, but if you really want solitude in the meadow and canyon runs of this river, book a May launch with an outfitter, before spring runoff, or a September date, after tourists have gone home. Funny how these periods coincide with the best fishing.

If you want to float the river without an outfitter, you must apply to the Montana Department of Fish, Wildlife, and Parks and enter the permit lottery before February 1 of the year you wish to float the Smith.

Nowhere is the river large. It averages maybe 50 yards across and, when water is running at the normal levels of 200 to 400 cfs, two to three feet deep. Boulder gardens are frequent as are right angle bends, particularly in the canyon section. No one in their right mind runs drift boats down this river—too many opportunities to slam into sharp rock outcrops. Rafters carry extra repair kits. Canoeists thread their way among obstructions. When the water falls in late summer, "Things get a little snuggly," says veteran guide Mike Reitz.

SMITH RIVER

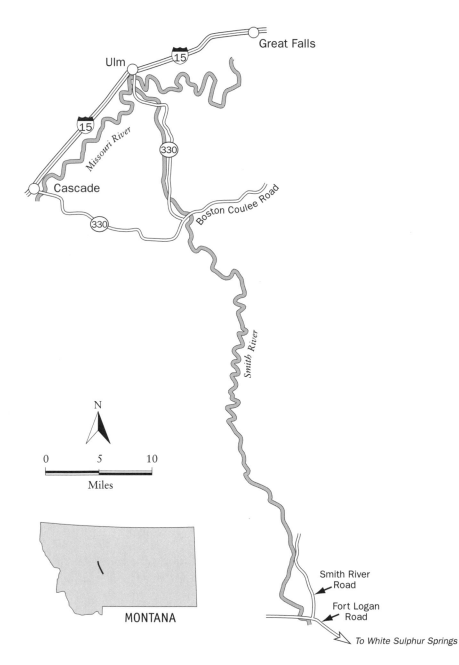

While golden stones come off in late May, salmon flies hatch in June, and there is good trico fishing in mid-July, this is not a dry-fly river *per se*. Sure, attractors will seduce strikes, but everyone fares better with wets. A Golden Stone attractor like a Stimulator with a #14 to #16 bead head, Pheasant Tail, or Gold Ribbed Hare's Ear on an 18-inch dropper is the preferred rig early on. Later, replace the Stimulator with a parachute hopper or fish nymphs exclusively. Strike indicators may be helpful in the long riffles that characterize the river. More rainbows than browns inhabit the upper reaches, but the ratio reverses the farther downstream one floats. Browns run bigger, averaging 16 inches or so to 12 inches for rainbows. A good day's fishing will bring one or two fish to net each hour you're on the river. Better anglers do better, and when the fish are "on" as they sometimes are, everyone does better.

Though a snowstorm may surprise you, May is probably the premier month on the Smith. Fish are rapacious as the water warms—warm water triggering activity among emerging aquatic insects. The meadows are turning green, and game seeking the tender shoots of emerging plants and grasses ventures into the lowlands. Few other anglers have yet tested the trout. Book a trip with a knowledgeable outfitter—typical floats run from three to seven days. Trying to cover 20 miles of river during each of three days and seriously fish at the same time is no fun for anyone. The better option is a five- or six-day package which will set you back about $2,500. Fly into Helena and rent a car or arrange for your outfitter to collect you. If you want to sample the Smith without floating it, you'll find some wadeable water at the Smith River access and bridges west of White Sulphur Springs.

RESOURCES

Gearing up: Montana River Outfitters, 923 10th Ave. N., Great Falls, MT 59401; 800-800-4350; www.mt-river-outfitters.com.

Accommodations: Great Falls Chamber of Commerce, 710 First Ave. N., Great Falls, MT 59405; 406-761-4434. Travel Montana, P.O. Box 7549, Missoula, MT 59807-7549; 800-VISIT MT; www.visitmt.com.

Books: *The Fly Fisher's Guide to Montana*, Greg Thomas, Wilderness Adventure Press, Gallatin Gateway, MT, 1997.

Fishing Montana, Michael S. Sample, Falcon Publishing, Helena, MT, 1999.

The Montana Angling Guide, Chuck Fothergill and Bob Sterling, Stream Stalker Publishing Co., Woody Creek, CO, 1988.

69 YELLOWSTONE RIVER, MIDDLE

Location: South-central Montana.
Short take: Everybody's favorite river, and the fishing is good, too.
Type of stream: Freestone.
Angling methods: Fly, spin.
Species: Cutthroat, brown, rainbow.
Access: Moderate.
Season: Year-round.
Nearest tourist services: Gardiner, Livingston.
Handicapped access: Some access along bank; best from drift boats.
Closest TU chapter: Joe Brooks.

RISING IN A MAGNIFICENT CALDERA of paint pots and smoking fumaroles, the river tumbles out of Yellowstone National Park at Gardiner and makes a headlong rush through Yankee Jim Canyon and into Paradise Valley, heading for Livingston about 60 miles below. At Livingston, the river swings east, and near Springdale it slows. The upper river is the province of cutthroats and rainbows. The deceptively deep canyon water holds browns of sizes too large to be imagined. Rainbows take over in the happy riffles of the central valley before giving way to browns below Livingston. Unfettered by major impoundments, the river flows swiftly on this leg of its 168-mile journey to the Missouri just over the North Dakota state line. Run-off swells the river with silty water from mid-May well into June and often July, depending on the snowpack. But normally, thereafter the river runs clear, except when torrential thunderstorms muddy up the Lamar and Gardner. Then the Yellowstone will take a day or two to clear.

From the town of Gardiner, at the north entrance to the park, down to Corwin Springs the river foams around boulders and races over ledges before it pools up, only to hurry on again. These waters contain the largest cutthroat population as well as vast numbers of Rocky Mountain whitefish. At Corwin, the river enters the four miles of Yankee Jim Canyon where huge boulders create Class III rips, the most challenging on the river. It's reported that the biggest brown trout may inhabit deep holes here, but they are extremely difficult to fish, thanks to the fast water. Experienced oars may guide drift boats through during periods of moderate flow, but most angling is from the bank, and spin anglers with heavy spoons have a decided advantage. The canyon ends at Miner Creek and the river begins to calm. Still pocket water and runs are productive.

Downstream from Point of Rocks, the Yellowstone takes a breather. There's little gradient through this agricultural valley and little structure to hold many fish. Floating it is the best way to cover the water. Scenery is spectacular and occasionally you'll pick up a fish. But more and better trout will be found below the Paradise access, just downstream from the bridge over Mill Creek. With its shifting, cobbled bottom,

YELLOWSTONE RIVER, MIDDLE

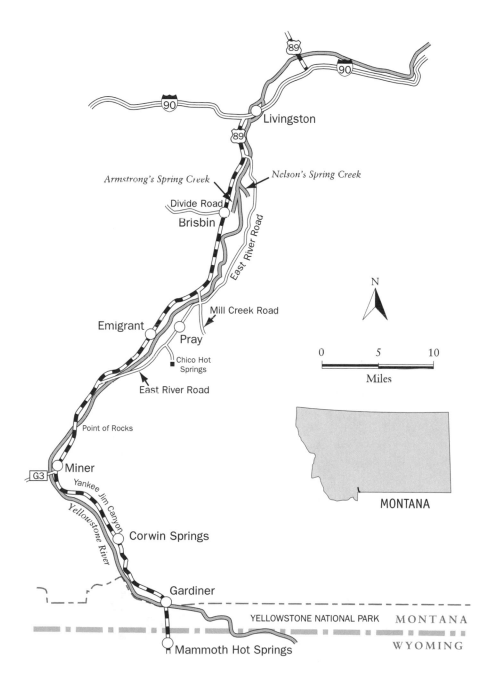

DENVER BRYAN

The Yellowstone River, flowing through the Paradise Valley, is a true western classic.

numerous turns and occasional islands, the mileage from here through Livingston is responsible for most of the middle Yellowstone's fame. Rainbows and browns predominate with an occasional, but rare, cutthroat. Hatches are reasonably consistent: midges in early spring, caddis in May, salmon flies in June and into July, hoppers in August and early September, then Blue-Winged Olives in mid-fall. Sculpins constitute a major portion of the diet of Yellowstone trout, and streamer ties that resemble these fat-headed minnows work very well. Big nymphs, Rubber Legs, Woolly Buggers, Matukas, and Muddlers all have their place. Don't stop fishing at Livingston; the run down to Springdale and beyond receives less pressure than the Paradise Valley and often yields bigger fish.

Access to much of the middle Yellowstone is easy. The state has established several launching points where wading anglers can enter the river. (Wading is best in August and September, when flows are lower.) U.S. Highway 89 runs alongside or close to the river for much of its course downstream from Gardiner, and motels, fishing lodges, bed-and-breakfasts, and restaurants abound.

In some ways, the middle run of the Yellowstone is the most public of the big western rivers. And it's under severe pressure. Landowners, anxious to protect their expensive real estate, are rip-rapping banks at an amazing pace in an attempt to constrain the river's peak run-off to the existing channel. But to rob the river of its natural floodplain is to increase velocity in the current bed, thus scouring it of aquatic insect larvae and nascent trout. Increasing channelization of the Yellowstone bodes ill for the river, not only for the fish, but for cottonwoods, willows, birds, and other animals of its riparian zone.

The upper Yellowstone is covered on page 260.

RESOURCES

Gearing up: Dan Bailey's Fly Shop, P.O. Box 1019, Livingston, MT 59047; 406-222-1673. The Master Angler, 107 S. Main St., Livingston, MT 59047; 406-222-2273. Yellowstone Angler, P.O. Box 660, Livingston, MT 59047; 406-222-7130.

Accommodations: Gardiner Chamber of Commerce, P.O. Box 81, Gardiner, MT 59030; 406-848-7971; www.gomontana.com/gardinerchamber.html. Livingston Chamber of Commerce, 208 W. Park St., Livingston, MT 59047; 406-222-0850. Travel Montana, P.O. Box 7549, Missoula, MT 59807-7549; 800-VISIT MT; www.visitmt.com.

Books: *The Fly Fisher's Guide to Montana*, Greg Thomas, Wilderness Adventure Press, Gallatin Gateway, MT, 1997.

Fishing Montana, Michael S. Sample, Falcon Publishing, Helena, MT, 1999.

The Montana Angling Guide, Chuck Fothergill and Bob Sterling, Stream Stalker Publishing Co., Woody Creek, CO, 1988.

70 FIREHOLE RIVER

Location: Yellowstone National Park, northwestern Wyoming.
Short take: The most exotic free-flowing river in the country, with trout to match.
Type of stream: Freestone.
Angling method: Fly.
Species: Rainbow, brown.
Access: Easy.
Season: Late May through mid-November.
Nearest tourist services: West Yellowstone, Montana.
Handicapped access: Possible to fish, but no formal access.
Closest TU chapter: Jackson Hole.

HALF AN HOUR AGO, you pulled into the parking lot, rigged your five-weight, struggled into your 'prenes, laced and tied your felt-soled boots, slung on your vest over that soft and warm fleece sweater, and walked down to the stream. You've held this scene in your mind for two years, since the last time you fished the Firehole, the time when the *baetis* were coming off in the snow and that rainbow—must have been a 20-incher—kept sipping along the grass next to the bank under Midway Bluff. You worked him with progressively smaller Blue-Winged Olives and tippets to match. The snow quit and the sun came out and turned the grass flats to tawny gold. At first you didn't notice the string of bison, breath smoking in the frosty air, amble down the trail from the bluff. But the splash of their crossing at the shallow above the steaming hot spring caught your attention and you turned to look. That, of course, is when the rainbow took your tiny fly, and so startled were you that you struck like it were a smallmouth. And an instant later when there was nothing there, you shivered and laughed, locking the vision deep in your memory to be visited later when days are gray and the nights so very long.

The Firehole has a special effect on anglers, perhaps induced by the faint odor of sulphur cast into the wind by scores of geysers and fumaroles. Rising in Madison Lake, the Firehole is a very thin stream and not worth fishing above Old Faithful and closed to fishing immediately below. At Biscuit Basin, the Little Firehole comes in from the west, cooling the main stem and providing a fishery for browns, rainbows, and cutthroat. Below the basin, the Firehole opens into a broad meadow. Here in the Midway and Lower Geyser basins, its waters are really too warm to fish from late July into August. But like the Little Firehole, the tributaries of Sentinel, Fairy, and Nez Perce creeks hold good, if hard-to-take, fish who've moved in to escape the heat.

The gradient quickens below Nez Perce Creek and the flat, often weedy bed of the meadow, stretch gives way to larger cobbles and boulders. The Grand Loop Road which has been following the river moves slightly east to a new route, but the old

FIREHOLE RIVER

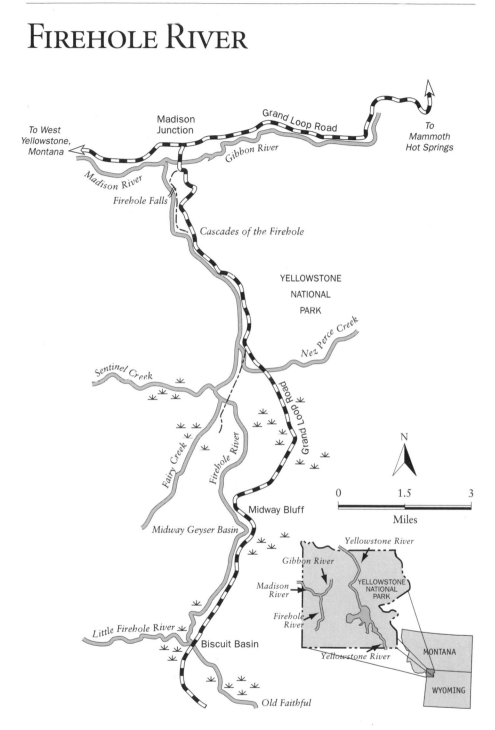

To West Yellowstone, Montana

Madison Junction

Grand Loop Road

To Mammoth Hot Springs

Gibbon River

Madison River

Firehole Falls

Cascades of the Firehole

YELLOWSTONE NATIONAL PARK

Nez Perce Creek

Sentinel Creek

Grand Loop Road

Fairy Creek

Firehole River

Midway Bluff

Midway Geyser Basin

N

0   1.5   3

Miles

Little Firehole River

Biscuit Basin

Old Faithful

Yellowstone River

Gibbon River

Madison River

YELLOWSTONE NATIONAL PARK

Firehole River

Yellowstone River

MONTANA

WYOMING

Anglers on the Firehole River in Yellowstone National Park have to be willing to share the water.

one turns off to the west at the top of Firehole Cascades. Here begins brawling water, frothing around goodly sized rock, creating deep eddies that are hard to fish well, but pay dividends in browns and rainbows of 14 inches and sometimes much better. A falls punctuates the river about a mile upstream from the junction with the Gibbon where the two waters give birth to the Madison.

The Firehole is extremely popular and its fish very well educated. Small dry flies—Hendricksons, Quill Gordons, Adams, Pale Morning Duns, Blue-Winged Olives and Midges can be quite effective when presented with a drag free float. Occasionally terrestrials produce in the meadow stretches, and streamers do well in fall, which is considered by most, the best time to fish this river.

RESOURCES

Gearing up: Madison River Outfitters, Inc. P.O. Box 398, 117 Canyon Street, West Yellowstone, MT 59758; 800-646-9644. Bud Lilly's Trout Shop, P.O. Box 530, 39 Madison Ave., West Yellowstone, WY 59758; 406-646-7801.

Accommodations: West Yellowstone Chamber of Commerce, P.O. Box 458, 30 Yellowstone Ave., West Yellowstone, MT 59758; 406-646-7701; wyellowstone.com. Travel Montana, P.O. Box 7549, Missoula, MT 59807-7549; 800-VISIT MT; www.visitmt.com.

Books: *Fishing Yellowstone National Park*, Richard Parks, Falcon Publishing, Helena, MT, 1998.

The Montana Angling Guide, Chuck Fothergill and Bob Sterling, Stream Stalker Publishing Co., Woody Creek, CO, 1988.

71 GIBBON RIVER

Location: Yellowstone National Park, northwestern Wyoming.
Short take: A small stream with as many moods as the weather.
Type of stream: Freestone.
Angling method: Fly.
Species: Grayling, brook, rainbow, brown.
Access: Easy.
Season: Late May through November.
Nearest tourist services: West Yellowstone, Montana.
Handicapped access: None.
Closest TU chapter: Madison-Gallatin.

FOR 38 MILES, THE GIBBON PLAYS TAG with the park's main loop road, but each time you see it, you think it's a different stream. Up above, below the three small ponds that birth and nurture it, the Gibbon sneaks under the Norris-Canyon road virtually unnoticed. But if you take the old road along the Virginia Cascades, there's the Gibbon. This wonderful run of pocket water is not heavily fished because its brookies and browns are smallish, yet willing. Anglers with three-weights can have much fun here.

So busy will you be watching traffic at Norris Junction, that you'll pay scant attention to the slow, marshy wetland over which the road crosses just east of the intersection. That too is the Gibbon, swinging first north then east through the 100 Spring Plain encircling the Norris Geyser Basin. Browns seem to like this slow water. At Elk Park, the still boggy river rejoins the Norris-Madison Junction Road, but heading south, it picks up energy in a series of rapids before slowing to meander through a broad meadow where elk always seem to graze. Small Adams, caddis, Cahill, and terrestrial flies will seduce the browns of this mileage. But its easy access means almost constant pressure. Among the best fishing is that of late May after run-off has flushed through the system.

Farther south past Monument Geyser Basin and Beryl Spring, the Gibbon picks up steam and begins hustling down an ever-tightening valley into a canyon that includes a thunderous falls. Above the falls, trout tend to be fairly small, averaging 10 inches or so. But below the waterfall they are larger, benefiting from deeper pools where the river flows hard against the bank in its course toward the Madison. This lower meadow is an idyll, resurging forest covers the slopes, the river flows clear over a varied bottom of slabs, gravel, and grass. Browns average 14 inches, and anglers share the water with occasional moose. The Gibbon is not a big-fish river except during the fall when spawning browns run up out of the Madison and halt at the base of the falls. These fish are trapped and know it. They're skittish as colts in the spring, but that primal urge holds them at the base of the falls. The first anglers who arrive on these waters with an early October's dawn will find fabulous fishing

GIBBON RIVER

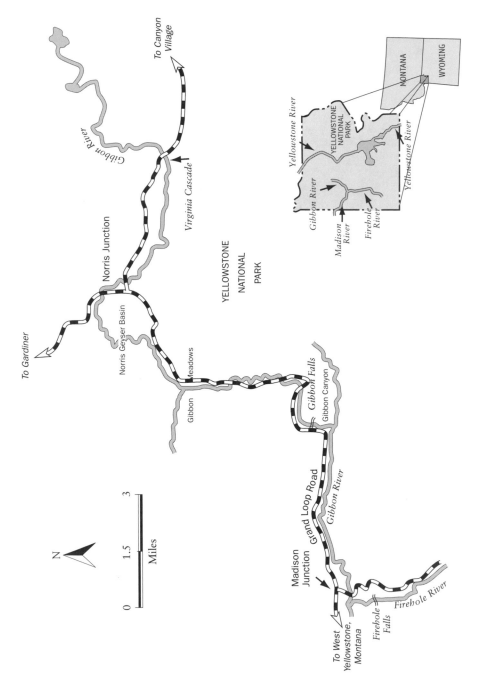

with streamers and nymphs. The second group of anglers will think these browns are stubborn as steelhead or Atlantic salmon—the fish of the proverbial thousand casts.

RESOURCES

Gearing up: Jacklin's Flyshop, 105 Yellowstone Ave., West Yellowstone, MT 59758; 406-646-7336.

Accommodations: West Yellowstone Chamber of Commerce, P.O. Box 458, 30 Yellowstone Ave., West Yellowstone, MT 59758; 406-646-7701; wyellowstone.com. Travel Montana, P.O. Box 7549, Missoula, MT 59807-7549; 800-VISIT MT; www.visitmt.com.

Books: *Fishing Yellowstone National Park*, Richard Parks, Falcon Publishing, Helena, MT, 1998.

The Montana Angling Guide, Chuck Fothergill and Bob Sterling, Stream Stalker Publishing Co., Woody Creek, Co., 1988.

72 GREEN RIVER, UPPER

Location: Western Wyoming.
Short take: There's more to the Green River than the Flaming Gorge tailwater.
Type of stream: Freestone, tailwater.
Angling methods: Fly, spin.
Species: Rainbow, cutthroat, brown.
Access: Varied.
Season: Year-round.
Nearest tourist services: Green River, Jackson.
Handicapped access: None.
Closest TU chapter: Upper Green River.

HIGH ON THE SLOPES of Stroud Peak in the Wind River Mountains, 50 miles by air from Jackson, rises the Green, one of Wyoming's most renowned trout rivers. Flowing first northwest, then south, the river rounds Big and Little Sheep Mountains on a journey that takes it some 200 miles across sage-brush steppe, through Fontenelle Reservoir, and into the top of Flaming Gorge Reservoir below the town of Green River. The glamorous water of the Green is, of course, the tailwater below Flaming Gorge Dam. But the upper reaches of the river offer challenging angling for rainbows and cutthroat in the 12-inch class and below Fontenelle Reservoir, larger browns and rainbows are found. The mountain waters of the Green have improved a great deal over the past few years, and it's certainly worth a look, especially if you're in Jackson and want to avoid the traffic on the Snake or in the national parks.

State Route 352 follows the curve of the upper reaches of the Green River from the boundary of the Bridger-Teton National Forest near Gypsum Spring to Green River Lakes Campground. The lakes themselves provide some angling for rainbows and mackinaws, and the campground is a jumping off point for backcountry trips to scores of alpine lakes beneath the glacier-capped peaks of the Wind River Range. If it's large numbers of fish or big fish you want, look elsewhere. Go, if only to soak in the scenery, and treat the fishing as a bonus. From the lakes down to Whiskey Grove Campground, the river flows around boulders set in a cobble bed. Wading is easy, fish take flies and lures readily. Yet size increases as elevation decreases and rainbows of a pound or two or more—even much more—are not out of the question.

U.S. Highways 189 and 191 cross the Green on Warren Bridge above the little hamlet of Bronx. Below the town are two miles of public water and a number of boat launching points for downstream floats. Most of the property in this area is in private hands, and ranchers are increasingly chary about permitting access. If the public access sections are too crowded, it never hurts to ask. And it's probably worthwhile; rainbows and browns average a foot or more in length. That's one of the reasons that floating the five miles or so from Warren Bridge to Daniel where US 191 and US 189 intersect is so popular, particularly with anglers from Jackson. The best

GREEN RIVER, UPPER

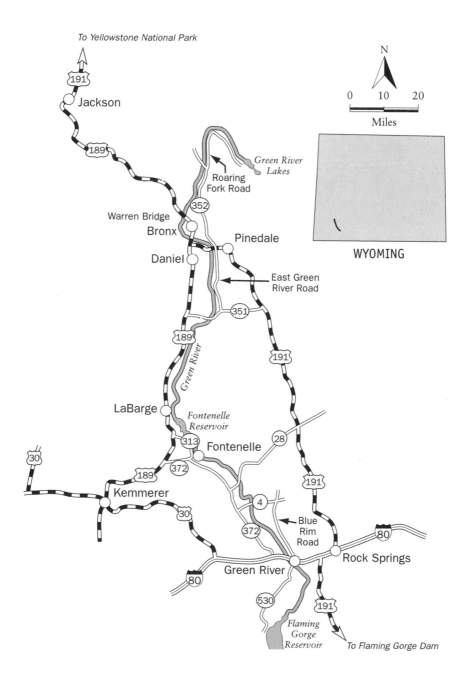

To Yellowstone National Park

191

Jackson

189

N

0   10   20

Miles

Green River
Lakes

Roaring
Fork Road

352

Warren Bridge

Bronx

Daniel

Pinedale

WYOMING

East Green
River Road

351

189

Green River

191

LaBarge

Fontenelle
Reservoir

313

Fontenelle

28

30

189   372

Kemmerer

191

30

4

372

Blue
Rim
Road

80

Green River

Rock Springs

80

530

191

Flaming
Gorge
Reservoir

To Flaming Gorge Dam

time to float is from July into early August. Any later, and this uncontrolled river may be too low. The 35 miles below Daniel are productive water, but public access is virtually nonexistent. You might be able to hook up with a guide who has permission to camp on private land along the route, and to do so might be worthwhile. Downstream from the confluence with the New Fork River, public access becomes a bit more prevalent, but float fishing remains the way to get the best from the river.

Fontenelle Reservoir impounds 20 miles of the Green. From the dam to Flaming Gorge Reservoir is a run of 74 miles. There's good public access below the dam, and here the water fishes well for rainbows and browns averaging 14 to 16 inches. The next 16 miles to the Big Sandy offer reasonably good angling—try #12 to #16 high-floating attractor patterns along the bank. Unfortunately, the feeder stream often lives up to its name and colors the river all the way down to Flaming Gorge. Most of this 16-mile run flows through the Seedskadee National Wildlife Refuge. TU's Rock Springs/Green River chapter has worked hard in cooperation with state and federal agencies to improve structure and habitat in this area. They also operate an effective wild fry stocking program. While fish in the refuge are very skittish because they are the prey of osprey, eagles, herons, and pelicans and angling is quite challenging, the size and quality of these fish make a float very worthwhile.

The lower Green River running through Flaming Gorge is described beginning on page 288.

RESOURCES

Gearing up: Wind River Sporting Goods, 420 Uinta Dr., Green River, WY, 82935; 307-875-82935. Outdoor Shop, 332 W. Pine, Pinedale, WY 82941; 307-367-2440.

Accommodations: Green River Chamber of Commerce, 1450 Uinta Dr., Green River, WY 82935; 307-875-5711. Pinedale Chamber of Commerce, P.O. Box 176 Pinedale, WY 82941; 307-367-2242.

Books: *Fishing Wyoming*, Kenneth Graham, Falcon Publishing, Helena, MT, 1998.

The Wyoming Angling Guide, Chuck Fothergill and Bob Sterling, Stream Stalker Publishing Co., Woody Creek, CO, 1993.

The Green River, Larry Tullis, Frank Amato, Portland, OR, 1993.

73 THE MADISON RIVER
IN YELLOWSTONE NATIONAL PARK

Location: Northwestern Wyoming.
Short take: Looks so easy, but it ain't.
Type of stream: Freestone.
Angling method: Fly.
Species: Brown, rainbow.
Access: Easy.
Season: Late May through early November.
Nearest tourist services: West Yellowstone, Montana.
Handicapped access: Near Madison Junction.
Closest TU chapter: Madison-Gallatin.

FROM THE JUNCTION of the Gibbon and Firehole Rivers, the Madison River flows happily along the park's west entrance road for about 14 miles. A drive along the road will show you elk, an occasional moose, anglers casting for browns and rainbows, a grizzly (on rare occasions), and other forms of wildlife indigenous to the park. These waters have been fished from the days that the idea for the park was hatched around a campfire at the head of the Madison in 1872. Then, the primary species was grayling. Just a good hoot and holler from West Yellowstone, with more fly fishing shops per block than any other tourist town in the west, the park section of the Madison sees more than its share of fishing pressure.

Make no mistake, though, this is productive water. Rich in dissolved minerals from its geothermally bred headwaters, the aquatic vegetation and insects thrive in the upper reaches. The uppermost reach near Madison Campground features runs, riffles, and undercut banks. Patches of watery weeds hold fish as well. In July and August this section is warmer than most other waters in the Park, thanks to inflows from the Firehole, and hatches of small mayflies and caddis are prolific. Below the campground, the road edges along the north side of the river to a bridge at Seven Mile Hole, where the two switch sides. About halfway between the campground and the bridge at Mount Haynes is a casting platform for physically challenged anglers. A little farther down the road, you'll note a section of stream where boulders are larger and the gradient just a bit steeper. Called Nine Mile Hole, this reach provides challenging wading for larger trout than those normally found in the riffles. At the base of Seven Mile Hole, try hoppers in August. Along the road are more than a score of pull-offs where anglers park to fish. Roughly half-a-mile from the West Entrance, a side road heads a mile north to Riverside. Called the Barns in reference to its former use as the site for the Union Pacific's Yellowstone tourist livery, three pools with gravel bottoms and good runs between are a favorite of West Yellowstone regulars who'll run out for an hour's angling if the hatch is right.

THE UPPER MADISON RIVER
IN YELLOWSTONE NATIONAL PARK

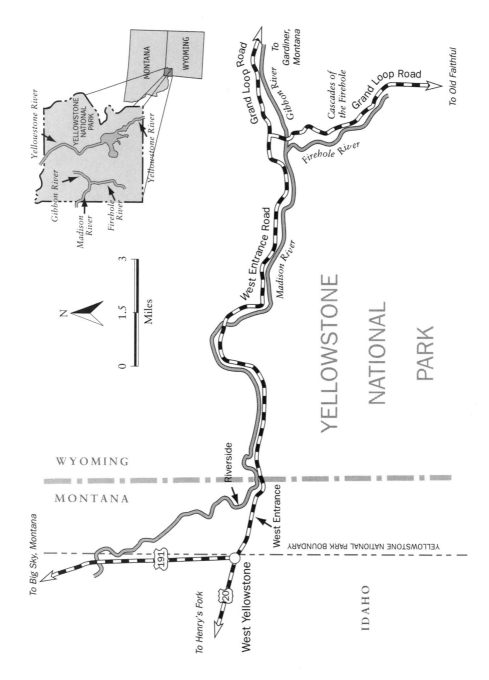

BARRY AND CATHY BECK

The Madison in Yellowstone National Park is acclaimed as a prime location for fall brown trout fishing.

The upper Madison produces mainly fish of 12 inches or so, and its proximity to a very heavily used access road precludes any chance of seclusion. But, owing to the nature of its feeder streams, this run of the Madison sheds its turgid meltwater earlier than the Yellowstone, Snake, or Fall rivers and is often fishable soon after the season opens in late May. In addition, come fall, when most of the tourists leave, spawning browns have begun to move up out of Hebgen Lake into the Madison. Streamers are the preferred ties for fishing this run. In the Barns pools, the drill is to fish them down and across, take a step downstream, and cast again—just like fishing for Atlantic salmon or steelhead. Browns of 16 to 18 inches are relatively common.

The nearby town of West Yellowstone, Montana, is served by an airport with commercial flights, though it may be less expensive to fly into Idaho Falls or Bozeman and rent a car. This really is a trouter's town. All roads lead to stellar water: Henry's Fork, the Madison, and the Gallatin. Within a couple hours' drive are the Yellowstone and the Snake and a hundred lakes and ponds. Accommodations are varied from exclusive angling lodges of rustic peeled log to motels with diners attached. Keep in mind that on the shoulders of the high tourist season, that is during spring and fall, rates are lower, anglers fewer, and the fishing is better.

The Madison River in Montana is described beginning on page 226.

255

RESOURCES

Gearing up: Madison River Outfitters, Inc., P.O. Box 398, 117 Canyon Street, West Yellowstone, MT 59758; 800-646-9644. Bud Lilly's Trout Shop, P.O. Box 530, 39 Madison Ave., West Yellowstone, MT 59758; 406-646-7801.

Accommodations: West Yellowstone Chamber of Commerce, P.O. Box 458, 30 Yellowstone Ave., West Yellowstone, MT 59758; 406-646-7701; wyellowstone.com. Travel Montana, P.O. Box 7549, Missoula, MT 59807-7549; 800-VISIT MT; www.visitmt.com.

Books: *Fishing Yellowstone National Park*, Richard Parks, Falcon Publishing, Helena, MT, 1998.

The Montana Angling Guide, Chuck Fothergill and Bob Sterling, Stream Stalker Publishing Co., Woody Creek, Co., 1988.

74 NORTH PLATTE RIVER

Location: Southeastern Wyoming.
Short take: Big, untamed river in the south; marvelous tailwaters to the north.
Type of stream: Freestone, then tailwater.
Angling methods: Fly, spin.
Species: Brown, rainbow.
Access: Moderate.
Season: Year-round.
Nearest tourist services: Saratoga, Casper, Rawlins.
Handicapped access: Informal access is possible in Saratoga.
Closest TU chapter: Platte Valley.

RISING IN A BOWL BETWEEN the Rocky and Medicine Bow Mountains in Colorado, the North Platte flows for some 30 miles before surging into Wyoming as a small but mature trout stream. Near the junction of the Encampment, another fine trout stream, the river enters the high plains and runs free until penned up by the big dam at the head of a gorge the Seminoe Mountains about 100 miles north of the border. Below Seminoe Dam is tiny Kortes Dam and downstream from that begins the fabled Miracle Mile. After stuttering through Pathfinder and Alcova reservoirs, the river continues as a trout fishery to Government Bridge, about 17 miles southwest of Casper.

With more than 150 miles of river, you'd need a month to see it all, let alone fish it. For fans of wild trout in natural waters, the upper reaches have much to offer. Entering the state in a not terribly narrow canyon, the river is about what you would expect; it runs through boulder gardens, down riffles, and occasionally through heavy rapids favored by whitewater enthusiasts during runoff from late May into, sometimes, July. Sixmile Gap Campground provides access to the river, and anglers' trails lead up and down the stream. Below the Medicine Bow National Forest, most of the land is in private hands, and public access becomes pretty well limited to campgrounds at Pickaroon, Bennett Peak, and Treasure Island.

Here the river starts its long trek across the plains, winding and meandering through a broadening valley. The bottom is cobble and here and there the river loops hard against banks of glacial till, undercutting them and dumping cottonwoods into the channel. Small bluffs of limestone rise from the river, and the float from Treasure Island Access to Saratoga is one of the river's best for rainbows and some browns. Saratoga, an unpretentious town with good accommodations, restaurants, and fly shops, straddles the river. While residents fish it, visitors frequently fail to do so, and they should.

From Saratoga north, most of the land is devoted to ranching, bridges are few, and formal public access is very limited. But once in a while ranchers respond favorably to a friendly request for permission. Otherwise, anglers must fish from boats.

NORTH PLATTE RIVER

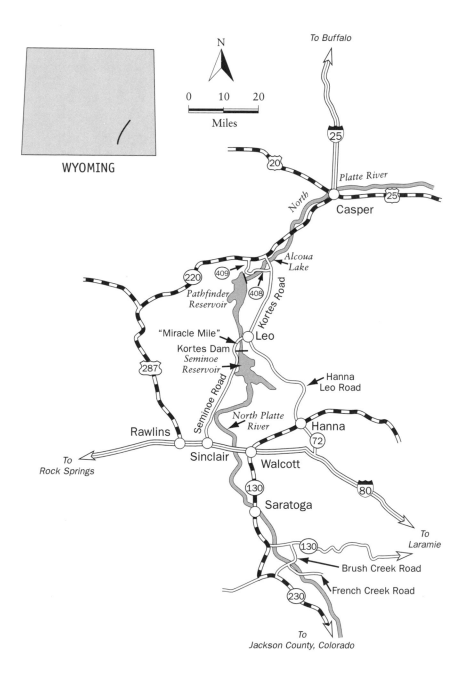

WYOMING

The fishing in this section is very good, but as the river progresses under the Interstate 80 bridge, it slows and deepens and the trout, while larger, become few and far between.

The outflow of Seminoe Dam sets up six miles of tailwater known euphemistically as the Miracle Mile. Spring and fall spawners move up from Pathfinder Reservoir and collect in the river channel. Fall, with its lower flows and bigger browns, is the most popular time, but fishing here really knows no season. Midges come off in winter (they brave the bitter weather even if you can't), and the usual mayflies and caddis hatch during warmer months. Most of the larger fish are taken with nymphs and streamers. Access is quite ample. Don't expect solitude, but you may be pleased by the spirit of camaraderie that prevails on this stretch.

While the Miracle Mile is known almost world-wide, the eight miles below Alcova Dam may hold more trophy sized fish. This is big, broad water, too deep to cross in waders. Fish nymphs, streamers, spinners, and spoons in fall when flows are lowest and big browns are on the prowl.

RESOURCES

Gearing up: Great Rocky Mountain Outfitters, Inc., 216 E. Walnut St., P.O. Box 1636, Saratoga, WY 82301; 307-326 8750. Bi-Rite Sporting Goods, 313 W. Cedar, Rawlins, WY 82301; 307-324-3401.

Accommodations: Rawlins-Carbon Chamber of Commerce, P.O. Box 1331, 519 W. Cedar, Rawlins, WY 82301; 307-324-4111. Saratoga-Platte Valley Chamber of Commerce, P.O. Box 1095, Saratoga, WY 82331; 307-326-8855.

Books: *Fishing Wyoming*, Kenneth Graham, Falcon Publishing, Helena, MT, 1998.

The Wyoming Angling Guide, Chuck Fothergill and Bob Sterling, Stream Stalker Publishing Co., Woody Creek, CO, 1993.

75 YELLOWSTONE RIVER, PARK SECTION

Location: Yellowstone National Park, northwestern Wyoming.
Short take: Riotous whitewater, deep pools, smoking springs.
Type of stream: Freestone.
Angling methods: Fly, spin.
Species: Cutthroat, brown, rainbow.
Access: Moderate.
Season: Late-May through early November.
Nearest tourist services: Gardiner.
Handicapped access: None.
Closest TU chapter: Joe Brooks, East Yellowstone.

THE SNAKE RIVER AND THE YELLOWSTONE rise on separate sides of the Two Ocean Plateau in the southeast corner of Yellowstone National Park. The Snake flows south and west and ultimately into the Pacific. Waters of the Yellowstone eventually reach the Gulf of Mexico, and the first part of their journey runs through the country's most dramatic geologic treasure. The land of the park was born of cataclysmic volcanic eruption—the latest 600,000 years ago (the rocks of the Appalachians date back 600 million years), which hurled 240 cubic *miles* of debris into the air, and collapsed the central cone into a caldera of 28 by 47 miles. The violence of its geologic past lingers in geysers, fumaroles, bubbling mud pots, and steaming springs. You will see, too, the legacy of the fires of 1988—feathery stands of fresh green lodgepole and aspen where once old-growth darkened the forest floor. The regeneration of a forest is, indeed, inspiring.

From the river's headwaters on the plateau to Yellowstone Lake is a distance of 30 utterly isolated miles. No roads and few trails probe this area. Native cutthroats of six inches or so ply these thin waters, except in the spring when bigger cutts enter the lower reaches that drain into the Southeast Arm of the lake. These runs occur in June, often before snow has melted from access trails and before the river opens in mid-July for fishing. You may find some of these larger cutts in the system in late July. If it's solitude you seek, and you don't mind a couple of days of strenuous hiking to find it, this may be your cup of tea.

Below Yellowstone Lake, the river flows through a broad, gentle run before reaching Chittenden Bridge at the head of the Grand Canyon of the Yellowstone. Cutthroat move out of the lake and into this water to spawn in June, and in July they begin returning to the deeper water. The season on this mileage opens July 15 and fishing remains very good for cutthroat into the first weeks of August. This area is subject to changing regulations; check at a visitor center or ranger station before wetting your line.

YELLOWSTONE RIVER, PARK SECTION

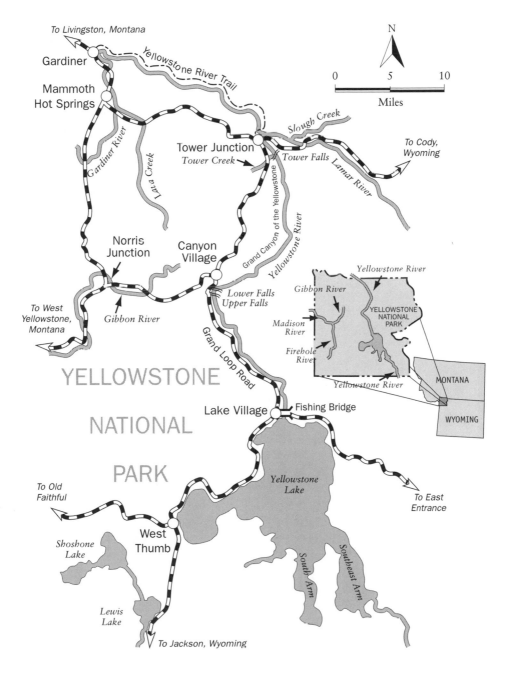

To Livingston, Montana

Gardiner

Mammoth
Hot Springs

Yellowstone River Trail

Gardiner River

Lava Creek

Tower Junction

Tower Creek →

Slough Creek

Tower Falls

Lamar River

To Cody,
Wyoming

N

0   5   10

Miles

Grand Canyon of the Yellowstone

Yellowstone River

Norris
Junction

Canyon
Village

Lower Falls
Upper Falls

Gibbon River

Grand Loop Road

Yellowstone River

Gibbon River

Madison River

Firehole River

YELLOWSTONE
NATIONAL
PARK

Yellowstone River

MONTANA

WYOMING

To West
Yellowstone,
Montana

Lake Village

Fishing Bridge

Yellowstone River

To Old
Faithful

*Shoshone
Lake*

West
Thumb

*Yellowstone
Lake*

South Arm

Southeast Arm

To East
Entrance

*Lewis
Lake*

To Jackson, Wyoming

Below Chittenden Bridge, the pace of the river quickens before the Yellowstone plunges over the Upper Falls (108 feet) and the Lower Falls (308 feet). The water between and below these falls is closed to fishing, and the first opportunity to fish the canyon is near the mouth of Sulphur Creek, about five miles down the Glacial Boulder trail from Inspiration Point. Sharp and steep, the lower quarter of the trail drops more than 1,200 feet in about a mile and a half. Cutthroats average about 14 inches in this section.

About mid-July, the salmon fly hatch reaches the mileage at Tower Falls. At the same time, melt is streaming out of the system and the river is becoming clear enough to fish. The falls are a barrier to cutthroat migrating upstream and fish in the runs downstream from the falls average about 13 inches or so. A relatively easy walk down to the river from the parking lot at Tower Store puts one on fishable water. A walk of a mile or so upstream will separate you from other, not-so-dedicated anglers.

The last reach of the Yellowstone within the park is the Black Canyon run. Plan to camp overnight if you wish to fish it. Most trails are too long and too arduous for a day trip, with the exception of the Rescue Creek Trail, which leads anglers to a big bend in the river and the northern terminus of the Yellowstone River Trail at White Lane in Gardiner.

In the national park, the Yellowstone is managed for wild cutthroats, though occasional brook trout and rainbows turn up below the falls downstream from the lake. Only artificial lures are permitted. Nymphs and streamers are most effective, but caddis, attractors like the Wulff and Stimulator, and terrestrials have their place as do light spoons for the spinning crowd. As the man says, though, there's more to fishing than fishing on the upper Yellowstone. You'll see elk and white pelicans and most likely at least one bison. Above all else, Yellowstone is a preserve, and angling here, when you're out of sight and earshot of others, is like fishing in a church.

The Middle Yellowstone is described beginning on page 240.

RESOURCES

Gearing up: Parks Fly Shop, P.O. Box 196, Gardiner, MT 59030; 406-848-7314.

Accommodations: Gardiner Chamber of Commerce, P.O. Box 81, Gardiner, MT 59030; 406-848-7971; www.gomontana.com/gardinerchamber.html. Yellowstone Park Hotels and Campgrounds, P.O. Box 165, Yellowstone National Park, WY 82190; 307-344-7311. Travel Montana, P.O. Box 7549, Missoula, MT 59807-7549; 800-VISIT MT; www.visitmt.com.

Books: *Fishing Yellowstone National Park*, Richard Parks, Falcon Publishing, Helena, MT, 1998.

The Montana Angling Guide, Chuck Fothergill and Bob Sterling, Stream Stalker Publishing Co., Woody Creek, Co., 1988.

SOUTHERN ROCKY MOUNTAINS

ARIZONA

COLORADO

NEW MEXICO

UTAH

76. COLORADO RIVER
77. ANIMAS RIVER
78. ROARING FORK
79. DOLORES RIVER
80. FRYINGPAN RIVER
81. GUNNISON RIVER
82. SOUTH PLATTE RIVER
83. SAN JUAN RIVER
84. GREEN RIVER, FLAMING GORGE

76 Colorado River

Location: Northern Arizona.
Short take: Quintessential tailwater. Huge rainbows. Best access by boat.
Type of stream: Tailwater.
Angling methods: Fly, spin.
Species: Rainbow.
Access: Limited.
Season: Year-round.
Nearest tourist services: Marble Canyon.
Handicapped access: At Lees Ferry ramp.
Closest TU chapter: Lees Ferry.

SINUOUS, COLD, AND VERY GREEN from deep and life-giving beds of aquatic mosses, the Colorado flows past 1,000 foot cliffs of rugged red sandstone on its 15.5 mile journey from Glen Canyon Dam to Lees Ferry, where it descends into the Grand Canyon. Eagles and condors soar above thermals rising along the canyon's vertical walls. But the slick river is, itself, eerily quiet. Since the closing of the dam in 1963 and their stocking in 1964, trout, exclusively rainbows, have thrived in the upper river. Water is of constant temperature, the flow, relatively constant. The river environment is wholly artificial, a long, frigid tailwater, in a hot and dry canyon where cloudbursts once turned the river into a churning brown slurry in a heat-beat. Since construction of the dam, no natural sediment has been introduced into the system save that from simulated flooding in the last half of the 1990s. The river runs clear as bottle glass to the mouth of the Paria River just below Lee's Ferry, that year-round fly-fishing mecca at the base of Vermilion Cliffs.

Millennia of flash floods down the Paria have pushed a gravel bar out from the west wall of the canyon creating a shoal where a party of Spanish explorers first tried to cross the river in 1776. John Wesley Powell, the one-armed Civil War vet turned geologist, camped on the bar after running his heavy wooden boats through and naming the canyon above. The gravel bar provides the only place where anglers without a boat can take advantage of this marvelous coldwater fishery. The bar above the mouth of the Paria stretches about a third of a mile. Shallow to the west, it deepens toward the main channel which flows hard against the eastern bank. Boulders of a foot or two in diameter fill the course and trout lie in pockets behind them.

The best way to fish this bar, as with the dozens upstream, is to work nymphs below strike indicators. Crustaceans constitute the primary food source here and scud patterns, particularly gray or tan in sizes #10 to #16 are most effective. Frequently a Brassie in #16 to #24 is fished on a 10- or 12-inch dropper below the scud. As you'd suspect, Hare's Ears, Pheasant Tails, Prince nymphs, San Juan Worms and Woolly Buggers in sizes from #10 to #16 will do the trick. During midwinter spawn, egg patterns also work well As for dry flies, midge hatches predominate with tiny black or olive being the most effective. However, imitators of midge clusters, par-

COLORADO RIVER

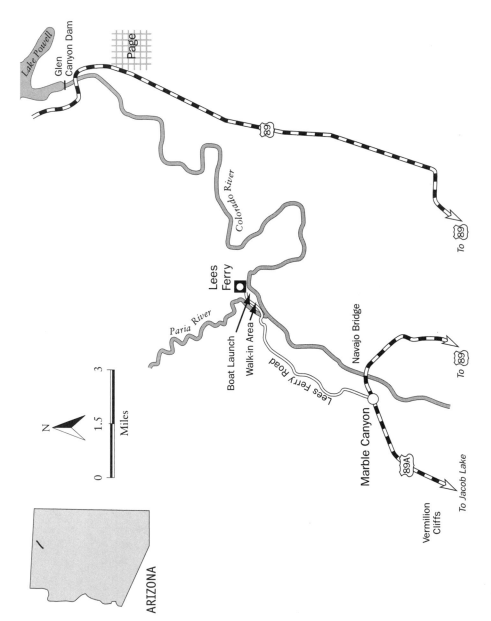

ticularly Griffith's Gnats and Grey Uglies, take more fish. During high flows, terrestrials attract rainbows. Spin fishers will find best success with brown or black jigs bounced along the bottom.

While you can park at a small parking pull-off and walk to this bar, you'll need

Scud imitations, drifted deep, do the trick on the Colorado River at Lees Ferry.

a boat for the long run upstream to the river's other bars. If you don't have your own, rent one from Lees Ferry Anglers at Vermilion Cliffs, a couple miles downstream from Lees Ferry. Boating gives you a shot at myriad eddies and shoals and places that fish well no matter what the river's stage. When flows are below 14,000 cfs, fishing is generally best. On a typical summer's day, due to peak power demands, flows can average 20,000 cfs or more. Winter flows are much lower and that, coupled with spawning and day-time highs in the 40s and 50s, make this an ideal time to fish the Lees Ferry reach of the Colorado.

In the town of Marble Canyon, just south of Lees Ferry, you'll find a motel, service station, store, and an airstrip. But fly fishers in the know head for Vermilion Cliffs, with its rustic, eccentric bar (its original 99 bottles of beer on the wall has grown to more than 180), funky river-rock motel, and extremely well stocked fly shop and guide service, Lees Ferry Anglers.

RESOURCES

Gearing up: Lees Ferry Anglers, HC 67 Box 2, Marble Canyon, AZ 86036; 800-962-9755.

Accommodations: Lees Ferry Lodge, Vermilion Cliffs, HC67 - Box 1, Marble Canyon, AZ 86036; 520-355-2231.

Books: *The Lees Ferry Angling, Boating & Historical Guide*, Dave Foster, Marble Canyon Books, Marble Canyon, AZ, 1992.

77 ANIMAS RIVER

Location: Southwestern Colorado.
Short take: Troubled by mine seepage above, the river below Durango is a "Gold Medal" river.
Type of stream: Freestone.
Angling methods: Fly, spin, bait.
Species: Brown, cutthroat, rainbow.
Access: Moderate to difficult.
Season: Year-round.
Nearest tourist services: Durango.
Handicapped access: Limited.

ANYONE WHO'S EVER DRIVEN NORTH from the New Mexico border on U.S. Highway 550 through Durango can't help but be taken by the stunning beauty of the Animas River. Below Durango, the river flows through a bed strewn with boulders, some as big as Volkswagens. From the junction of U.S. Highway 160 north to the center of town, the river looks as pretty as it fishes. For that reason it was awarded "Gold Medal" status by the Colorado Department of Wildlife in 1997. The Animas was the first river to achieve that status, and to do so it had to maintain 60 pounds of trout and carry 12 trout of 14 inches or more per acre.

In downtown Durango, US 160 turns left, crossing the Animas. From that bridge downstream to Purple Cliffs, a distance of about 3 miles, is a special regulations area. Artificial flies or lures must be used and anglers may retain only two trout per day. Each of those must be at least 16 inches in length. Browns are the dominant species, but Tasmanian strain rainbows, some Colorado cutthroat, a few cuttbow hybrids, and a smattering of brook trout inhabit these waters. Virtually all of the fishing on the Animas is concentrated in the area from Durango south for seven or eight miles.

Why? While the river rises in Denver Lake between Seigel and Houghton Mountains, a pair of 13,000 footers 70 miles north of Durango, its headwaters basin was intensely mined. Heavy metals leached from tailings into the river, effectively throttling aquatic life. Yet the inflow of unpolluted tributaries dilutes the concentration of the heavy metals and fishing in the river improves from Tenmile Creek south. This creek, itself, is a reasonably good fishery for 8- to 12-inch rainbows, as are the Ruby, Needle, and Noname, but the only way you can reach them is by hooking a ride on the Durango and Silverton Railway, a narrow gauge excursion line that runs through the Animas River gorge. Catch the 8:15 A.M. from Durango, fish mid-day, and ride the 3:00 P.M. back to town. Other tributaries including Florida River and Basin, Jackson, Hermosa, Elbert, Bear, Canyon, Tank, and Cascade Creeks offer good angling for small wild trout as well.

With a drainage basin that's 85 miles long and bounded on both sides by more than a dozen 13,000-foot peaks, the Animas is a quintessential run-off stream. Warm

ANIMAS RIVER

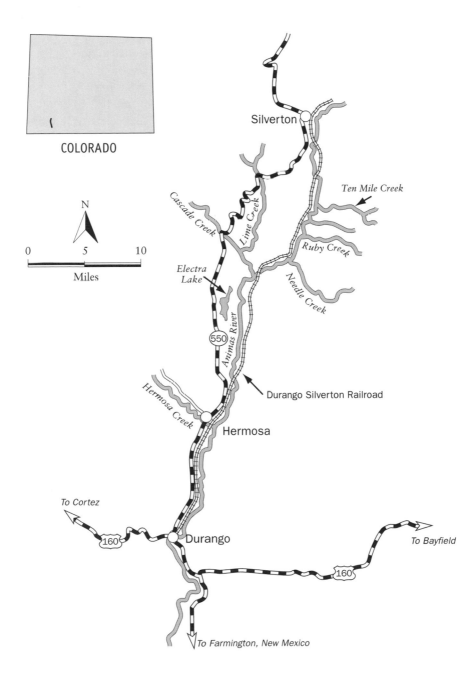

COLORADO

N

0   5   10
Miles

Silverton

Ten Mile Creek

Cascade Creek

Lime Creek

Ruby Creek

Electra Lake

Needle Creek

Animas River

550

Durango Silverton Railroad

Hermosa Creek

Hermosa

To Cortez

160

Durango

To Bayfield

160

To Farmington, New Mexico

and sunny days in February, March, and April provide good fishing, particularly with midges and streamers, but in May and June chalky brown meltwater flows into the system. Rafters and kayakers have a ball, but anglers look for clearing feeder streams. Usually the main stem is fishable again by the first of July, but that depends on the snow pack, daily temperatures, and additional precipitation. Early in the season, it's possible to float the river, but later on the most effective method relies on good waders of either neoprene or Gore-Tex. A wading staff is recommended, as are cleats on wading shoes. The big boulders are, in a word, very slippery.

Standard spinners, spoons, and small plugs work well for spin fishers, and while there's no signature hatch on this river, Tom Knopick of Duranglers, a fly shop in Durango, says that after the run-off passes, it's "caddis, caddis, and more caddis." Trudes, Humpys, and Stimulators also take fish. Pre-run-off patterns include Blue-Winged Olives and midges, and sculpins and other streamers. Tackle should be none too delicate for the mileage in town and below. Durangler's John Flick says that Animas River 'bows and browns have scant regard for leader smaller than 4X. And he reminds us that a past state record brown of 23 pounds was caught below the US 160 bridge in town.

RESOURCES

Gearing up: Duranglers, 801 B Main Ave., Durango, CO 81301; 970-385-4081. Gardenswartz Sporting Goods, 863 Main Ave., Durango, CO, 81301; 970-247-2660.

Accommodations: Durango Chamber of Commerce, 111 S. Camino del Rio, P.O. Box 2587, Durango, CO 81301; 800-525-8855.

Books: *The Colorado Angling Guide*, Chuck Fothergill and Bob Sterling, Stream Stalker Publishing Co., Woody Creek, CO, 1989.

78 ROARING FORK

Location: Central Colorado.
Short take: Highways run along it, but fish, some large, run in it. And don't overlook the tributaries.
Type of stream: Freestone.
Angling methods: Fly, spin.
Species: Brown, rainbow, brook, cutthroat.
Access: Moderate.
Season: Year-round.
Nearest tourist services: Aspen.
Handicapped access: In Aspen.
Closest TU chapter: Ferdinand Hayden.

ROARING FORK (WHICH IS A FORK OF THE COLORADO RIVER and not to be confused with the Roaring Fork, a creek that flows into Lake Granby) is a trouter's delight. More than 75 miles of river, all but 10 miles of it wadeable, makes a bee-line from headwaters in Independence Pass west by northwest to the Colorado at Glenwood Springs. Bees, contrary to what the metaphor suggests, never fly in completely straight lines. And Roaring Fork tends to bend a bit here and there. But it is not one of those meandering streams—far from it.

The upper reaches of the river are fairly thin and steep. Small rainbows, brook trout, and cutthroats make up the population as the river pushes down from cascade to pool to cascade again. Some anglers fish this mileage and do reasonably well. Anglers are fewer and the terrain encourages solitude. You won't discover much peace and quiet on the stretch below McFarlane Creek which enters the river four miles above Aspen. Spanning a dozen or so miles, the water from McFarlane Creek to upper Woody Creek Bridge, eight miles below the town, is designated a catch-and-release fishery. About half of this section is open to the public but less than well marked. Private portions aren't well marked either.

Roaring Fork earns its name as it enters its first major canyon just below the mouth of Maroon Creek. Numerous boulders roil the water in this section, but an abandoned rail bed-turned-hiking/biking path, eases access considerably. Artificial lures and catch-and-release are the rules here. Nymphs work better than dries with the exception of the early evenings of late summer.

Roaring Fork exits the canyon at upper Woody Creek (also known as True Smith) Bridge. The river runs shallower, but is still quite swift, and wading will provide some interesting moments even if you're wearing cleats and using a staff. Trout, browns mainly, are somewhat smaller than their siblings in the canyon above. The bottom in this run contains more gravel and hatches are better. The river is still too small to require a drift boat, and most anglers fish it afoot, working caddis, Green Drakes, little yellow stones, or Pale Morning Duns. A dozen miles downstream from Woody

Roaring Fork and Fryingpan River

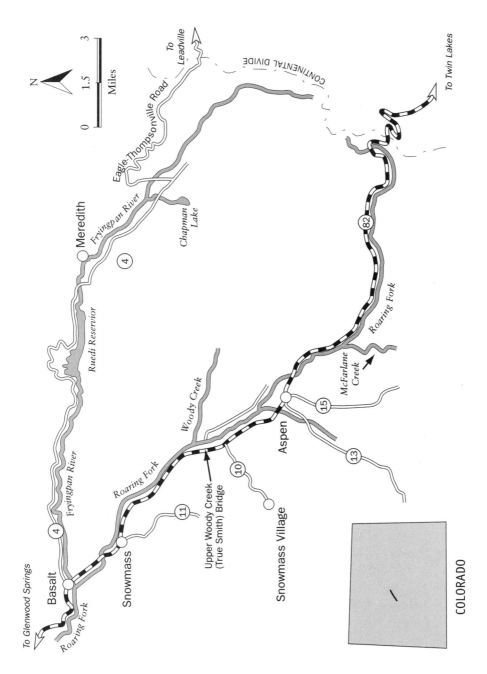

Creek, the Fryingpan enters from the north, and its heavy waters change the nature of Roaring Fork.

No longer is it really wadeable, and public land is mixed with private. Telling one from the other is difficult. Anglers fishing via shanks mare will find access to the river at Hooks Siding, Catherine, Carbondale, Westbank, and Sunlight Bridges. But better fishing will be from a drift boat, firing casts into pockets behind rocks within a foot or two of the bank. Gravel bars, so conducive to pull-out-and-wade fishing on rivers like the South Fork of the Snake, are limited. You'll catch scores of trout—the largest will top 15 inches or so—and your casting arm will ache; all signs of a very good day.

Roaring Fork is a wild river and its flows are unimpeded by any dams. The river runs heavy with snowmelt from mid-May through June. Anglers, being sensible creatures, switch their affection to the Fryingpan tailwaters below Reudi Dam when the Fork is unfishable. During pre-run-off, Blue-Winged Olives and little buckskin caddis will turn the trick as will Mepps, Panther Martins, and small crankbaits for spinning anglers. A hatch of yellow stones brightens July and August. Drew Reid of Roaring Fork Anglers recommends a #15 (read: a sparsely dressed #14) Little Yellow Stone. Things slow a bit in August, but pick up again toward the end of the month as waters cool. Best action in fall comes with BWOs and such streamers as a black Flash-a-Bugger or Pearl Zonker. By the end of November, fish have become too lethargic for much activity, but even in midwinter, skiers who happen to have a light rod, waders, and a box of midges may have fun at high noon on a sunny day.

On Roaring Fork, TU's Ferdinand Hayden Chapter plays an important role. Over the years, members have established drop structures to aerate the flow, and the chapter was instrumental in securing federal wild river and state catch-and-release designations for the Fork. Chapter president Bill Gruenberg doesn't call many meetings. Instead he fills out grant applications soliticing funding for habitat improvement projects from that portion of lottery revenues allocated to recreation. When the chapter conceives of a project, they often find the money as well as local and state partners to make it happen.

RESOURCES

Gearing up: Roaring Fork Anglers, 2114B Grand Ave., Glenwood Springs, CO 81601; 970-945-0180. Snowmass Outfitters, P.O. Box 6068, Snowmass Village, CO 81615; 970-925-4287.

Accommodations: Aspen Chamber of Commerce, 425 Rio Grande Place, Aspen, CO 81611; 800-262-7736. Basalt Chamber of Commerce, P.O. Box 514, Basalt, CO 81621; 970-927-4031. Glenwood Springs Chamber of Commerce, 1102 Grand Ave., Glenwood Springs, CO 81601; 970-945-6589.

Books: *The Colorado Angling Guide*, Chuck Fothergill and Bob Sterling, Stream Stalker Publishing Co., Woody Creek, CO, 1989.

79 DOLORES RIVER

Location: Southwestern Colorado.
Short take: Once a turgid warmwater river, but construction of McPhee Dam created a tailwater that offers technical and intellectual challenges for the most experienced angler.
Type of stream: Tailwater.
Angling methods: Fly, spin.
Species: Rainbow, brown, cutthroat.
Access: Moderate.
Season: Year-round.
Nearest tourist services: Durango.
Handicapped access: None.
Closest TU chapter: Five Rivers.

EVERYONE, ALMOST, WANTED McPhee dam to be built on the Dolores River, a slow, sluggish stream that flowed down from the San Juans and across the desert. The resulting impoundment would add recreation to an economy struggling with declining mining and forestry industries. Cold water releases from below the earth-fill structure would create a brisk tailwater trout fishery that would complement arid alpine fishing on the headwaters of the river east of the town of Dolores.

The dam was closed in 1983, trout were immediately stocked—rainbows, browns, and cutthroat—and by 1987, the 12 miles from McPhee Dam to Bradfield Bridge carried all the promise of a fine, albeit small, tailwater. Efforts by Trout Unlimited, the Colorado Division of Wildlife, and the USDA Forest Service enhanced this mileage by creating wing dams to deflect flow and through selective plantings to improve the riparian zone. The river and its trout, especially cutthroat, responded with vigor. In the last half of the '80s, the Dolores was widely revered as much for its large, eager fish as for the solitude among the cottonwoods at the base of high sandstone bluffs.

But in 1990, disaster struck. Then, according to Durango fly-shop owner Tom Knopick, more than 100 days of 20 cfs flows, the minimum flow required to maintain the coldwater fishery under the required Environmental Impact Statement, stripped the river of 50 percent of its trout population. Low flows proved especially lethal to larger fish. The issue, in times of drought, is preserving the coldwater fishery in McPhee Lake, while not sacrificing the tailwater. Because of its greater recreational (read: economic) impact the reservoir comes first, before the outflow. Optimal flows for the river should run in the 150 to 250 cfs range. Now, summer releases are about half of that and in the fall, they drop to one third. Reservoir managers are making every effort, however, to prevent the 20 cfs runs that decimated the fish population.

Just when the trout population was beginning to improve, whirling disease was discovered to have infected the river. The discovery, made in October 1997, was the

DOLORES RIVER

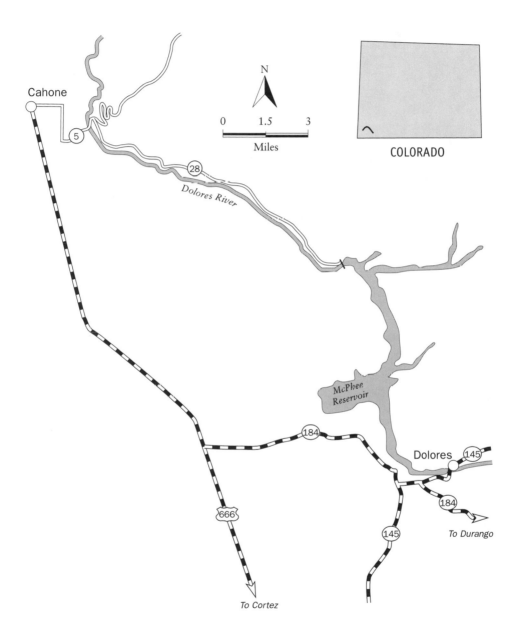

Below McPhee Dam, the Dolores provides a year-round, highly-technical tailwater challenge.

second half of the double whammy for the Dolores. The river's younger classes of trout were most affected. Larger fish seem somehow more resistant. That's all the more reason to use single, barbless hooks when fishing these tailwaters.

Is the fishing reasonable? Yes, according to Knopick. Fish are scattered, though the mileage immediately below the dam is most productive, and spooky. Water is often low and clear. Long thin leaders and light spinning lines with tiny lures are most effective. Browns have adapted best to this environment. You'll find a few rainbows, but cutthroats are very rare. The river fishes best from the end of run-off in late June through September. Evenings offer better fishing than mornings or mid-day.

Is fishing this river wise? There are anglers who would hold that any fishing adds more pressure to an already stressed population. Others would say that tailwater ecologies are artificial, a kind of long-term variation on the old put-and-take theme. And some would wonder about including the Dolores among profiles of the top 100 trout streams in the country. But if we had not, fewer anglers would know its story.

RESOURCES

Gearing up: Duranglers, 801 B Main Ave., Durango, CO 81301; 970-385-4081.

Accommodations: Durango Chamber of Commerce, 111 S. Camino del Rio, P.O. Box 2587, Durango, CO 81301; 800-525-8855.

Books: *The Colorado Angling Guide*, Chuck Fothergill and Bob Sterling, Stream Stalker Publishing Co., Woody Creek, CO, 1989.

80 FRYINGPAN RIVER

(See map on page 272)

Location: Central Colorado.
Short take: A favorite tailwater for huge rainbows. Crowded in summer, much less so in spring and fall.
Type of stream: Tailwater.
Angling methods: Fly, spin.
Species: Rainbow, brown, brook.
Access: Easy to moderate.
Season: Year-round.
Nearest tourist services: Basalt, Aspen.
Handicapped access: Below Reudi Dam.
Closest TU chapters: Ferdinand Hayden, Aspen.

A NARROW FINGER OF THE Williams Mountains juts westward from the Continental Divide, separating the Fryingpan and Roaring Fork drainages. Roaring Fork is a wild river, undammed in its entirety. But when it's flowing high, wide, and handsome with run-off or discolored from cloudbursts, you'll find fishing in the "Pan." The Fryingpan gathers its first waters above the 13,000-foot level of Deer Mountain on the divide. Just upstream from the confluence with Granite Creek, the Fryingpan's flow is diverted into the Boustead and Carlton Tunnels which run under the Continental Divide to feed the Arkansas River. From Granite Creek to the head of Reudi Lake, County Route 4 follows the river, providing ample access to its pocket waters. Don't overlook fishing from belly boat or beach in Chapman Reservoir.

The creation of Reudi Lake in 1968 bred the fine tailwater fishery we know today. Nearly 14 miles of cold, clear waters flow from beneath the dam, nourishing a diverse biomass that includes healthy populations of caddis, mayfly, and crustaceans. Known as the Toilet Bowl, the big pool at the base of the Reudi Dam holds lunker rainbows of 10 pounds or better. You can see them, and—if your frustration level allows it—cast mysis shrimp imitations to them 'til one of them takes. In the section immediately downstream from the dam are two ramps for physically disabled anglers.

Below the dam, the river flows through a series of riffles and pools, coursing over a sandstone and shale bed that's littered in spots with large granite boulders. Seldom more than 40 feet wide, and with flows averaging about 100 cfs, the river is easily waded. Because of the way it was deposited as thin beds of sands and muds, rock in the Fryingpan tends to be more slabby than bouldry. With little sediment entering the system, except in the vicinity of the Seven Castles, the river is seldom discolored during rains. The river is both a dry-fly and nymph fisher's dream. Green drakes, which start about July 4 and continue for the next 10 days, might be considered the signature hatch on the Fryingpan. Blue-Winged Olives come off from mid-March through mid-May and again from early September into early November. Caddis are not quite as prolific as on the neighboring Roaring Fork, but they are the primary insect of summer. July and August also sees hatches of little yellow stoneflies. Midges hatch all year long. Streamers are not overly popular on this river, but nymphs including scuds, Gold-ribbed Hare's Ear, Muskrat, Renegade, Pheasant Tail and Green Caddis Larvae are very effective. Designated a "Gold Medal" stream by the Colorado Department of Wildlife, the Fryingpan is for the most part a catch-and-release river, and fly fishing is the most common technique. Still, spin fishers find success with small gold and silver Mepps, Panther Martins, and Rooster Tails.

The first four miles below the dam are the most easily reached, and the river receives plenty of attention. In this section, crowding is an increasing problem, and anglers seeking solitude would do better to plan angling for spring or fall. As is the case with all rivers bounded by private land, access to lower reaches is becoming more of a challenge as well. TU and other local and state organizations are working to secure easements, and some progress is being made. Private land is often posted and public land is reasonably well identified with signs. When in doubt, of course, ask.

The town of Basalt is a good jumping off point for fishing this river. You'll find accommodations, from motels to four-star guest ranches, throughout the valleys of the Roaring Fork and Fryingpan. Best bet for the traveling angler: Fly to Aspen or Denver and rent a car, and plan to spend two weeks after Labor Day.

RESOURCES

Gearing up: Fryingpan Anglers, 123 Emma Rd., Unit 100, Basalt, CO 81621; 970-927-3441.

Accommodations: Basalt Chamber of Commerce, P.O. Box 514, Basalt, CO 81621; 970-927-4031.

Books: *The Colorado Angling Guide*, Chuck Fothergill and Bob Sterling, Stream Stalker Publishing Co., Woody Creek, CO, 1989.

81 GUNNISON RIVER

Location: Central Colorado.
Short take: Above Gunnison, a classic freestone stream with good access. Black Canyon, wild and strenuous access, not for the faint of heart.
Type of stream: Freestone, tailwater.
Angling methods: Fly, spin.
Species: Brown, rainbow, cutthroat, brook.
Access: Easy to extremely difficult.
Season: Year-round.
Nearest tourist services: Gunnison, Montrose.
Handicapped access: None.
Closest TU chapter: Gunnison.

THE GUNNISON RIVER is really two vastly different fisheries. The upper stretch is a classic sub-alpine freestone stream. The lower mileage rushes through Black Canyon and Gunnison Gorge and is accessible only by float or hikes down very steep ravines. In between the two is a chain of four deepwater lakes which are good fisheries.

At the little hamlet of Almont, the East and Taylor rivers join to form the upper Gunnison. From Almont to the town of Gunnison, the river flows across a high plateau along a route lined with cottonwoods. Most of this property is private, but above the town the Colorado Division of Wildlife has secured two leases, the Van Tyul and Redden, which allow anglers access to this classic stretch of brown and rainbow trout water. The former is the better water, and it is located midway between the Colorado Highway 135 bridge north of town and the U.S. Highway 50 bridge to the south. The Redden lease is farther upstream, and includes about one-half mile of shoreline on the outside of a bend. The upper river has not been as hard hit by whirling disease as the lower river, yet the disease has taken its toll. To mitigate the impact, the Gunnison TU chapter has purchased and stocked disease-free rainbows from a private hatchery. This TU chapter also works hand-in-glove with state and federal agencies to acquire public access to streams in the upper Gunnison Basin.

The upper section begins to fish well with those first sunny days of March with midday midge hatches. An initial spate of melt—snows up to 10,000 feet—blows through during the last two weeks of April, and then the river settles down and clears for two weeks. The main melt begins in May, peaks about the tenth of the month, and has cleared the system by the twentieth, about the same time of the first major hatch of stoneflies. Caddis begin about the same time, and they're followed a month later by green drakes and gray drakes. After the grays come *baetis* which last into November. Nymphs are seldom fished in this river because dry fly action is relatively consistent, and because tributaries provide a plethora of dry-fly angling opportunities.

GUNNISON RIVER

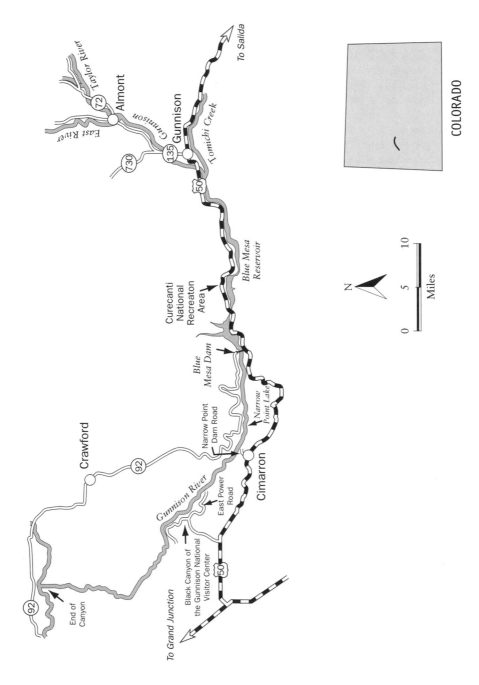

COLORADO

To Salida

Taylor River

72 Almont

Gunnison

Gunnison

135

East River

730

Tomichi Creek

50

Blue Mesa Reservoir

Curecanti National Recreaton Area

Blue Mesa Dam

Narrow Point Lake

Crawford

92

Narrow Point Dam Road

Cimarron

Gunnison River

East Power Road

92

End of Canyon

Black Canyon of the Gunnison National Visitor Center

50

To Grand Junction

N

0   5   10

Miles

If you come up from Montrose on US 50, you'll drive up Iron Springs Draw on Route 347 and cross Jones Summit, which opens onto Vernal Mesa. "Where's the river?" you'll wonder, until you see the deep chasm that rends the mesa; 2,000 feet below is the river. A boulder-strewn bed that crosses ledge after ledge, the Gunnison in the gorge offers superb nymph fishing for big trout. The rainbows you catch, if you're lucky, will be 16 inches or better. Smaller fish have fallen victim to whirling disease. Plans are underway to restock the river with disease free fingerlings. Browns now predominate, and you'll catch a lot of them in the 10- to 12-inch range. Aside from a great hatch of golden stoneflies in early June, most fly fishers throw nymphs and streamers. Spin fishers use small minnow-like plugs, spinners, and spoons.

Between the walls of the gorge, falcons soar on the thermals, and little tufts of wildflowers struggle where pockets of soil have accumulated in cracks in the deep brown rock. If you want to fish the gorge, you have two options. You can climb down one of six short, steep trails: Tomichi, Gunnison, or Warner, all descending from the South Rim in Black Canyon of the Gunnison National Monument lands, and Chukar, Bobcat, or Duncan in the Bureau of Land Management section downstream. Each trail leads to about a half-mile of fishing. The Ute Park Trail is much easier, but three times as long. It lands you at a campground with three miles of river frontage. This is the departure point for 2- and 3-day trips that float the lowest 14 miles of the Gunnison.

RESOURCES

Gearing up: High Mountain Tackle and Fly Shop, 115 S. Wisconsin St., Gunnison, CO 81230; 970-641-4243. Cimarron Creek Anglers, 317 E. Main St., Montrose, CO 81401; 970-249-0408.

Accommodations: Gunnison Area Chamber of Commerce, 500 E. Tomichi Ave., Box 36, Gunnison, CO 81230; 800-274-1501.

Books: *The Colorado Angling Guide*, Chuck Fothergill and Bob Sterling, Stream Stalker Publishing Co., Woody Creek, CO, 1989.

82 SOUTH PLATTE RIVER

Location: Central Colorado, south of Denver.
Short take: Want to know an educated trout? Those in the South Platte have seen flies so often they can tie 'em. Why do they still take? They're curious about new patterns; just like everyone else.
Type of stream: Canyon tailwater.
Angling methods: Fly, spin.
Species: Rainbow, browns.
Access: Moderate.
Season: Year-round.
Nearest tourist services: Denver.
Handicapped access: None.
Closest TU chapters: Collegiate Peaks, Cheyenne Mountain.

IN THE SPRING OF 1990, TU-Colorado won a huge victory over ever-thirsty developers and the Corps of Engineers, who conspired to drown 21 miles of "Gold Medal" trout water, some of the richest in the state. Thanks to unstinting efforts by the energetic Charlie Russell of Denver, TU's Conservationist of the Year in 1989, the Environmental Protection Agency ruled that the Corps' plans would have unacceptably adverse effects on fish, wildlife, and recreation. Colorado trouters battled against the dam for more than a decade. Joining the fray to preserve the river were the National Audubon Society, the Environmental Defense Fund, and the National Wildlife Federation. Among other impacts, reduced flows would have threatened whooping and sandhill cranes and other species as diverse as the prairie white-fringed orchid and the razorback sucker. In the end, it was this coalition of kindred interests that killed the project.

What was saved? First, the victory was a wake-up call for TUers and developers alike. The message was clear. Persistent grassroots efforts can derail even the slickest political deals. No longer do water interests have automatic *carte blanche*. Second, the win ensured that thousands of anglers will have a chance to cast to some of the most persnickety trout in the West. About an hour south from downtown Denver, the South Platte flows through Cheesman Canyon. Cheesman Dam releases cold water into the canyon. The river fishes best when flows are between 100 and 200 cfs. Twice that amount constitutes normal high water, but flows can reach 2,000 cfs. At 700 cfs the river becomes extremely dangerous. Call 303-831-7135 on a touch-tone phone, punch in "1," then an asterisk, then "40" and another asterisk. You'll hear the most recent flow at Deckers, just below the mouth of the canyon.

You'll find good sized browns in this water, and many rainbows. The latter are now being stocked to counteract the effects of whirling disease. While stocking has been a way of life for the sections downstream from Deckers, it's been three generations since non-wild fish have been introduced to the canyon. Nymphing is the most

SOUTH PLATTE RIVER

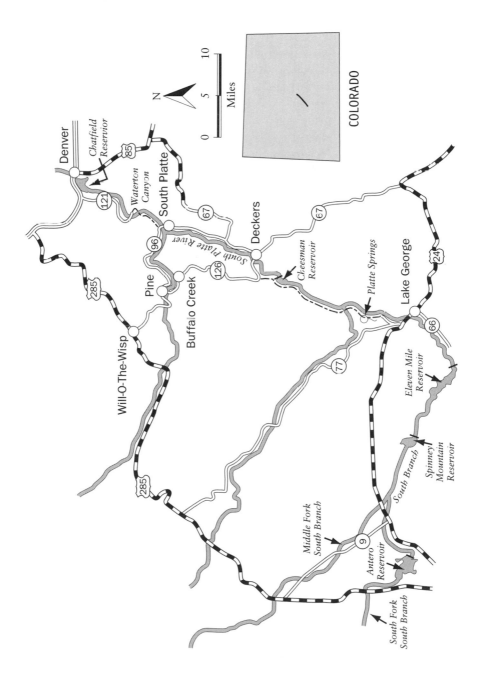

COLORADO

Miles

N

Denver

Chatfield Reservoir

85

South Platte

Waterton Canyon

121

67

96

Deckers

South Platte River

126

Cheesman Reservoir

67

Platte Springs

Lake George

24

Pine

285

Buffalo Creek

Will-O-The-Wisp

66

77

Eleven Mile Reservoir

South Branch

Spinney Mountain Reservoir

285

Middle Fork South Branch

9

Antero Reservoir

South Fork South Branch

effective technique. Seven to eight-foot leaders are the name of the game with a second fly-fished on an 18-inch dropper. Longer droppers make it difficult to feel the subtle take of these finicky trout. Your box should contain the Miracle Nymph, Brassie, Black Beauty, Pheasant Tail, and RS2. Sparse ties work better, generally speaking, than full bodied versions. Sizes are tiny, #18 to #22. For dries, fish Blue-Winged Olives in spring and fall, Tricos in late summer, caddis on summer evenings. Yellow Sallies and PMDs also produce in midsummer.

The Gill Trail, named for early lodge owners along the river, runs the length of the canyon's catch-and-release section. From the trailhead, there's an easy 20-minute walk to the stream. Access to the fabled canyon water requires a 20 minute walk from the Gill Trail Parking Lot which is off Colorado Highway 126 south of Deckers. You can also access the river by driving to Cheesman Dam and hiking down to the river, but the trail gradient is very steep.

While the famous water on the South Platte is found in Cheesman Canyon, the trout fishery provides sport all the way to the Platte Canyon at Waterton, virtually in Denver's suburbs. Also the river and its tributaries above Spiney Mountain Reservoir, and below Spiney Mountain and Elevenmile Lakes Wilderness are very popular catch and release fisheries.

RESOURCES

Gearing up: Denver boasts a number of tackle shops, all of which can provide timely and accurate information about the South Platte. Anglers All, 5211 S. Santa Fe Dr., Littleton CO 80120; 303-794-1104. The Denver Angler, 5455 W. 38th Ave. Unit E, Denver, CO 80212; 303-403-4512.

Accommodations: Woodland Park Chamber of Commerce, P.O. Box 9022, Woodland Park, CO 80866; 719-687-9885.

Books: *The Colorado Angling Guide*, Chuck Fothergill and Bob Sterling, Stream Stalker Publishing Co., Woody Creek, CO, 1989.

83 San Juan River

Location: Northern New Mexico.
Short take: Best rainbow water in the United States? That's up to you.
Type of stream: Tailwater.
Angling methods: Fly, spin.
Species: Rainbow.
Access: Easy.
Season: Year-round.
Nearest tourist services: Navajo Dam.
Handicapped access: Texas Hole.
Closest TU chapter: Rio Grande.

HERE'S A RIDDLE: Why were San Juan rainbows called "rattling trout?" Answer: "Because they gorged on freshwater snails." Second Riddle: "Why do San Juan trout no longer rattle?" Answer: "They ate all the snails." Snails invaded the San Juan River soon after the Navajo Dam was closed in 1962. And stocked rainbows dined on them as if they were *escargot*. Now, of course you catch them on fine little flies—Blue-Winged Olives, gray caddis, Pale Morning Duns, Brassies, and San Juan Worms.

Though rainbows and browns are found for a couple dozen miles below the dam, it's the first ten miles that attract virtually all anglers. And of that, 3.75 miles of "Quality Water" along New Mexico Route 511, gets most of the attention. From the base of the dam, the channel braids among numerous willow-capped islands in the Upper and Lower Flats sections. During low flows of winter and early spring, you'll find good dry-fly fishing with Midge patterns. When run-off swells the river in May and June, the water spreads out into high-water channels in the willows. As long as it is clear enough to fish, and it often is, you can work each of these little runs as if it were a tiny creek. Short, accurate casts are a must, as is stealth. Later as the water level falls, the riffles and pools in the main stem become accessible to wading anglers. The flats sections are apt to get crowded even in winter when daytime temperatures can reach the 50s. But somehow there always seems to be room for everyone. And if this section seems too populated for your tastes, try the quarter-mile no-kill section immediately below the dam.

If wading is not your style, or you've planned a stay of several days, take the 14-mile float from the dam to the town of Blanco. This will carry you to flats and bars generally inaccessible to wading anglers. You'll get an opportunity to dredge Woolly Buggers and other big wet streamers and nymphs down where large, seldom-caught browns and rainbows hide.

It's possible to stay in Aztec or Bloomfield at nice motels and dine in chain restaurants. But if you want the real flavor of this place, hang out at Chuck Rizuto's or Abe's and try to teach the bartender at the Sportsman how to make a martini. This is a funky desert town where everyone carries rod tubes in the car and more waders

SAN JUAN RIVER

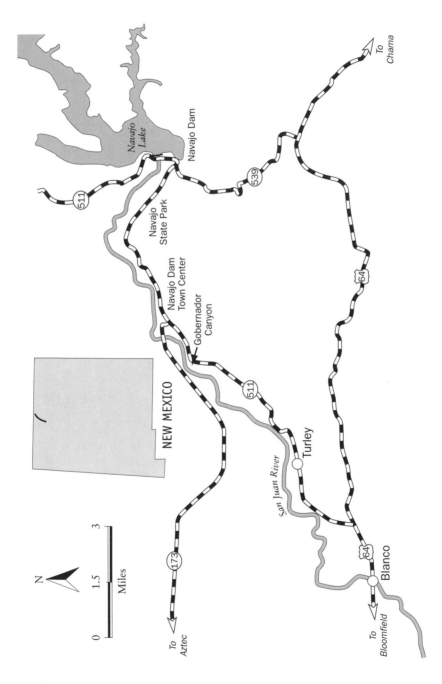

than work clothes are hung outside to dry. Durango is the closest airport with good commercial service, and if you fly in there, plan to visit the Animas and Dolores Rivers as well.

RESOURCES

Gearing up and accommodations: Abe's Motel and Fly Shop, P.O. Box 6429 Navajo Dam, NM 87419; 505-632-2194. Rizuto's Fly Shop and Resort, 1796 Hwy 173, Navajo Dam, NM 87419; 505-632-3893.

Books: *Fly Fishing in Northern New Mexico*, Craig Martin, Ed., University of New Mexico Press, Albuquerque, NM, 1991.

84 GREEN RIVER, FLAMING GORGE

Location: Northeastern Utah.
Short take: Clean, cold, productive; what more could you want?
Type of stream: Tailwater.
Angling methods: Fly, spin.
Species: Brown, rainbow, cutthroat.
Access: Difficult.
Season: Year-round.
Nearest tourist services: Dutch John.
Handicapped access: Little Hole.
Closest TU chapter: Flaming Gorge.

THE ARCH OF FLAMING GORGE DAM is thrust against the walls of Red Canyon by the pressure of 100 miles of impounded water from the Green River. The lake is famous for huge browns and kokanee salmon, but the tailwater below is known among anglers throughout the world for its river-run browns, cutthroats, and rainbows. Unlike the big tailwater on the Colorado between Glen Canyon Dam and Lees Ferry, the Green below Flaming Gorge is accessible by foot. For 11 miles, a well maintained trail follows the north bank of the river and leads anglers to a dozen rapids and flats. Even in periods of low flow, crossing the river is very difficult. But wading and casting along the edge is quite productive.

Most who fish the river float it, launching just below the dam and floating the 7.5 miles to Little Hole, a takeout and picnic ground maintained by the USDA Forest Service. This is the most famous section of the river, the most heavily fished, and the most favored by rafters and tubers, whose exuberant shouts ring throughout Red Canyon on hot summer weekends. The best time to be on this stretch is any time other than weekends from June through August. Even if your schedule places you on the river on a Saturday or Sunday during the summer, fishing toward the bank will yield very nice fish (browns averaging 16 inches and 'bows and cutthroats of 15 inches or so). A second float, from Little Hole to Browns Park, is also popular and productive. But cloudbursts trigger flash floods from Red Creek, which comes in from the north about halfway down this stretch, and pumps fine, orange sediment into the river. The last stretch of the best water, the 13 miles from Browns Park to Swallow Canyon, reportedly contains large fish. Yet after a heavy thunderstorm, fine sediment from Red Creek hangs in the slower moving lower section. Sometimes days are required before it clears.

The Green experiences reasonably predictable and constant flows. Gone, by and large, are the daily fluctuations which used to raise the river from 800 cfs to 4,500 cfs and then drop it back again. Instead, the river runs between 2,500 and 3,000 cfs

GREEN RIVER, FLAMING GORGE

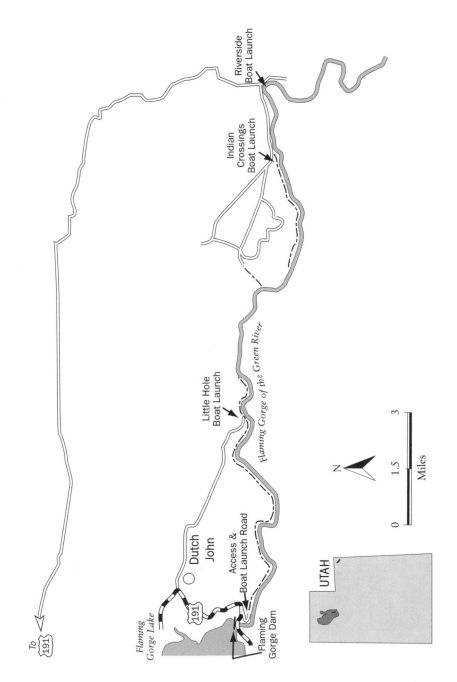

Riverside Boat Launch

Indian Crossings Boat Launch

Flaming Gorge of the Green River

Little Hole Boat Launch

N

0   1.5   3

Miles

Dutch John

Access & Boat Launch Road

Flaming Gorge Lake

191

Flaming Gorge Dam

To 191

UTAH

The Green River below Flaming Gorge Dam is easily reached by a foot trail along its entire length.

during the winter, rising to about 4,000 cfs in May. In late June or early July, flows drop back to about 1,800 cfs, where they are maintained through the fall.

While primarily fished with flies, spinning anglers do very well with quarter- and eighth-ounce leadhead jigs in black and ginger. For flyfishers, the season begins with midges in February and March, shifts to Blue-Winged Olives from March into May, big cicadas in May, and then terrestrials—hoppers, crickets, ants. Isolated hatches of Pale Morning Duns and tricos come off in July and August. And later, coinciding with spawning runs of browns in the fall, is an excellent hatch of Blue-Winged Olives. Nymphs and scuds, particularly when fished below a big dry that serves as a strike indicator, can be very effective. Sizes tend to be small—#16 to # 26.

Accommodations in Dutch John are limited. Flaming Gorge Lodge, with its fly and tackle shop, is the center of most activity. Many anglers who come to fish the Green River as a destination will fly into Salt Lake City and rent a car. While the river is open year-round, the months of January and February may see numerous road closings. Flaming Gorge Lodge operates from mid-March through November.

RESOURCES

Gearing up and accommodations: Flaming Gorge Lodge, 155 Greendale, US 191, Dutch John, UT 84023; 435-889-3773.

Books: *The Green River*, Larry Tullis, Frank Amato, Portland, OR, 1993.

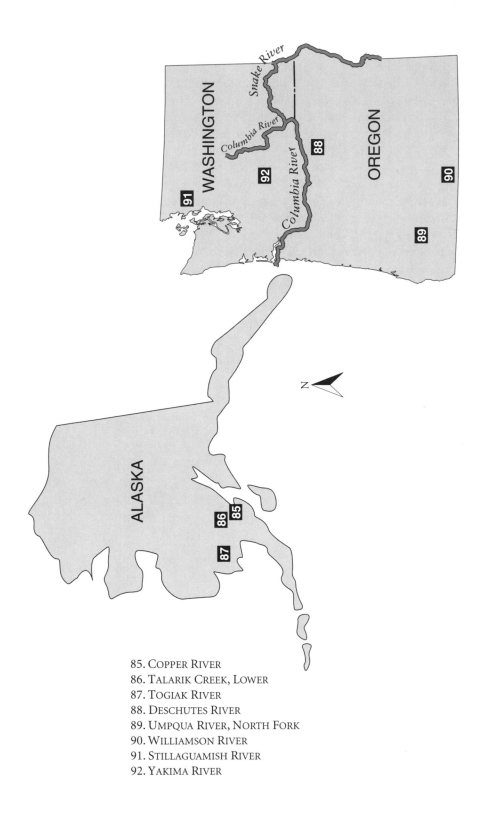

85. Copper River
86. Talarik Creek, Lower
87. Togiak River
88. Deschutes River
89. Umpqua River, North Fork
90. Williamson River
91. Stillaguamish River
92. Yakima River

NORTHWEST

ALASKA

OREGON

WASHINGTON

85 COPPER RIVER

Location: South-central Alaska; southwest of Cook Inlet, across from Homer.
Short take: Alaska has two Copper Rivers. Glacier-fed, the first carries some steelhead and rainbows in its tributaries, the second is the one everybody raves about.
Type of stream: Freestone.
Angling method: Fly.
Species: Rainbow, Pacific salmon.
Access: Restricted.
Season: June through September.
Nearest tourist services: Private lodges.
Handicapped access: Fishing from a boat is possible; otherwise no access.

ALRIGHT, THE FIRST THING YOU GOTTA KNOW about the Copper River in Alaska is that there are at least two of them. The closest one to civilization flows into Prince William Sound in a big delta east of Cordova. The other is a much smaller river that drains a trio of lakes in the narrow isthmus that separates Iliamna Lake from the salty waters of Iliamna Bay, at the southwest end of Cook Inlet.

The former is more challenging and if you're making the trek to Alaska by car from the Lower 48, it might just be worthwhile to poke around on that Copper's tributaries before heading into Anchorage and points west.

The far more famous Copper is the object of our attention here—the one down in the Iliamna region. Mack Minnard calls it "a beautiful piece of water with all the attributes of a first-class rainbow river." He should know. An Alaska Fish and Game biologist, he worked in the drainage for 18 years. It's one of the few rivers that sees hatches of mayflies, stoneflies, and caddis. Stoneflies—mahogany in #6 and #8 and lime greens in #16 and #18—begin to come off in mid-June. They're followed by Yellow Sallies (#14 and #16) toward the end of the month. Caddis appear in the full range of colors and sizes. By early July, mayflies and stoneflies have faded, but there's caddis activity into the end of the month.

By the third week of July, topwater action virtually ceases. Sockeye are the first of Alaska's five salmon species to spawn in the river, and their eggs, maturing in gravelly redds have attracted the interest of rainbows. Soon the rainbows are feeding on the bottom like hogs at a trough. So guess which patterns are most effective? Eggs. In virtually any color. And flesh flies, combed-out strips of orange yarn tied on a hook. You may also stir up some action with mouse patterns, big Matukas, and Muddlers. Most rainbows run in the 12- to 20-inch range, but the number of 24-inch fish is large enough so most anglers play one or two while they're on the river. The farther the season goes, the fatter the fish. July and August are peak months for salmon on the river but that, too, begins to pale as the weeks slide into September and the 'bows are at their largest.

COPPER RIVER

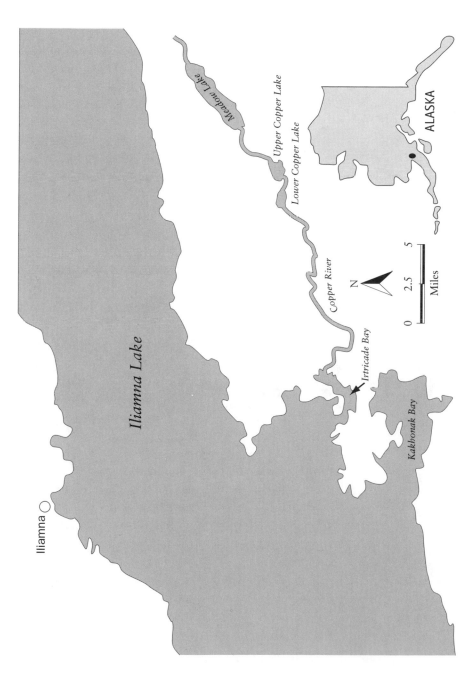

Rainbows of twenty-four inches are the draw on the Copper River in the Iliamna region of Alaska.

Thirteen miles of the Copper, from its mouth on Intricate Bay up to a set of 50-foot falls, are navigable. The drill here is to jet-boat upstream, then drift down, fishing runs around gravel bars and undercut banks, and the heads and tails of slick pools. Anyone can boat up the river. The banks, however, are private property and trespassing is prohibited except within the normal high water marks that define the river's main corridor. Wading is OK, but a trip into the bush is not.

You won't find much freelance activity on this river. Flown or boated in from lodges such as Goll's and Gerkin's, most anglers fish with guides. In the last two decades, fishing pressure on the river has more than trebled. Some, like Gerkin, believe that the Copper suffers from overfishing and declining runs of the salmon that bring trout into the system. His argument is that the increasing commercial salmon catch is limiting the numbers of salmon that come into the Copper, thus causing decreases in the amount of food—eggs and decaying flesh—on which rainbows feed. It's true that in the late 1970s, the Copper was in serious trouble from disease-plagued salmon. And in 1990, the river became a special management area permitting only catch-and-release fly fishing. Despite years of study, the full relationship between the rainbows and salmon is not well understood. Fisheries biologists are now advocating that the escapement rate for salmon be stabilized at 4 to 8 million salmon per season as opposed to a former system that allowed rates to vary between 2 and 18 million per year.

The prognosis for the Copper River is good. Subject, of course, to vagaries of weather, the river should continue to fish well. With no limit on the number of anglers, the number of days of solitude on the river will be few indeed. Does that make a difference in the quality of your angling experience? That's up to you. The story is the same on most of the established rainbow and salmon fisheries in the forty-ninth state and elsewhere. Big fish draw crowds, and if they get to be too much for you, head up above the falls and play with the grayling (12 to 20 inches) for a while.

RESOURCES

Gearing up: Lodges carry local flies and lures, but otherwise, fill your tackle boxes before you come.

Accommodations: King Salmon Visitors Center, P.O. Box 298, King Salmon, AK 99613; 907-246-4250.

86 TALARIK CREEK, LOWER

Location: About 50 miles west of Iliamna.
Short take: Huge 'bows at the Rock.
Type of stream: Freestone.
Angling method: Fly.
Species: Rainbow, some sockeye.
Access: Difficult.
Season: April through October.
Nearest tourist services: Iliamna.
Handicapped access: None.
Closest TU chapter: None.

LOWER TALARIK CREEK is Alaska's premier fishery for rainbows measured in pounds and not inches. It's also one of Alaska's shortest fisheries. A channel of maybe three quarters of a mile divides a pair of lagoons. In this channel, which looks like it might have been cut by the Corps of Engineers, anglers from a dozen or more lodges in the Iliamna region vie for spots to cast to rainbows. The channel is a feed trough and these rainbows are hogs. They gorge on sockeye salmon flesh and eggs and almost anything else you care to throw at them. They're big, passive fish used to having the current bring them dinner. Get there at the right time on virtually any day from mid-August into September, and you'll catch so many 5- to 9-pound 'bows that you'll wonder whether you'll ever be happy again on your home stream with its stock of 9-inchers. Don't worry. Winter will intervene with its snow and sleet and endless doldrums, and by April you'll be more than ready to pick up a willowy rod and toss #16 Hendricksons or 1/32 ounce Roostertails to your local trout. But in your mind will be that one that broke you off in the Talarik. That's the one you'll remember.

Centuries of storms pounding up Lake Iliamna have built a massive bar between the lake and the waters of the Lower Talarik. Along the north side of the bar runs the channel between the two lagoons. The waters of the lake lap the south side of the bar. The mouth of the creek moves along the face of the bar, perpendicular to the axis of the lower lagoon. Spring and fall storms plug the old mouth with sand and cobble. When the storms abate, the river pushes a new breach in the bar. One never knows from one year to the next whether it will move, and if it does, where it will be. The rock in the channel is always there, and behind it is where most anglers try to fish.

There is, however, more to the Lower Talarik than the short hot stretch at its mouth. Sockeye spawn in the length of the river which runs more than 15 miles back into the hills. Above the uppermost lagoon, the river forks. The west fork is the smaller of the two and, according to the temperate advice of an Alaska fish biologist, "is bear country. Stay the heck out!" The east branch is a different story. You'll

Talarik Creek, Lower

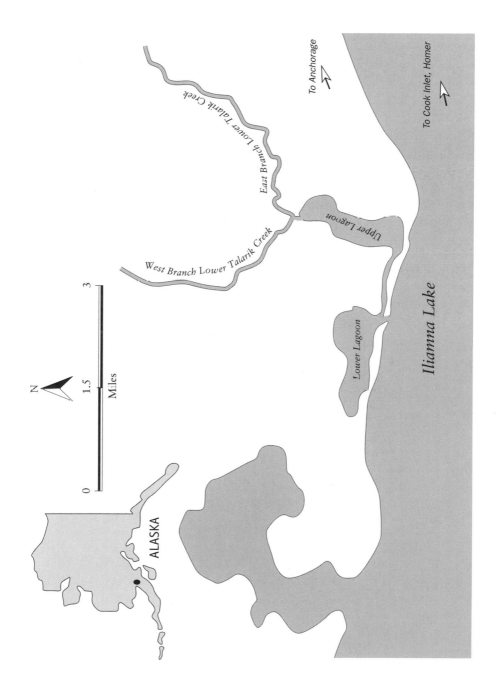

encounter bears there too, but not so many. This is the longer of the two forks. It rises in a pod of lakes and flows about 15 miles to the confluence. Only one or two parties float this water each year. They take grayling, char, salmon, and rainbows, but the 'bows are not as large as those at the mouth.

Closed to angling by means other than fly fishing, the Lower Talarik is thought to be one of few places where rainbows may winter over in a stream rather than returning to the depths of the big lake. The Nature Conservancy, with help from a potpourri of public and private organizations including the Orvis Company, has purchased 155 acres that includes the mouth of the Lower Talarik. It is a marvelous wetland community of eagles and harriers and tundra swans, of bear and caribou, of wolves and red foxes, and of sockeye and the rainbow trout they nourish. The Alsaka Fish and Game Commission is also considering the creation of the Lower Talarik Special Use Area. This would limit camping near the creek's mouth. Their concern, and one shared by many guides and lodges, is that ever-increasing angling pressure may one day erode the quality and uniqueness of one of Alsaka's finest rainbow fisheries.

While Lower Talarik is a very fine rainbow river, it's hard to reach without the services of a lodge or guide with a plane. For a less expensive alternative, Tony Route, author of a number of books about fishing in Alaska, suggests the upper reaches of the Kenai above Skilak Lake. Here the Kenai resembles large rivers of the West. Rainbows run in the fall as they do on the Talarik, but you can drive to it, camp, or stay in an inexpensive motel, and fish it from the bank if that's your pleasure.

RESOURCES

Gearing up: Best to stock up before leaving home. Lodges can supply local patterns.

Accommodations: King Salmon Visitors Center, P.O. Box 298, King Salmon, AK 99613; 907-246-4250.

87 Togiak River

Location: Western Alaska.
Short take: A popular river for all five Pacific salmon.
Type of stream: Freestone.
Angling methods: Fly, spin.
Species: Salmon.
Access: Limited.
Season: May through September.
Nearest tourist services: Dillingham.
Handicapped access: None.

RISING ON THE WESTERN SLOPES of the Wood River Mountains, the Togiak drains the southeastern quadrant of the Togiak Wildlife Refuge. With 4.2 million acres, the refuge is about the same size as Connecticut and Rhode Island combined. It is a barren land of steep mountains, broad, swampy river valleys, bears and birds, and, yes, hordes of mosquitoes. But who cares a whit for that buzzing sound in your ears when your drag's screaming and your rod's bent to the breaking point and you've got maybe a dozen more turns before your spool is bare? That's king salmon fishing and that's why the Togiak is so popular.

Kings are the first of the five species of Pacific salmon to enter this river system. They appear in mid-June. About ten days later they'll reach maximum numbers which will hold for the following month. But by early August they're gone. Typical fish are in the 35-pound range, but 50-pounders are common enough. At the same time the kings are running, you'll also find chums and sockeye or red salmon of ten pounds or so. Pinks, the smallest of the salmon, enter the river in late July and a week or two later, the cohos or silvers begin their runs. Known for their slashing, leaping runs, silvers fish best from early in the second week of August into the third week of September. Occasional rainbows and Dolly Varden are taken from the Togiak, but they do not constitute as major a recreational fishery as they do on the other rivers in the refuge, the Kanetok and Goodnews.

Slow, gentle, and broad with few riffles, the Togiak is an easy float. Anglers drift from pool to bar in the best water that runs from the refuge boundary 20 miles or so upstream. Below the boundary is land controlled by native peoples. Fishing is permitted, but camping along the banks is not. Most of the sport fishing activity is focused on the upper mileage, and anglers usually employ guides or fish from private lodges located in areas served from Dillingham or Goodnews Bay. When the kings are running, the river sees a lot of boat traffic. In fact, 98 percent of all kings taken from the Togiak are caught from boats. Like all major rivers in Alsaka, the Togiak runs high and off-color with meltwater in the spring. The peak of run-off varies quite a bit, more than a month in some years. The river does not fish well when it's dirty with sediment. During the silver run late in the season, the river has dropped

TOGIAK RIVER

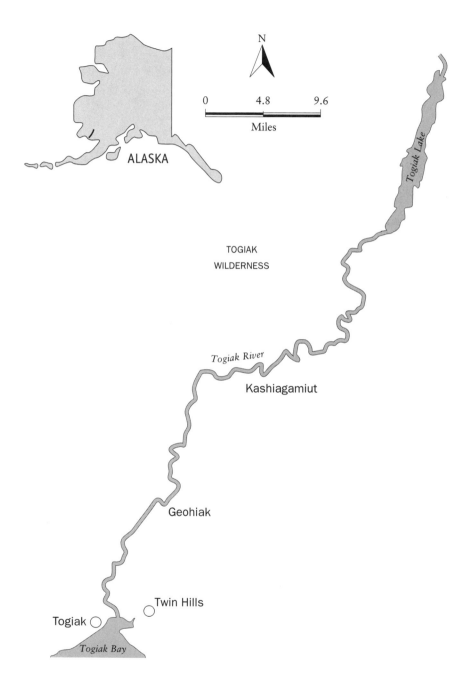

N

0   4.8   9.6

Miles

ALASKA

Togiak Lake

TOGIAK
WILDERNESS

Togiak River

Kashiagamiut

Geohiak

Twin Hills

Togiak

Togiak Bay

and there is some, but not much, wade fishing. There's no magic lure, other than personal stamina, for fishing for these great salmon. Spinners and spoons serve hardware hurlers as well as green, red, orange, blue, and flashing flies work for fly fishers. The key to successful salmon fishing is having a good drag on your reel and knowing just how much tension your rod and reel can stand.

The Togiak is very popular for salmon, but the other two rivers that flow out of the refuge, the Kanetok and the Goodnews, offer swifter flows and larger populations of rainbows. Unless your mission is strictly salmon, it might be worthwhile to spend a day on the Goodnews, if only to rest your arm.

RESOURCES

Gearing up: Buy tackle in Anchorage or at home before you leave.

Accommodations: Dillingham Chamber of Commerce, P.O. Box 348, Dillingham, AK 99576; 907-842-5115.

Books: *Flyfishing Alaska*, Anthony Route, Johnson Books, Boulder, CO, 1995.

88 DESCHUTES RIVER

Location: North-central Oregon.
Short take: Wild steelhead, indigenous hybrid 'bows, and a stunning canyon.
Type of stream: Freestone.
Angling methods: Fly, spin.
Species: Steelhead, redside.
Access: Moderate.
Season: Year-round.
Nearest tourist services: Maupin.
Handicapped access: Below Maupin.
Closest TU chapter: Deschutes River.

THE LITTLE DESCHUTES RISES on the north side of the Mount Thielsen Wilderness, across the divide from the headwaters of the North Fork of the Umpqua. Its sister fork, the main stem of the Deschutes, has its origins in Little Lava Lake and flows through a pair of lakes, Crane Prairie and Wickiup, before tumbling over Pringle Falls and meeting the Little Deschutes near Sun River west of U.S. Route 97. The upper waters offer reasonably good angling for brooks, browns, and rainbows, and might be worth a look if you're in the vicinity of Crater Lake and have decided not to fish the Umpqua. The season is only open from June through August. The middle section of the river begins at Bend and beats a course north-northeastward into Lake Billy Chinook. Aggressive agricultural usage all but dewaters the middle section in summer. You'll find some winter fishing here, but unless business takes you there, there's better angling downstream.

Three dams just west of Madras control the river's releases into its final bed—the mileage that's so popular for steelhead and "redside" trout, a hybrid rainbow and cutthroat that's indigenous to the river and well adapted to the water's high alkalinity. It's the chemistry of the water that enables the growth of an unusually healthy community of aquatic insects. So massive are the hatches of caddis, mayflies, and stoneflies, that minnows do not constitute as major a portion of the trout's diet as elsewhere. With about 2,500 fish per linear mile, the river is rich with trout. Among the most important hatches are the salmon flies and golden stones of May and June, PMDs of late May though August, Blue-Winged Olives in February, June, and October; and October caddis. Caddis hatch throughout the main part of the season, and midges come off both winter and summer.

Steelhead enter the river in June, after a laborious journey up the Columbia. The Corps of Engineers, in its infinite wisdom, ferry steelhead through locks at dams via barge. Not only do a number of wild, streambred steelhead make it back, but also returning are hatchery fish (so designated by the missing adipose fin) and a number of confused steelhead which may be disoriented by the barge ride and think the Deschutes is the Salmon, the Snake, or some other river. While steelhead remain

DESCHUTES RIVER

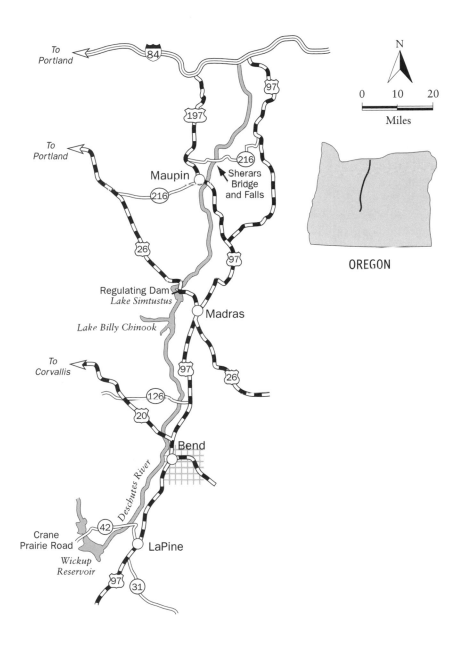

To Portland

84

97

197

To Portland

216

Maupin

Sherars Bridge and Falls

216

26

97

N

0   10   20

Miles

OREGON

Regulating Dam
Lake Simtustus

Lake Billy Chinook

Madras

97

26

To Corvallis

126

20

Bend

Deschutes River

42

Crane Prairie Road

Wickup Reservoir

LaPine

97

31

in the river into December, the prime months are September and October. That's when most anglers hit the river, and there is simply no better time. Rafting, a plague in the summertime, fades on weekdays with the close of the vacation season. High pressure cells keep skies blue, and in the sunlight the contrast between the cool, dark, occasionally olive-tinged river, a thin screen of green brush along the banks, and the reddish yellow-brown of basalt cliffs along the river's course can be absolutely stunning.

Fishing is not good all of the time. How could it be? But the odds of taking steelhead in the Deschutes are probably better than in the Umpqua simply because anglers can work more productive water in a day. Float the river through the canyon below Maupin and look for ideal runs, then beach the boat, climb out, and cast. Wear your waders because fishing from a boat is illegal. From Sherar Falls to Pelton Regulation Dam, only barbless hooked, artificial lures may be used. On the mileage from the falls to the first railroad trestle, bait may be used, but thereafter downstream to the mouth, the artificial-only rule applies. All the favorite steelhead patterns have their advocates here, but there's little to equal the excitement of a 10-pound chromeside smashing a waking Bomber.

The largest town in this neck of the woods is Maupin, about midway between the dam and the river's mouth. There a few tackle shops and bed-and-breakfasts cater to anglers. You'll find motels and restaurants as well. What you won't find is an airport with commercial flights. Your best bet is to fly to Portland, rent a car, and plan to fish the Deschutes for a week.

RESOURCES

Gearing up: Deschutes Canyon Fly Shop, 599 S. Hwy 197, P.O. Box 334, Maupin, OR, 97037; 541-395-2565. Deschutes River Outfitters, 61115 S. Hwy. 97, Bend, OR 97702; 888/315-7272; www.deschutesoutfitter.com.

Accommodations: Maupin Chamber of Commerce, P.O. Box 220, Maupin, OR 97037; 541-395-2599.

Books: *Fishing in Oregon's Deschutes River*, Scott Richmond, Flying Pencil Publications, Scappoose, OR, 1993.

Fishing in Oregon's Best Fly Waters, Scott Richmond, Flying Pencil Publications, Scappoose, OR, 1998.

89 UMPQUA RIVER, NORTH FORK

Location: Southwestern Oregon.
Short take: Zane Grey's favorite river is still the best.
Type of stream: Freestone.
Angling methods: Fly, spin.
Species: Steelhead.
Access: Moderate.
Season: Year-round.
Nearest tourist services: Roseburg.
Handicapped access: Yes.
Closest TU chapter: Middle Rogue Steelhead.

REPORTEDLY ON HIS WAY TO CAMPBELL RIVER to fish for Tyee, Zane Grey paused at the confluence of Canton and Steamboat Creeks, in the then unspoiled watershed of the North Fork of the Umpqua. The year was 1932. Logging had yet to strip towering firs from the high Cascades to the northwest of Crater Lake. Grey and his entourage returned annually, drawn by heavy runs of summer steelhead, the best then, as now, in the continental United States. His camps were spotless and well organized and often equipped with a make-shift fighting chair where he worked out, practicing for his battles with marlin. It was in his camp on this river that he suffered the stroke in 1937 from which he died two years later.

Once ravaged by silty run-off, today the Umpqua is almost the river of the days when Grey fished it. Though lakes have been impounded in its headwaters, the river still flows cold and as green as jade through the black rock canyon where he fished it. Steelhead, fewer now, make annual runs. Summer fish start in June and are in the system until October. The winter run begins in January and reaches its peak in February before tailing off in March. The 32 miles from Rock Creek upstream to Soda Springs Dam is fly-fishing-only, catch-and-release water. Below Rock Creek, general rules apply.

The river is narrow in the mileage upstream from Rock Creek. You might say it flows through a gorge of slab rock, chutes, occasional gravel bars, and runs so deep that, though the water is very clear, you'll never see the bottom. It is good water, ideal for an eight-weight. Most of the year water levels are stable, but in spring and fall rains, or late or early snow can rise the river precipitously. Most of the pressure on the river comes in summer when the steelhead are a little smaller. In summer, approximately 2,400 wild fish and twice that number of stockers are found in the river. But the best fishing is in winter, when gray skies and blustery days drive snow in your eyes as you cast. The steelhead of winter run larger, and anglers are many times fewer. Purists on the river use floating lines with non-weighted flies. Others depend on sinking lines and heavy flies to get down to where big steelhead lie. The patterns that produce fish on the North Fork of the Umpqua are larger by a size or

Umpqua River, North Fork

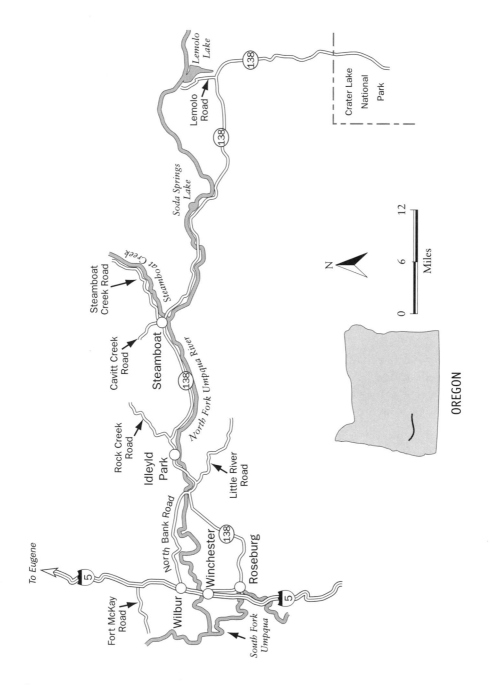

Steamboat Creek was the first tributary of the North Umpqua to capture Zane Grey's imagination.

two than those used on other steelhead rivers. Among favorites are streamers in black, gray, brown and purple; Green Butt Skunk, Muddlers, and the Bucktail Caddis. The best time of the angling day is early morning, after the fish have had a night's rest.

If you fish for summer steelhead, there's a chance that you'll hook a sea-run cutthroat. These must be released immediately. The river is closed to all taking of any kind of trout, a situation that's likely to prevail for the next few years.

Accommodations abound in the valley downstream around Roseburg, a small city a few miles south of the Interstate 5 bridge over the river. And up in the river valley, on the spot where Zane Grey spent his last summer, sits the charming Steamboat Inn. This is the quintessential streamside fishing lodge: gourmet meals, well appointed rooms with porches over looking the river, excellent fishing library, and an excellent tackle shop. The lodge is the focal point for efforts to protect the watershed, and owners Jim and Sharon VanLoan spearhead a worldwide network of activists.

RESOURCES

Gearing up: Blue Heron, 109 Hargis Road, Idleyld, OR 97447; 541-496-0488. Steamboat Inn, 42705 N. Umpqua Hwy., Steamboat, OR 97447; 800-840-8825 (yes this is a lodge but it sells tackle too!).

Accommodations: Roseburg Chamber of Commerce, 4105 SE Spruce St., Roseburg, OR 97470; 541-672-2648.

Books: *Fishing in Oregon's Best Fly Waters*, Scott Richmond, Flying Pencil Publications, Scappose, OR, 1998.

90 WILLIAMSON RIVER

Location: South-central Oregon.
Short take: The river where big 'bows come to chill out. (And so should you.)
Type of stream: Spring-like creek.
Angling methods: Fly, spin.
Species: Rainbow.
Access: Difficult.
Season: May through October.
Nearest tourist services: Chiloquin.
Handicapped access: Yes.
Closest TU chapter: Klamath Basin.

THIS IS THE RIVER THAT YOU HATE TO LOVE. Take a look at it: ledges, choppy riffles, glassy glides, aquatic fronds waving in the current, grassy banks, willows, everything that wonderful water should be. But it is clear air. Trout can see you. They can see your line and leader and tippet. Those with better-than-average vision can probably count the wraps on the head of your fly. You're getting the picture. Long fine tippets. Flies fished delicately, riding high on their hackles, drifting just below the surface, or riding above the substrate. Patience. Have patience.

And what of the trout? Rainbows run up the Williamson from Upper Klamath Lake to spawn. But then the season is closed. The big rainbows—a 20-inch fish won't raise much in the way of congratulations here—slip into the Williamson when summer sun and air temperatures warm the lake to intolerable levels. Evaporation increases its alkalinity. Trout feel stressed and they seek the Williamson's cool waters for relief. They begin moving up into the river in late June or July. That is, if the weather is seasonally hot. With a cool, cloudy summer, they may not move up at all. That leaves anglers three choices: work over the resident population of smaller fish, test the limits of your frustration by trying to find and get a bite out of one of the denizens that lie secure behind that brush tangle under the bank, or pack up your gear and make tracks south to any one of Northern California's spring creeks, which will likely be fishing more charitably.

Most of the best of the Williamson—that section of five miles or so from Chiloquin to below the U.S. Highway 97 bridge—is held privately. Little of the best of the Williamson can be accessed on foot. The most effective technique is to float it, but even then, boat access points are severely limited and most require a fee. That's the price of admission.

Anglers wedded to dry-fly fishing may not be as successful here as those willing to chuck nymphs and other sub-surface patterns. Most effective are streamers such as Woolly Buggers and Zonkers and big nymphs. Fished across and down on a sink-tip line, with a slow pull-and-pause retrieve, these flies can be deadly. Try them also in the subsurface film. The glory hatch must be *Hexagenia limbata* in the mileage

WILLIAMSON RIVER

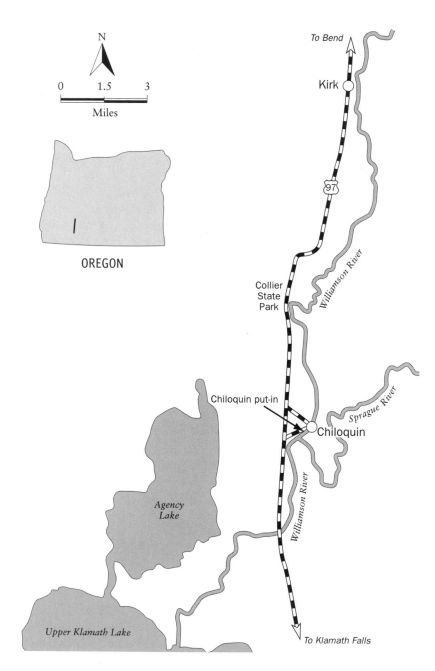

N

0   1.5   3
Miles

OREGON

To Bend

Kirk

97

Williamson River

Collier
State
Park

Chiloquin put-in

Sprague River

Chiloquin

Agency
Lake

Williamson River

Upper Klamath Lake

To Klamath Falls

below Chiloquin. Cast drys or subsurface variations toward the bank. Tricos may do the trick in August and September, but remember that you're fishing a 6X or 7X tippet when you strike a fish that could weigh three or four pounds. *Callibaetis* are prevalent early in the season and again as the season draws to a close. Caddis are numerous on the river, and the big, orange October caddis hatch is a great *finis* to the season. And you don't want to overlook hoppers in August and early September.

The secret to catching fish on the Williamson is to move slowly, fishing each lie thoroughly; too many anglers fish it at a very fast clip. That may work on the Yellowstone, but not here. As demanding as a limestone stream and as difficult as a freestoner with scores of conflicting currents, the Williamson requires your full concentration. If you have only one day to fish the river, good luck. If you have a few days to learn its ways, it will indeed be the toughest river you'll ever love.

RESOURCES

Gearing up: Williamson River Anglers, Junction of Hwys 62 & 97, Chiloquin, OR 97624; 541-783-2677.

Accommodations: Klamath Basin Chamber of Commerce, 701 Plum St., Klamath Falls, OR 97601; 541-884-5193.

Books: *Fishing in Oregon's Best Fly Waters*, Scott Richmond, Flying Pencil Publications, Scappose, OR, 1998.

91 STILLAGUAMISH RIVER

Location: Western Washington.
Short take: A pair of mountain rivers with trout and steelhead.
Type of stream: Freestone.
Angling methods: Fly, spin.
Species: Cutthroat, Dolly Varden, salmon, steelhead.
Access: Moderate.
Season: Year-round.
Nearest tourist services: Seattle.
Handicapped access: No.
Closest TU chapter: Stillaguamish Valley.

IT'S CALLED THE "STILLY" by those who know and love it, this short fork of a river that rises in the Mount Baker National Forest northeast of Seattle. Forming among the ridges and peaks of a band of low mountains dominated by a trio of 5,000 footers, the headwaters of the North Fork of the Stillaguamish follow a route that looks like a question mark with the dot at the point where it leaves the highlands. From there it enters a an ever-broadening valley, picking up tributaries along the way, until it joins the South Fork just above the Washington Route 9 bridge at Arlington. With few meanders, the Stilly then flows west, crossing beneath Interstate 5 and entering Port Susan Bay just north of Warm Beach.

The Stillaguamish is not known as a great trout river, though its sea-run cutthroats have made an amazing recovery. The fame of this fishery is staked to summer and winter runs of steelhead. Winter steelhead enter the system in late November or early December and offer good fishing into April. Good fishing, that is, if you can stand the cold rains, sleet, and snows of a Pacific Northwest winter. Anglers are allowed to fish from boats from the mouth of the river up to the Washington Route 530 bridge at Cicero. Above that point, fishing from floating devices is prohibited. Cicero marks the midpoint in the fly-fishing-only water from the junction of the North and South Forks upstream to Swede Haven. This mileage contains the river's best steelhead water, deep runs with a few submerged boulders, riffles, rapids and pools. Typical steelhead flies—Perils, the Skunks, and Bombers—get results on both wild fish and those that have been stocked. In summer, the steelhead run comes with those balmy days of June and continues through September.

You'll also find chum salmon in the Stilly. Typically, they run in November and December and fishing is permitted up to the river's forks. While fishing for trout is permitted in the lower reaches of the river all year, it's only open from December through February above the Warm Beach-Stanwood Highway. The South Fork of the Stillaguamish has some resident trout, and fishing for them is allowed from June through February as far upstream as Granite Falls, where the Mountain Loop Highway crosses.

STILLAGUAMISH RIVER

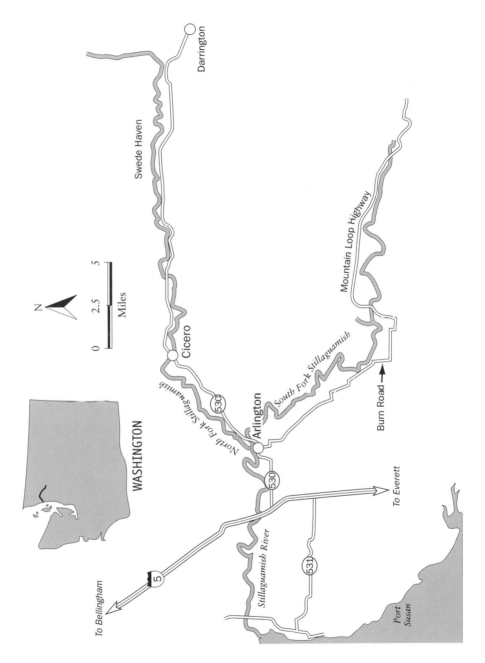

Darrington

Swede Haven

Mountain Loop Highway

South Fork Stillaguamish

Burn Road

Cicero

North Fork Stillaguamish

530

Arlington

530

WASHINGTON

To Bellingham

5

To Everett

Stillaguamish River

531

Port
Susan

N

0   2.5   5
Miles

Is the North Fork of the Stilly a destination river? That's a good question. But with Skagit and Sauk in the neighborhood, an angler could do worse than an early April week in northwest Washington.

RESOURCES

Gearing up: Orvis Seattle, 911 Bellevue Way NE, Bellevue, WA 98004; 425-452-9138. Avid Angler Fly Shoppe, 1174 First Avenue Northeast, Seattle, WA 98125; 206-362-4030.

Accommodations: Snohomish County Visitor's Bureau, 909 SE Everett Mall C-300, Everett, WA 98208; 245-348-5802.

Books: *Steelhead Water,* Bob Arnold, Frank Amato Publications, Portland, OR, 1993.

92 Yakima River

Location: Central Washington.
Short take: Wade in spring and fall, but float all summer.
Type of stream: Freestone.
Angling methods: Fly, spin.
Species: Rainbow, cutthroat.
Access: Easy to moderate.
Season: Year-round.
Nearest tourist services: Yakima, Ellensberg.
Handicapped access: No.
Closest TU chapter: Yakima.

RISING IN THE SNOQUALMIE WILDERNESS, the headwaters of the Yakima are captured in three impoundments—Keechelus, Kachess, and Cle Elum—before being released into the river channel for its run of about 30 miles to Roza Dam. At Roza, deep in the Yakima Gorge, the river's flow is diverted for agricultural use. Just the opposite of most western rivers, the Yakima flows low in the spring and high in summer. Wadeable until early June, the river must be fished from a watercraft (without a motor) until farming needs diminish in the first weeks of September.

While there is some fishing in the tailwaters of each of the three dams, primary trout waters begin where the waters meet up near the town of Cle Elum. Here the river follows a forested course around gravel bars and into pools with some pocket water. It widens and breaks into the open in the farmland around Ellensburg, but at Thrall, the river enters a high canyon. It is not so much that the river drops from a plain into a gorge in the manner of the Colorado at Lees Ferry; rather, a high arid plateau rises on either side of the river. Through the gorge runs Washington Route 821 and, on the other side of the river, the Burlington Northern rail line. In this steep valley, the river retains its primary character, though pocket water and large boulders are more prevalent. Most of the mileage from Yakima to Ellensburg flows through public lands, but upstream of Ellensburg much of the land is private. At Horlick, the river enters a short wooded canyon which opens at Cle Elum.

Despite their unusual nature, flows in the Yakima are consistent enough to generate good hatches. March browns begin to come off from mid-March into June. You'll also find some golden stones, and the first of the caddis that will be on the river until November. Pale morning duns are prevalent from mid-May into mid-July, overlapping with the salmon fly hatch which comes into its own in July. *Baetis* are available spring and fall. In the early part of the year, use #18 to #20 and plan to go one size smaller in the fall. In addition, terrestrials and normal streamers—the Wooly Bugger for instance—work quite well. And midges continue to hatch throughout the winter.

Though quite scenic and with trout averaging 12 to 15 inches, the Yakima could be a destination stream for traveling anglers. More likely though, is the possibility

YAKIMA RIVER

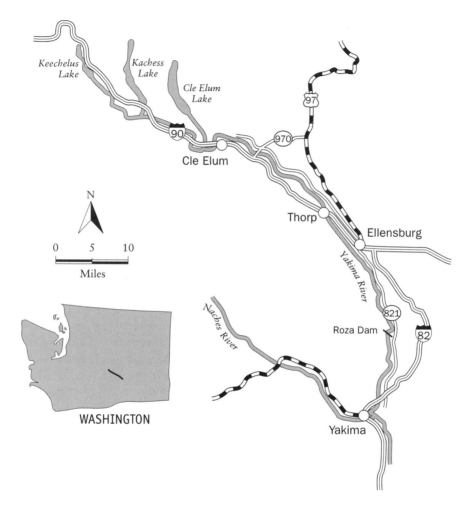

that traveling anglers will fish it when touring in the vicinity of Mount Rainier, Mount St. Helens, and other volcanic peaks of the Cascades. Ellensburg, centrally located at the junction of Interstates 82 and 90, provides a range of accommodations. And the upper reaches of the Yakima are not much more than an hour's drive from Seattle on I-90.

RESOURCES

Gearing up: Gary's Yakima River Fly Shoppe and Outfitters, 1210 W. Lincoln St., Yakima, WA 98902; 509-457-3474.

Accommodations: Yakima Chamber of Commerce, 10 N. 9th St., Yakima, WA 98901; 509-248-2021; www.yakima.org.

SOUTHWEST

CALIFORNIA

CALIFORNIA

93. FALL RIVER
94. HAT CREEK
95. HOT CREEK
96. MCCLOUD RIVER
97. OWENS RIVER
98. SACRAMENTO RIVER
99. SAN JOAQUIN RIVER, MIDDLE FORK
100. SMITH RIVER

93 FALL RIVER

Location: North-central California.
Short take: Clear and cold spring creek with good hatches. You must float; there's no place to wade.
Type of stream: Spring creek.
Angling methods: Fly, spin.
Species: Rainbow.
Access: Difficult.
Season: Late April through November.
Nearest tourist services: Redding, Fall River Mills.
Handicapped access: By boat.
Closest TU chapter: Sierra.

RISING IN THE THOUSAND SPRINGS AREA of Northern California, the Fall River meanders through a broad valley of tawny grassland and pine. To the south and west are a chain of little mountains—Fort, Soldier, Haney—which poke up a couple thousand feet above the valley floor. (These are, indeed, little mountains because Mount Shasta's snow-capped cone towers 10,000 feet above these peaks, dwarfing them and giving them the appearance of mere foothills.) Gradient on the Fall River is not steep; it seems to belie its name except at its junction with the Pit at the town of Fall River Mills.

While the Shasta National Forest comes close to the river, the Fall's actual course runs through private lands and access is severely limited. Even if you could walk to the river, wading would be very difficult. Thick beds of aquatic grasses wave to and fro and the bottom beneath them is soft. Floating, generally in flat-bottomed prams powered by twin electric motors, is the only way to fish the river. Cal Trout maintains a launching ramp with limited parking at the Island Road Bridge, and California Fish and Game has a launch site on Pacific Gas & Electric property where McArthur Road crosses Fall River a couple miles below its confluence with the Tule. Numerous fishing lodges have property on the river. Some, like Rick's Lodge near the headwaters, are full-service and others, such as The Fly Shop's Riverside, are cottages that are rented by the day or longer. All of the lodges provide access to the river.

The upper third of Fall River, the five miles from the springs to Spring Creek bridge, is the only mileage lined with trees. When the river opens in late April, pale morning duns begin to hatch. The hatch improves into late June and then fades only to rise again in late September. Green drakes are plentiful as well. July brings tricos which continue into October. You can find little Blue-Winged Olives most any time on the upper section. Duane Milleman, fly-fishing guru at The Fly Shop in Redding, reports solid midday hatches around Island Road Bridge, even on days when the air temperature passes the century mark.

FALL RIVER

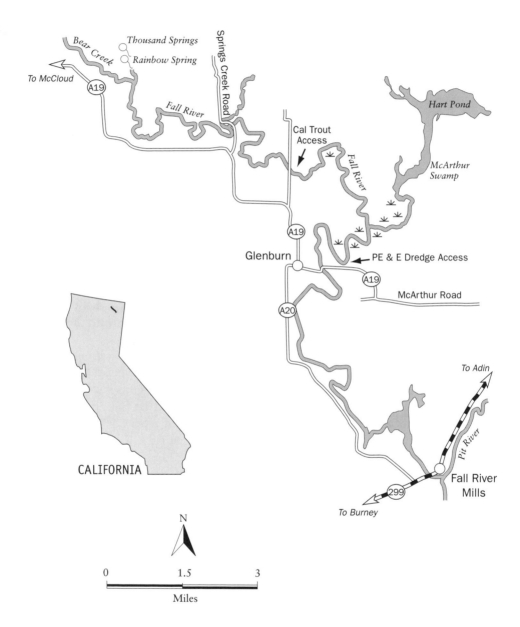

CALIFORNIA

N

0   1.5   3

Miles

On the lower section of the river, downstream from Island Road to the Tule River, you'll find more tan caddis hatches than on the upper section. Anglers fishing caddis dries or pupae are almost guaranteed a fish during those gentle evenings of high summer. On the lower river, from the Tule River to McArthur Road Bridge, *Hexagenia limbata* come off from mid-June through July. Fish nymphs and pupae as the sun sets, and then go dry after dark.

This is rainbow water where fish average 18 inches or so. Water clarity demands long, fine leaders of 5X or 6X and #14 to #20 flies. Often, anglers will have success using a pile cast, dropping a dry a good ways above a trout's feeding station, straightening the leader, and flipping a couple of coils of line out so that the fly and leader can float down to the fish without a drag. The trick is to drift the fly over the fish, but not the fly line, else your fish will vanish. The valley is apt to be windy, so plan on at least a five-weight system.

RESOURCES

Gearing up: The Fly Shop, 4140 Churn Creek Road, Redding, CA 96002; 530-222-3555; www.flyshop.com. Shasta Angler, 43503 Hwy. 299E, Box 430 Fall River Mills, CA 96028; 530-336-6600.

Accommodations: Rick's Lodge, Star Rt. Glenburn, Fall River Mills, CA 96028; 530-336-5300. Fall River Valley Chamber of Commerce, P.O. Box 475, Fall River Mills, CA 96028; 530-336-5840.

Books: *California Blue Ribbon Trout Streams*, Bill Sunderland and Dale Lackey, Frank Amato Publications, Portland, OR 1998.

94 HAT CREEK

Location: Northern California.
Short take: Wild trophy trout waters are both highly technical and suited for novices. Upper reaches offer good put-and-take fishing.
Type of stream: Freestone, then tailwater spring creek.
Angling methods: Fly, spin.
Species: Rainbow, brown.
Access: Easy.
Season: Late April through mid-November.
Nearest tourist services: Hat Creek, Fall River Mills, Burney.
Handicapped access: Yes

RISING ON THE SLOPES OF Lassen Volcanic National Park, Hat Creek is a bustling little freestone stream that hustles down the mountain and breaks into the valley floor below Old Station. There it slows and begins to meander through meadows where livestock, fenced from the creek, graze. Banks are laden with heavy brush, which sweeps the water and provides cover for browns and rainbows. In the upper reaches, Hat Creek is a put-and-take stream, heavily stocked. There is, however, some natural reproduction. Mileage in the park and the abutting Lassen National Forest is open to public angling but once bounded by private land, access becomes limited to guests in the lodges along its course.

Inflows from bubbling springs of the Rising River, which joins Hat Creek just south of Cassel, cools the river to consistent temperatures and changes its nature from a freestone meadow stream to a spring creek. Highly alkaline, the water supports a wealth of aquatic life resulting in myriad hatches and substantial populations of crustacea. Cassel sits astride the creek. Upstream of the town is a long shallow forebay impounding the intake for the Hat #1 generating plant for Pacific Gas & Electric. Open to bait as well as artificial angling, the forebay and Lake Baum below exhibit many of the characteristics of the famed three-mile stretch upstream from Lake Britton. Bait (crickets, night crawlers, salmon eggs) and lure (small minnow-like crank baits, spinners, and spoons) anglers are very successful on the forebay and Lake Baum, and fly anglers who are willing to launch a flat-bottomed boat or raft can do quite well.

But it's the state-designated Trophy Trout mileage below Hat Powerhouse #2 that draws the raves. The first 200 yards below Lake Baum is a classic freestone riffle, a fine piece of easy water that can make any nimrod seem like a pro. Nymphs—Pheasant Tails, beadhead Hare's Ears, or similar—fished close to the bottom of the two to three-foot deep pocket water consistently take fish. A hatch of little yellow stones in June or tricos from July through August will be most productive for dry-fly anglers on the fast water.

HAT CREEK

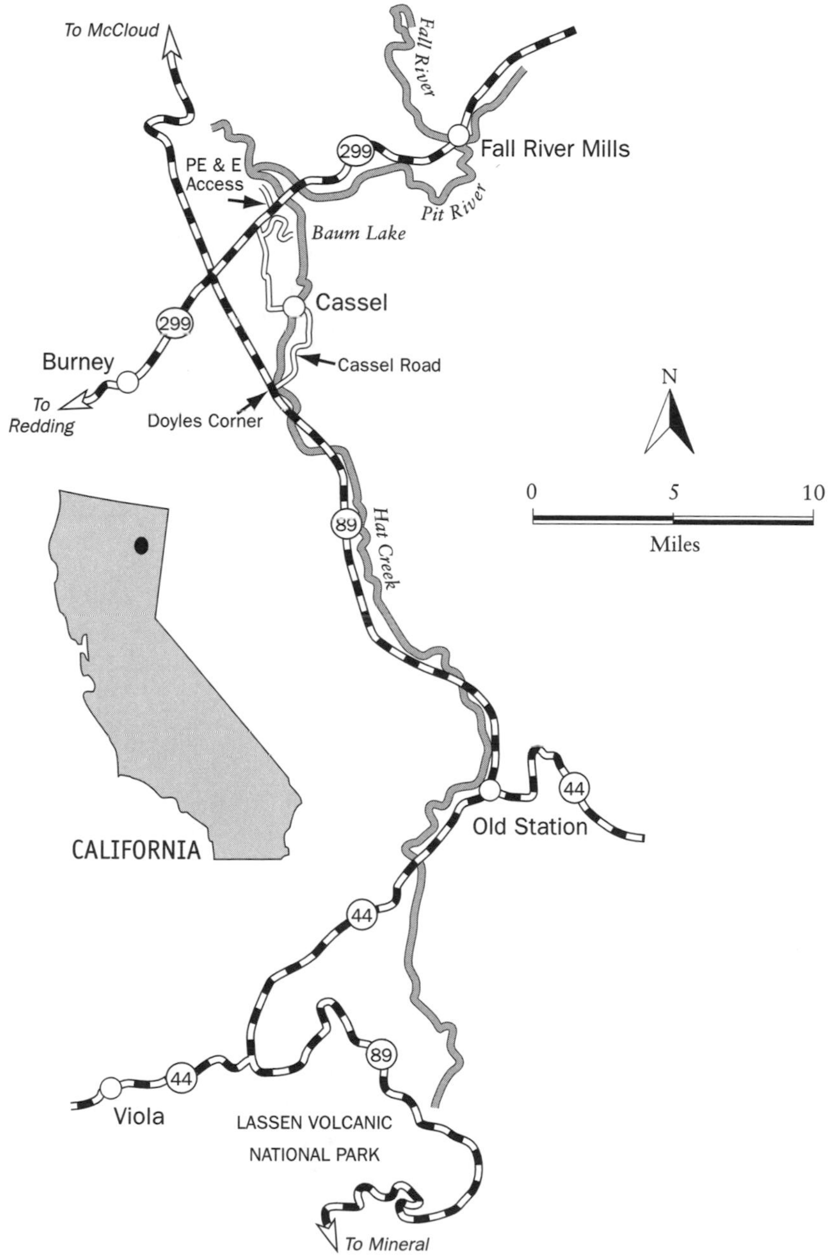

To McCloud

Fall River

PE & E
Access

299

Fall River Mills

Pit River

Baum Lake

Cassel

299

Burney

Cassel Road

To
Redding

Doyles Corner

89

Hat Creek

N

0   5   10

Miles

CALIFORNIA

Old Station

44

44

89

44

Viola

LASSEN VOLCANIC
NATIONAL PARK

To Mineral

The alkaline waters of Hat Creek support prolific insect populations—and the trout that eat them.

After the Powerhouse Riffle, Hat Creek slows and comes into its own. Sandy-bottomed with beds of aquatic mosses and grasses that wave in the steady current, the creek dons the trappings of the quintessential spring creek. Hatches are numerous and often two or three species are coming off at once. The first of the major hatches is the salmon fly which begins with the opening of the season in April and continues into May and sometimes, June. Green drakes appear in May and June. You'll see them on days of wind-driven drizzle. The little sister sledge is also an early hatch that runs into July. As summer advances, smaller mayflies—pale morning and evening duns—draw trout. Tricos reach their peak in midsummer; anglers who master the trico hatch do so with long, 6X or 7X leaders and precise casting. At times a whole day will be virtually devoid of rising fish, only to have all hell break loose right at dusk. Cooling fall weather brings caddis in such numbers (and of such small size) that they're hard to believe.

Below the slick spring creek water is a final mile of deep pools transected by ledge rock. You'll find fewer fish here, but those you encounter will be larger than most others in the creek.

The Trophy Trout section of Hat Creek and, to lesser degree, the three miles above it are some of the most technically challenging water in the West. Floats must be drag free. Successful anglers use presentations that place the fly in the feeding lane well above the trout. The leader and tippet should lie upstream from the fly. And the fly should be lifted off the water before the line puts the trout down. To be consistently successful, you'll need to be able to deliver a fly 50 feet with accuracy and finesse. Nine-foot, three- to five-weight rods allow delicate presentations, yet have ample power to fight 20-inch fish.

Hat Creek's quality is no accident. Thirty years ago, TU's Burney and San Francisco Chapters joined forces with Pacific Gas & Electric and the California Department of Fish and Game to create this trophy trout fishery. It stands as a monument to shared vision and cooperation among anglers, a utility, and state government. Hat Creek will be crowded, that you can bet on. But anglers are developing a kind of etiquette. The old business of two casts' distance between anglers is about right, and asking permission to walk downstream of an angler nymphing in the riffles is *di riguer*. You'll find boats on Baum Lake, but not on the three-mile section of trophy water. The river is too small and too short to make them necessary.

RESOURCES

Gearing up: Vaughn's Sporting Goods, 37307 Main St., Burney, CA 96013; 530-335-2381; e-mail: vaughnfly@sport4u.com; www.vaughnfly.com. Rising River Fly & Tackle, 21549 Cassell Rd., P.O. Box 30, Cassel, CA 96016; 530-335-2291.

Accommodations: Burney Chamber of Commerce, 37088 Main St., P.O. Box 36, Burney, CA 96013; 530-335-2111.

Books: *California Blue Ribbon Trout Streams*, Bill Sunderland and Dale Lackey, Frank Amato Publications, Portland, OR, 1998.

95 HOT CREEK

Location: Eastern California near Mammoth Lakes.
Short take: Not much public water, but what there is can't be beat.
Type of stream: Spring creek.
Angling method: Fly.
Species: Rainbow, browns.
Access: Limited.
Season: Year-round.
Nearest tourist services: Mammoth Lakes.
Handicapped access: None.
Closest TU chapter: Mammoth Flyrodders.

HOT CREEK IS APTLY NAMED. It's not just the quality of the fish, a multitude of browns and rainbows of 14 inches-plus, but cold runoff from the high mountains around Mammoth is tempered and enriched by seeps from scores of geothermal springs. The creek rises in a little valley across the ridge from Antelope Springs. It follows a weedy channel for more than two miles before it is joined by the waters of Mammoth Creek, itself something of a trout stream. Hot Creek then courses past a hatchery, runs through a short stretch of meander, and enters Hot Creek Ranch, a fly-fishing ranch with miles of prime (and private) dry-fly water.

Below the ranch are two miles of creek that are open to the public but restricted to catch-and-release fly-fishing only. For the first half mile or so, the upper section maintains the character of the ranch. Tight meanders snake through a broad, grassy valley, but soon the ground begins to fall to the east as the stream enters a gentle canyon containing a mile-and-a-half of fishable water. Composed of weathered volcanic rock, the sides of the canyon are initially steep. The floor of the canyon is grassy, and a well trodden footpath follows the river, which has gained velocity. Riffles break sleek runs, and here and there are submerged boulders that provide some structure. You won't find any pocket water or plunge pools in this mileage, just gentle curves heavy with aquatic grasses streaming in the current. The vegetation, undercut banks, and an occasional block of rock provide cover for big 'bows. For the angler, there is none. No trees, no bushes, not even any high grass. Stealth, delicate presentations of dries, precise casts to rising fish, these are the harbingers of success on Hot Creek. But as the day lengthens, mountain winds gather intensity; by mid-afternoon, the 3-weight with which you started has given way to a 5 or 6. Runoff raises water in Hot Creek from late May through June. Plan to fish earlier or later in the season.

The most productive fly on Hot Creek is probably a #18 Blue-Winged Olive, followed by similarly sized Hot Creek Caddis, CDC Caddis, and the Olive Cripple. While nymphing is a no-no on the ranch, no one will throw you off the public section if you're tossing Pheasant Tails with or without Beadheads in sizes #16 and #18. While

HOT CREEK

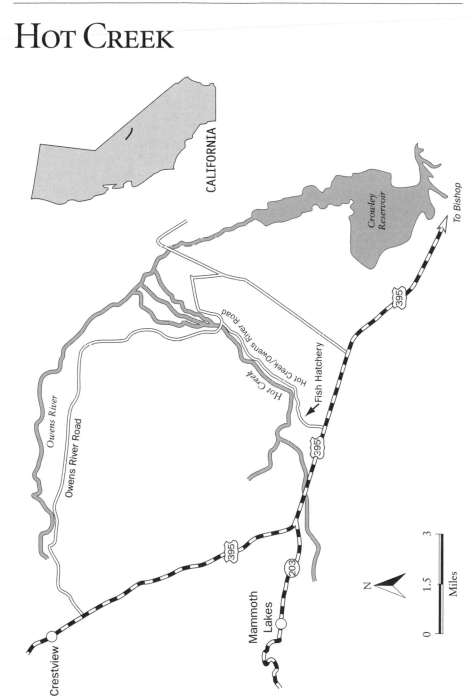

CALIFORNIA

Crowley Reservoir

To Bishop

395

Fish Hatchery

Hot Creek/Owens River Road

Hot Creek

Owens River

Owens River Road

395

395

203

Mammoth Lakes

Crestview

N

0   1.5   3

Miles

small flies carry the day here, too many anglers overlook Olive or Black Woolly Buggers in sizes as large as a #4. Fished upstream and worked through structure just fast enough to keep them above the weeds, this old standby can fool good trout. But you have to be on your toes, for these well educated fish spit out flies as soon as they taste them.

Running a hundred or so yards south of the creek, but following its course, is Owens River Road. Along it are a number of turn-outs from the first parking area close to the top of the public water to the last, where bathers seeking respite in the soothing waters of the hot spring often park. Each of these little side roads leads to a path that slips down the gentle canyon side to the flat valley of the creek. The stream is almost always crowded, but somehow there always seems to be room for one more. If you fly into this area, you'll get a good look at Hot Creek while your plane lands at Mammoth Lakes Airport, roughly a mile-and-a-half south of the river.

RESOURCES

Gearing up: Kittredge Sports, 3218 Main St., Mammoth Lakes, CA 93546; 760-934-7566. The Trout Fly, P.O. Box 7819, Gateway Center Mall, Mammoth Lakes, CA 93546; 760-934-2517. Trout Fitters, Shell Mart Center, Mammoth Lakes, CA 93546; 760-924-3676.

Accommodations: Mammoth Lakes Chamber of Commerce, Box 123, Mammoth Lakes, CA 93546; 760-934-2712.

Books: *California Blue Ribbon Trout Streams*, Bill Sunderland and Dale Lackey, Frank Amato Publications, Portland, OR, 1998.

Flyfisher's Guide to Northern California, Seth Norman, Wilderness Adventure Press, Gallatin Gateway, MT, 1997.

96 McCloud River

Location: North-central California.
Short take: California's premier trout fishery. The Nature Conservancy water offers the best bet.
Type of stream: Freestone above the dam, tailwater below.
Angling methods: Fly, spin, bait.
Species: Rainbow, brown.
Access: Moderate.
Season: Late April through mid-November.
Nearest tourist services: Lodges and tackleshops.
Handicapped access: Yes.
Closest TU chapter: Redding Red Bluff.

MOST OF US HAVE CAUGHT McCLOUD TROUT, only we don't know it. This river, which along with the Sacramento, Squaw, and Pit, feeds Lake Shasta, was the source of those initial rainbow eggs that were gathered in 1874 and shipped to the East and Midwest. Raised in hatcheries, the resulting fish provided the breeding stock that introduced rainbow trout to anglers who knew only feisty native brookies. In return the McCloud received immigrant browns before the turn of the last century, and it's this combination of big browns and rainbows, along with spectacularly wooded canyon water, that makes the McCloud so special.

Rising in Dead Horse Canyon, the McCloud flows for about 56 miles before reaching Lake Shasta. In the 1960s, a reservoir impounded the river about 30 miles downstream from its headwaters. As is typical of dams, this one is both blessing and curse. It provides cool, clear, and stable flows for about 20 miles of glorious water, the mileage that everyone dreams about when they think of McCloud River trout. The impoundment traps much of the glacial sediment which would otherwise silt the river when the snows of Mount Shasta, at 14,000 feet, begin to melt in July. And it provides a haven for big browns and rainbows, which enter the upper river to spawn in winter and spring. Unfortunately, the dam diverts much of the flow into the Pit River in the next watershed to the east and the result has been low flows that have brought to virtual extinction one of the southernmost populations of Dolly Varden in the United States.

For 30 miles above McCloud Reservoir, the river is a classic freestone stream. Much of the river is shadowed by the McCloud Loop Road, and California Highway 89 generally runs along its course. At Algoma, the uppermost access, the river is not much wider than a healthy hop. The California Department of Fish and Game, in an attempt to encourage native populations of Red Band rainbows, is only stocking brook trout above Middle Falls. Fishing pressure is heavy as it is on sections immediately below Four-Mile Flat and Skunk Hollow. The eastern terminus of the loop road begins at Cattle Camp. The large pool here marks the start of some of the best public fishing on the upper river. While you may encounter some small wild fish, in

McCloud River

the main brook trout are of the put-and-take persuasion. Below 40-foot Middle Falls, and at the plunge pool below Lower Falls, 8- to 14-inch rainbows are released. Here the Loop Road circles back to CA 89, and downstream the river soon enters the Hearst estate, which is closed to public angling all the way to the reservoir.

The dam on the reservoir spills water into the lower river at a rate of 150 to 220 cfs. Heavily shaded, the river works through hefty boulders of basalt creating deep pockets and runs that hold trout. From the dam downstream about five miles to

Ladybug Creek, the river runs through Shasta National Forest and the road to Ah Di Na campground puts you in the middle of this fine stretch of public water. Below are several miles of Nature Conservancy water. The upper three miles are open only to ten rods per day. Reservations can be made up to two weeks in advance by calling 415-777-0487. Five rods are reserved in advance and five are open on a first come, first served basis. Fishing generally does not begin until 7:30 A.M. and closes at sunset. Because of restricted access, this is arguably the best public section of the river. Below a section of a few miles where no fishing is permitted, the stream is in private hands of the McCloud River Club and Bolli Bokka Club. The latter rents a few lavish, yet rustic furnished camps and provides guide service on the river upstream from Shasta Lake.

The McCloud is most productively fished with nymphs, and angling is quite technical. The most effective strategy is to dead-drift nymphs through three zones in the flow: the upper zone to seduce trout that may come up aggressively, a mid-zone for those not so eager, and then the bottom where most of the biggest trout lie. Dick Galland, who's fished this river for decades, recommends a four- or five-weight rod loaded with the next heaviest double-taper line. Leaders and tippets should match water depth, velocity, and fly size. Among the most effective nymph patterns are: Black Rubberlegs, Golden Stones, October Caddis, Prince and PTs. He also recommends Woolly Buggers, Marabou Leeches, and Woolhead Sculpins. Dry flies take a back seat here, but May brings good hatches of golden stone and salmon flies. The little yellow stone is consistent from June through September when October caddis come in. You'll also encounter PMDs and green drakes early in the season and blue-winged olives in the fall. Midges hatch throughout the season.

Something of a seasonal river, the McCloud fishes well in May and June, before being discolored by glacial melt. (Some anglers believe that when the river runs a chalky green, trout are less wary and more apt to take artificials, and indeed such has proven to be the case.) But the best action occurs in October and November, when large lake-run browns move into the river to spawn. Fishing pressure picks up then as well, but the public water in the canyons of the McCloud is not easily fished and to reach the best water, one must clamber or over rocks and remain ever cautious of rattlesnakes. Needless to say, the number of anglers declines rapidly as distance from parking lots increases.

RESOURCES

Gearing up: Mitchell Barrett, Redsides McCloud, 110 Squaw Valley Rd., P.O. Box 69, McCloud, CA 96057; 530-964-2044. Dick Galland, Clearwater House, P.O. Box 90, Cassel, CA 96016; 916-335-5500.

Accommodations: McCloud Chamber of Commerce, P.O. Box 372, McCloud, CA 96057; 877-964-3113; www.mtshasta.com/mccloud/mccloud.html.

Books: *California Blue-Ribbon Trout Streams,* Bill Sanderland and Dale Lackey, Frank Amato Publications, Portland, OR, 1998.

The Fly Fishing Guide to Northern California, Wilderness Adventure Press, Gallatin Gateway, MT, 1997.

97 OWENS RIVER

Location: East-central California.
Short take: Two big runs of spawners on the upper mileage and lots of greedy juveniles in the lower gorge make this as fine a piece of trout water as there is in California.
Type of stream: Spring creek, tailwater.
Angling methods: Fly, spin.
Species: Brown, rainbow.
Access: Moderate.
Season: Late April through mid-November; gorge is open all year.
Nearest tourist services: Mammoth.
Handicapped access: Yes.
Closest TU chapter: Mammoth Flyrodders.

LIKE SO MANY STREAMS, there's a big difference whether you're above or below. Above Crowley Lake, the Owens is one kind of river, a gentle stream that meanders through a wide and shallow glacial valley between mountains that brush 9,000 feet or more. Below Crowley Lake is the 16-mile gorge, one of the greatest restoration projects in the annals of coldwater fisheries.

Some history: In 1913, the first Los Angeles aqueduct diverted water from the Owens River to the city some 300 miles to the south. Forty years later, the water from the gorge section—a 3,000 foot drop in 20 miles—was diverted into penstocks to generate power leaving thousands of brown trout to suffocate in pools of stagnant water. Three decades later in 1985, John Sullivan, a TU member who remembered the gorge in its days as wild trout fishery, wrote an opinion piece for the *Los Angeles Times* calling for the rewatering of the gorge. The work of scores of volunteers was rewarded in 1991 when water, albeit a mere trickle, began again to flow into the channel of the gorge.

Plunging from one pocket to another down a very steep gradient with a flow of something less than 90 cfs, the gorge section is little, but good, water. Brown trout in the 8- to 10-inch class pack the river, feeding on steady hatches of mayflies and caddis. Midge and *baetis* hatches are good all winter. Nymphing is not necessary. Trout readily rise to duns, spinners, and emergers in the surface film. The full course of the gorge is accessible, but only by foot. Parking exists near each of the three powerhouses on the section. Trails descend the 300 feet from the flat top of the canyon to stream level. At the base of the gorge, the Owens tails out into Pleasant Valley Lake where the water rapidly warms and becomes habitat for bass.

No doubt about it, return of water to the Owens River Gorge is a stunning victory for trouters. Yet the river above Crowley Lake has also benefited from the work of TU volunteers. Repair of riparian habitat and fencing are stabilizing habitat for resident browns and big spawners that run up the river from the lake. Rising in Big Springs, the upper mileage of the river is, indeed, a spring creek. Save the few weeks

OWENS RIVER

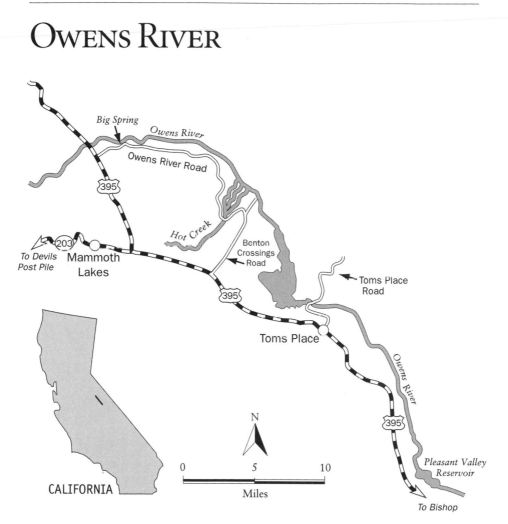

Big Spring

Owens River

Owens River Road

395

Hot Creek

To Devils
Post Pile

203

Mammoth
Lakes

Benton
Crossings
Road

Toms Place
Road

395

Toms Place

Owens River

395

CALIFORNIA

N

0   5   10

Miles

Pleasant Valley
Reservoir

To Bishop

of spring snow-melt in late May and June, this section of the river sees consistent flows throughout the year. Alpers Owens River Ranch, which rents cottages, and the former Arcularius which, now under new ownership, does not, controls access to about six and a half miles of the river. Below the posted land, the river runs a few miles to the lake and this section includes the mouth of another of California's stellar fisheries, Hot Creek.

Before the start of the fishing season in late April, spawning rainbows run up from Crowley into the Upper Owens, and other rainbows and browns come up to spawn in the fall. You can see them on their redds. Some of the veteran anglers who've worked this water for decades are content to give spawning fish a pass. Spring fishing is largely a matter of working nymphs—Gold-ribbed Hare's Ear and Pheasant

C. LARRY PROSOR

Peaks scratching 9,000 feet stand sentinel over the meadows of the Upper Owens River valley.

Tails are favorites—and streamers, such as a peacock and black Woolly Buggers. Toward the end of May or early June, spawners have begun to move back down the river to the lake. Dry-fly action, largely caddis with some mayflies, heats up in early July, but fish tend to be much smaller, averaging 10 to 12 inches during the height of summer. Terrestrials are very effective in the meadow section. When autumn comes, brood fish return to the river. Fish big Matukas and Woolly Buggers, and tighten your Gore-Tex against blowing drizzle and snow. Winter comes early to this valley in the high Sierra.

RESOURCES

Gearing up: The Trout Fly, P.O. Box 7819, Gateway Center Mall, Mammoth Lakes, CA 93546; 760-934-2517. Kittredge Sports, 3218 Main St., Mammoth Lakes, CA 93546; 760-934-7566. Trout Fitters, Shell Mart Center, Mammoth Lakes, CA 93546; 760-924-3676.

Accommodations: Mammoth Lakes Visitors Bureau, P.O. Box 48, Mammoth Lakes, CA 93546; 888-466-2666; www.visitmammoth.com.

Books: *Flyfisher's Guide to Northern California*, Seth Norman, Wilderness Adventure Press, Gallatin Gateway, MT, 1997.

California Blue Ribbon Trout Streams, Bill Sunderland and Dale Lackey, Frank Amato Publications, Portland, OR, 1998.

98 SACRAMENTO RIVER

Location: Northern California, at the head of Lake Shasta.
Short take: Thirty-five miles of outstanding trout water, easily accessible from Interstate 5 and the railroad grade that follow the river.
Type of stream: Freestone.
Angling methods: Fly, spin, bait.
Species: Rainbow.
Access: Easy and ample.
Season: Late April through mid-November.
Nearest tourist services: Dunsmuir.
Handicapped access: None.
Closest TU chapter: Redding, Red Bluff.

RAILROADS FOLLOW THE RIVER. So it is with the 35-mile stretch of the Upper Sacramento between Lakehead and Cantara. Here, the Upper Sac tumbles through a canyon and down a boulder strewn course, ever widening and smoothing into riffles and runs as it gathers strength from numerous creeks: Soda, Castle, Flume, Shotgun, Slate, and Dog. The Union Pacific's main north-south line runs along the river's course as does Interstate 5, yet the pounding of train and truck traffic is muted by aspens, pine, and spruce along the river's course.

Before 1991, angling here, whether with fly, spinner, or bait, for rainbows and browns was among the finest in the West. But a derailment at Cantara Loop just above Dunsmuir pitched a tank car loaded with 13,000 gallons of the pesticide metam-sodium into the river. Leaking chemicals poisoned the stream, killing a million fish and virtually all other aquatic life. There were doubts that the river would ever return to its former prominence. Yet, California Game and Fish officials decided to eschew heavy stocking, preferring that the river heal itself. And it has.

By 1995 the population of trout, largely rainbows that have migrated up from Lake Shasta below Lakehead, reached more than 4,000 per mile, where it seems to have plateaued.

The Sacramento drains Mount Shasta and neighboring peaks. Early in the season, from April into May, the river is fishable with conventional fly and spinning tackle. But in mid- to late May the river begins to rise with snow melt from the mountains and it is generally difficult to fish into June. Then, levels lower and the river becomes a paradise. During the warmer months of July and early August, fishing slows with rising water temperatures. It is best, then, from Mossbrae Falls, a veil of spring seeps that plunge into the river a mile and a half upstream from the bridge at Shasta Retreat, to Cantara. Most fish run between 9 and 14 inches, but 20-inch rainbows are not uncommon. Revered for their scorching runs, these rainbows, it is believed, are genetically linked to steelhead that ran this river system before the construction of Lake Shasta Dam in the late 1930s and early 40s.

SACRAMENTO RIVER

The mileage from Soda Creek (Exit 726) upstream to Scarlet Way Bridge, near but not at Exit 733, is stocked and anglers may retain fish. Otherwise, the Upper Sac is an artificial-lure, catch-and-release river. Spin anglers will find that Mepps, Panther Martins, Rooster Tails and similar spinners, fished slowly so blades flutter rather than spin along the bottom, will be very successful. Larger, heavier lures work better in periods of high flow. It's important to get down to where the fish lie.

Fly fishers tend to use weighted stonefly nymphs, fished with strike indicators, early in the season. Also Bird's Nest, Hare's Ear, Prince, Pheasant Tail and variations of beadheaded caddis pupae and larvae bring success. Caddis is the primary fly in this system. When water is warm, fish morning and evening with black or elk-hair patterns in sizes from #16 to #22. June sees hatches of green drakes and salmon flies as well as some pink cahills. Blue-Winged Olives come off when the water cools in September and you'll find midges all season. While fishing slows during the middle of the day, stimulators and similar patterns can draw strikes when fished blindly in the riffles of the lower section, and don't overlook terrestrials—hoppers, ants, crickets and similar fodder. A four- or five-weight rod with weight forward floating line is ample for the Upper Sac. And in the narrow water of Soda Creek, an ability to roll cast will aid anglers confronted with brushy banks.

Access to the river is more than ample. Every two or three miles along I-5 from Lakehead to Azalea, a hamlet near Lake Siskiyou above Dunsmuir, there's an exit. Side roads either cross the railroad leading to private retreat developments or stop at the tracks. Anglers park outside gates (they may be open when you arrive, but padlocked when you're ready to leave) and walk in. A stroll of half a mile or so from the parking area will take you away from most other anglers. Campers will enjoy sites at Castle Crag State Park and at Sims Road, about eight miles downstream. Fly and tackle shops as well as motels, restaurants, banks, and retail stores are all handy in Dunsmuir.

RESOURCES

Gearing up: Ted Fay Fly Shop, 4310 Dunsmuir Ave., Dunsmuir, CA 96025; 530-235-2969. Dunsmuir Flyfishing Co., 5839 Dunsmuir Ave., Dunsmuir, CA 96025; 530-235-0705.

Accommodations: Dunsmuir Chamber of Commerce, P.O. Box 17, Dunsmuir, CA 96025; 800-386-7684.

Books: *California Blue Ribbon Trout Streams*, Bill Sunderland and Dale Lackey, Frank Amato Publications, Portland, OR, 1998.

Flyfisher's Guide to Northern California, Seth Norman, Wilderness Adventure Press, Gallatin Gateway, MT, 1997.

99 SAN JOAQUIN RIVER, MIDDLE FORK

Location: Eastern California, across the mountains from Mammoth Lakes.
Short take: Two wild trout fisheries, split by the put-and-take waters around the Devil's Postpile.
Type of stream: Freestone.
Angling methods: Fly, spin.
Species: Rainbow, brown, brook, golden, rainbow/golden hybrid.
Access: Easy to extremely difficult.
Season: Late April through October.
Nearest tourist services: Tackle shops, accommodations in Mammoth Lakes.
Handicapped access: None.
Closest TU chapter: Mammoth Flyrodders.

CALIFORNIA WEARS ITS GEOLOGY ON ITS SLEEVE. If you don't agree, just have a look at Yosemite or to the south and a little west, the Devil's Postpile. This textbook example of pipe-like stems of basalt towers over the upper reaches of the Middle Fork of the San Joaquin, one of fewer than three dozen designated wild trout waters in the state. Access to this section of the river is quite limited. Winding up from Mammoth Lakes, Postpile Road swings south of 9,200-foot Minaret Summit before turning north to the cutoff that leads to Agnew Meadows. Continuing to descend, the one-lane road with turn-outs passes campgrounds at Soda Creek, Pumice Flats, and Minaret before breaking east around the Postpile and the parking at Reds Meadow. This road is closed to entering private vehicles from 7:30 A.M. (more or less) to 5:30 P.M. If you plan to fish, and want to drive in, get there early. You can leave whenever you wish. Otherwise, you'll have to use the shuttle bus which leaves from the gate below Minaret Summit.

Once you've transported yourself into this wilderness, what do you find? Rainbows, brookies, browns, goldens, and that hybrid rainbow/golden with flanks as orange as flame azalea and bellies to match. The river along the three campgrounds is heavily stocked with rainbows. This stretch of two miles is essentially tumbling pocket water. Above Soda Springs Campground begins four miles of Wild Trout water that runs up to the outflow of Shadow Lake. And good fishing extends another four miles or so to the headwaters of the Middle Fork in Thousand Island Lake. You'll have to walk in on the anglers' trail that departs from Agnew Meadows. A twenty minute walk, about a mile, will get you above most other rod wielders. From there you'll work plunge cascades, plunge pools, and riffles through the alders in between. The river is not large here and trout are not particularly wary. In fact, a #14 caddis or a tiny Panther Martin will catch fish all day. A big rainbow will run 15 inches, but most are in the 10-inch class.

SAN JOAQUIN RIVER, MIDDLE FORK

Shadow
Lake

Rosalie
Lake

Agnew
Meadows

Soda Creek Campground
Pumice Flat
Minaret Falls

Devils Postpile

Rods
Meadows

Rainbow Falls
Lower Rainbow Falls

Mammoth
Lakes

Minaret Summit Road

Middle Fork San Joaquin River

Miller
Crossing

Minards Road

To Oakhurst

N

0   1.5   3

Miles

CALIFORNIA

Wild trout water picks up again at the northern boundary of Devil's Postpile National Monument and continues for about three miles to Lower Rainbow Falls. The first section of this was burned in the late '80s and lacks shade. Cover for fish is not as great as it is lower down the river. Hike through this land where lodgepole pines are just about as tall as you are and head for the timber that shields the river from the sun. There, you'll pick up bigger fish; 10- to 12-inchers are more common, and the angler who invests the hours can net all five species, a grand slam in this neck of the woods. A fairly passable trail leads to Rainbow Falls, and a half-mile further, to the lower falls. Below the falls, the trail peters out, but the fishing improves. With few trails crossing the river and no campgrounds on its banks, the river becomes the province of those few anglers willing to bushwhack to backcountry trout.

High run-off, as you would suspect, plagues the Middle Fork into late June, and in some years, mid-July. Then water begins to recede and the fishing picks up. Despite the low flows of fall, fishing in September and October can be glorious. Hatches on the river are not particularly consistent. Fly boxes should contain Elk Hair Caddis, Royal Wulffs, Humpies, PMDs, Light Cahills, and a few Green Drakes in case you happen to hit that one day of the year when it's drizzly and they decide to come off. Blue-Winged Olives work in the fall. Peacock Hurl nymphs, beadheads of various descriptions, Flash-back and Pheasant Tails all take their share of fish.

Mammoth Lakes is headquarters for fishing this neck of the woods and that, of course, puts you in the catbird seat for a shot at the Owens and Hot Creek. Can you think of a better place to hear September's song?

RESOURCES

Gearing up: The Trout Fly, P.O. Box 7819, Gateway Center Mall, Mammoth Lakes, CA 93546; 760-934-2517. Kittredge Sports, 3218 Main St., Mammoth Lakes, CA 93546; 760-934-7566. Trout Fitters, Shell Mart Center, Mammoth Lakes, CA 93546; 760-924-3676.

Accommodations: Mammoth Lakes Chamber of Commerce, Box 123, Mammoth Lakes, CA 93546; 760-934-2712.

Books: *Flyfisher's Guide to Northern California*, Seth Norman, Wilderness Adventure Press, Gallatin Gateway, MT, 1997.

100 SMITH RIVER

Location: Northernmost coastal river in California.
Short take: Premier chinook fishery, also known for great steelhead, but upper reaches are difficult to access.
Type of stream: Freestone/tidal estuary.
Angling methods: Bait, spin, fly.
Species: Chinook, steelhead, cutthroat.
Access: Moderate to difficult.
Season: October through March.
Nearest tourist services: Tackle shops, motels.
Handicapped access: By boat.

RISING IN THE SISKIYOU MOUNTAINS, a finger of the Coast Range, the Smith River is California's longest undammed river. Its drainage covers more than 325 miles, though only the lower reaches—the 15 miles or so from the estuary to the junction of the Smith's Middle and South Forks, and about 15 miles up each of those forks—are considered prime fisheries. The river sees some of the finest runs of chinook salmon and steelhead (state records for both came from the Smith) in the country, and it's also home to cutthroat, some of which reside in the river year-round while others run to salt. Once heavily logged, most of the watershed is made up of parks: The Smith River National Recreation Area to the north, Six Rivers National Forest to the south, and the Jedediah Smith and Del Norte State Parks in between. Magnificent redwoods, sitka spruce, giant rose-bay rhododendron, and lush ferns frame the rivers.

About half-a-mile south of the junction of County Road 427 and U.S. Highway 199, the South and Middle Forks of the Smith merge. Float trips begin here in September through December for chinook and in December through March for steelhead. Similar tactics are used for both species in this section. Roe, perhaps with a bit of bright red or orange yarn tied to the hook as an attractor, cast with enough weight (3/8 to 1 ounce) to get it to the bottom is the most commonly used strategy. Back trolling small Wiggle Warts, Hot Shots, and similar plugs in black, blue, red, and green with silver or gold bellies is also effective. Fly fishing is difficult in this stretch; it's hard to work a fly down where the fish lie.

But the two forks of the river are another matter indeed. From the confluence with Patrick Creek west to the confluence with the South Fork, the Middle Fork flows through a series of runs, plunges, and pools only to run and plunge again. US 199 follows the Middle Fork closely. Drive the route, look for water that suits you, find a pull-off and fish. Access to the South Fork is a bit more difficult. While South Fork Road (CR 427) runs along the river, the stream itself flows through a gorge which you'll have to scramble down if you wish to fish it. You'll find more pocket water and fewer cascades and pools than on the Middle Fork. Good salmon flies for

SMITH RIVER

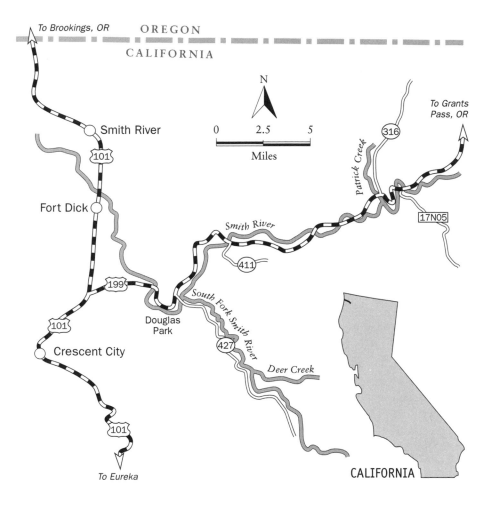

both forks include the Golden Goose, Green Goose, and Boss. Steelhead seem to favor such ties as the Purple Peril, Silver Hilton, and Limey early in the season with Polar Shrimp, General Practitioner, Brad's Brat, and Popcicles doing better later. Cutthroats from 8 to 17 inches are also found in these waters, but numbers are not as high as other inland streams. They provide better sport in summer than in winter, but then they and all other fish must be released immediately and unharmed. The summer closure is designed to protect steelhead and salmon smolts that are working their way downriver to the sea.

The best salmon and steelhead fishing comes when the river is running low and clear. That's a challenge on the Smith. Winter rains provide the spates of fresh water that draw salmon and steelhead up into the system. And the Smith fishes poorly when water is high and discolored. Successful anglers try to time their journeys to the watershed for two or three days after a good rain. Weather and water reports are available from Ed Moon at Smith River Outfitters. Accommodations are available in Crescent City and the closest major airport is in Eureka, about 75 miles south.

RESOURCES

Gearing up: Smith River Outfitters, P.O. Box 830, Smith River, CA 95567; 707-487-0935.

Accommodations: Crescent City/Del Norte County Chamber of Commerce, 1001 Front Street, Crescent City, CA 95531; 707-464-3174.

Other information: Smith River National Recreation Area, U.S. Highway 199, P.O. Box 288, Gasquet, CA 95543 707-457-3131.

Books: *California's Smith River,* George Bundick, Frank Amato Publications, Portland, OR, 1993.

INDEX

Page numbers in **bold** refer to maps.

ABOUT THE AUTHOR

Raised in the valleys beneath the Great Smokies, John Ross acquired a rod and reel from his granddad and has wandered trout streams ever since. He is the author of several sporting travel books including the *Sports Afield Guide to North America's Greatest Fishing Lodges* and is travel columnist for *Sporting Classics* magazine. He lives with his wife Katie and their little brown spaniel in Upperville, Virginia, near a nameless spring creek that holds a growing population of wild trout and a few wood ducks.

FALCON GUIDES ® Leading the Way™

HIKING GUIDES

Best Hikes Along the Continental Divide
Hiking Alaska
Hiking Arizona
Hiking Arizona's Cactus Country
Hiking the Beartooths
Hiking Big Bend National Park
Hiking the Bob Marshall Country
Hiking California
Hiking California's Desert Parks
Hiking Carlsbad Caverns
  and Guadalupe Mtns. National Parks
Hiking Colorado
Hiking Colorado, Vol. II
Hiking Colorado's Summits
Hiking Colorado's Weminuche Wilderness
Hiking the Columbia River Gorge
Hiking Florida
Hiking Georgia
Hiking Glacier & Waterton Lakes National Parks
Hiking Grand Canyon National Park
Hiking Grand Staircase-Escalante/Glen Canyon
Hiking Grand Teton National Park
Hiking Great Basin National Park
Hiking Hot Springs in the Pacific Northwest
Hiking Idaho
Hiking Maine
Hiking Michigan
Hiking Minnesota
Hiking Montana
Hiking Mount Rainier National Park
Hiking Mount St. Helens
Hiking Nevada

Hiking New Hampshire
Hiking New Mexico
Hiking New York
Hiking the North Cascades
Hiking Northern Arizona
Hiking Olympic National Park
Hiking Oregon
Hiking Oregon's Eagle Cap Wilderness
Hiking Oregon's Mount Hood/Badger Creek
Hiking Oregon's Three Sisters Country
Hiking Pennsylvania
Hiking Shenandoah
Hiking the Sierra Nevada
Hiking South Carolina
Hiking South Dakota's Black Hills Country
Hiking Southern New England
Hiking Tennessee
Hiking Texas
Hiking Utah
Hiking Utah's Summits
Hiking Vermont
Hiking Virginia
Hiking Washington
Hiking Wisconsin
Hiking Wyoming
Hiking Wyoming's Cloud Peak Wilderness
Hiking Wyoming's Wind River Range
Hiking Yellowstone National Park
Hiking Zion & Bryce Canyon National Parks
Wild Montana
Wild Country Companion
Wild Utah

■ *To order any of these books, check with your local bookseller
or call FALCON ® at **1-800-582-2665**.
Visit us on the world wide web at:
www.FalconOutdoors.com*

FALCON®

Discover the Thrill of Watching Wildlife.

The Watchable Wildlife® Series

Published in cooperation with Defenders of Wildlife, these high-quality, full color guidebooks feature detailed descriptions, side trips, viewing tips, and easy-to-follow maps. Wildlife viewing guides for the following states are now available with more on the way.

Alaska	Massachusetts	Oregon
Arizona	Montana	Puerto Rico &
California	Nebraska	Virgin Islands
Colorado	Nevada	Tennessee
Florida	New Hampshire	Texas
Idaho	New Jersey	Utah
Indiana	New Mexico	Vermont
Iowa	New York	Virginia
Kentucky	North Carolina	Washington
	North Dakota	West Virginia
	Ohio	Wisconsin

Watch for this sign along roadways. It's the official sign indicating wildlife viewing areas included in the Watchable Wildlife® Series.

■ *To order any of these books, check with your local bookseller or call FALCON at 1-800-582-2665.*

www.FalconOutdoors.com

FALCON®

Are you a
TU Member?

If so, "thank you," because your support helped make this book possible. If you're not yet a TU member, won't you think about joining today? We would love to have you as a member, whether you fish or not! Please consider becoming the newest member in the leading organization in North America working to protect these "100 best" trout streams—and thousands more just like them. After all, healthy streams benefit everyone, not just anglers.

TU membership offers lots of benefits... whether you're a novice or a seasoned pro. All members receive *Trout*, TU's award-winning color magazine. You'll get four issues a year, full of conservation news, updates on TU activities, grassroots success stories, fishing destinations recommended by "The Budget Angler," and how-to fishing tips from master anglers. When you join TU, you automatically become a member of a local chapter. Chapters meet regularly to share information about fishing hot spots from Maine to The Bahamas; learn about threats and opportunities facing trout streams and what you can do to help; plan work days on their home waters; organize events for fun and fundraising; and, of course, swap a few fish tales and learn how to tie the latest fly patterns. Looking for a fishing partner? Many chapters sponsor fish-with-a-friend programs that connect members in search of fishing companions.

Perhaps the biggest benefit of TU membership is the satisfaction of knowing you're working to shape a healthier future for trout and salmon—not to mention creating more and better fishing spots!

TU offers ten membership categories that allow individuals and businesses to contribute to TU's mission at the conservation support levels of their choosing: *an annual membership starts at just $30.* For more membership information, call *1-800-834-2419,* or join online today at our website: **www.tu.org**